George E. Weare

Edmund Burke's Connection with Bristol, from 1774 till 1780

With a prefatory memoir of Burke

George E. Weare

Edmund Burke's Connection with Bristol, from 1774 till 1780
With a prefatory memoir of Burke

ISBN/EAN: 9783337094270

Printed in Europe, USA, Canada, Australia, Japan

Cover: Foto ©ninafisch / pixelio.de

More available books at **www.hansebooks.com**

Edmund Burke's

CONNECTION WITH

Bristol,

From 1774 till 1780;

WITH

A Prefatory Memoir of Burke,

BY

G. E. WEARE,

Author of "Collectanea relating to the Bristol Friars Minors (Grey Friars) and their Convent."

PRINTED AND PUBLISHED BY
WILLIAM BENNETT, 43, BROAD STREET, BRISTOL

MDCCCXCIV.

Preface.

THE famous Election in the year 1774, is certainly the most exciting of the many interesting Parliamentary Elections at Bristol. It has a history all its own, and the many-sided details certainly deserve a permanent record, which the writer, to the best of his ability, has endeavoured to supply.

The writer's knowledge of the details of the various Parliamentary contests at Bristol, has been gained by a life-long desultory application to the subject; his earliest recollections including information as to old election episodes and customs; he has from time to time—in bygone years—made frequent visits to aged Citizens long since passed away, with a view to obtain information derived from personal recollections, and in some cases from traditions, ("recollections" and "traditions" are frequently worth listening to, but should be accepted with caution) and the information thus obtained has been found useful on many occasions.

The writer has in his possession a number of books, pamphlets, original broadsides, old newspapers, newspaper cuttings, MS. notes, &c.,—the whole forming a considerable collection relating to Bristol Elections—from which, and from other authentic sources of information, the facts relating to Burke's election at Bristol, and his subsequent parliamentary connection with the City, have been derived.

The broadsides and other election literature connected with the 1774 Election have a distinct interest, because it is not only a fact that in some cases the original broadside, from which the copy has been transcribed, is the only one known to exist, but in the composition of some of the replies to the attacks made upon Burke during the progress of the poll, there are sentences and phrases which might, with little fear of contradiction, be marked as being contributions from his own pen, or dictated by him. It would also be easy to mark some of the clever compositions of Hannah More, and in at least two or three cases, there are visible signs of the vigorous style of Richard Champion.

Preface—continued.

In connection with the compilation of this work, I am desirous at the close of my task, to return my best thanks to all those who have proffered encouragement and assistance, including of course, all those who have kindly subscribed to the work. In particular, I am under obligations to the Rev. A. B. Beavan, (Preston); Mr. John Latimer, Mr. William George, Dr. Garnett (British Museum); Mr. R. E. M. Peach, (Bath); Mr. H. B. Bowles, Mr. H. H. Gregory, Mr. J. E. Pritchard, the City Treasurer, (Mr. J. T. Lane); Mr. E. Norris Mathews (City Librarian), and Mr. E. Tilling (Assistant Librarian); Mr. L. Ackland Taylor, (the Librarian of the Bristol Museum Library), and Mr. W. Vaughan, (the Manager of the Commercial Rooms).

I am particularly anxious to place on record a most interesting—and to me the most pleasant—episode incidental to the production of this work. By singular good chance I have been able to secure the active interest--which has been of real service in the compilation—of two of the grandsons of Richard Champion, viz.: Mr. Richard Champion Rawlins (London) who has kindly rendered all the assistance in his power, and through whose intervention no less than four of Richard Champion's great grandsons, all living at a distance from Bristol, have subscribed for copies of the work; and Mr. J. H. Rawlins (Liverpool), who was good enough to make a special journey from Liverpool to Weston-super-Mare to see me.

My special thanks are due to Mr. Hugh Owen, F.S.A., for granting me permission to use the information contained in his important work, "Two Centuries of Ceramic Art in Bristol," and also for the use of his valuable plates. Mr. Alfred Trapnell, whose rare collection of China is well-known, has also rendered good service, and the publisher has availed himself of his kind offer to bear the cost of two engravings of certain pieces of the Burke Service— the sucrier, cream jug, and a cup and saucer, from the originals in his possession, and the tea-pot from an illustration of the original.

G. E. WEARE.

16, ELLENBOROUGH CRESCENT,
   WESTON-SUPER-MARE,
      October 1894.

LIST OF ILLUSTRATIONS.

Portrait of Edmund Burke, from an engraved portrait, painted by Sir Joshua Reynolds, in 1775. (The frame and scroll-work have been reproduced from a Pamphlet published in 1775.) - Frontispiece.

	Page.
A Freeman's Copy, with the Sheriffs Marks a *fac-simile* (reduced) of the original - - - - - -	82
The Candidates Agents taking the Freemen to the Poll (a *fac-simile* (reduced) of the original caricature.) - - -	85
Specimen of the Staves issued by Cruger's Committee (length 2ft. 6in.) - - - - - - -	85
The Chairing of the Members - - - -	91
The Harford-Lloyd Plaque - - - -	100
The Burke-Nugent Plaque - - - -	101
Portrait of Richard Champion - - - -	103
Portrait of Judith Champion, *neé* Lloyd - - -	105
The Burke Tea Pot - - - - -	107
,, Tea Service (Specimens of) - -	109
Portrait of Joseph Harford - - - -	112

A Prefatory Memoir
of
Edmund Burke.

HIS birth—early days—education—enrolment of his name at the Middle Temple—arrival in London in 1750—friendship with Garrick—visits to Macklin's "School of "Oratory" in Covent Garden—friendship with Peg Woffington—publication, in 1756, of his two works, the "Vindication of "Natural Society" and "A Philosophical Inquiry into the Origin "of the Sublime and Beautiful"—health broken down—visits to Bath and Bristol—reference to a work, "An Account of "the European Settlements in America"—in 1757 he quits the law and devotes himself to literature—connection with Dodsley and the Annual Register in 1759—connection with Wm. Gerard Hamilton as Secretary in 1761—formation of the Literary Club at the Turk's Head in 1764—commencement of his Parliamentary career in 1765—first Speech in the House of Commons, 1766—views on the differences between Great Britain and the American Colonies—appointment, in 1771, as Agent for the State of New York—Speech on American Taxation in April, 1774—the Canada Bill—the Prorogation of the Parliament in June, 1774.

BEFORE entering into the details of Edmund Burke's connection with Bristol, it has been thought desirable, with a view to lead up to the history of the celebrated Parliamentary Election of 1774, when Henry Cruger and Edmund Burke displaced the old members for the City, Lord Clare and Matthew Brickdale, to give a résumé of a few of the important events in the literary and political life of Burke, up to the time of his election at Bristol, (the only contested election, by the way, he was ever engaged in), special attention being paid to his views on the differences which had arisen between Great Britain and the American Colonies, which formed the reason for his selection as a Candidate.

It may be as well to point out that, in the compilation of this work, no attempt has been made to write a biography of the illustrious Edmund Burke, (the writer would think twice before rashly undertaking such a task), and the prefatory memoir has been written for the purpose of refreshing the memories of some readers, and to impart to others, those who may not have carefully read the history of Burke's career, a little information, which, it is hoped, may not be considered uninteresting or irrelevant.

Burke was born in Dublin, in the early part of 1727. His father was a Protestant, his mother belonged to a respectable Roman Catholic family, the Nagles of Castletown Roche.

In his boyish days, Edmund's delicate state of health was a source of uneasiness to his parents. He had probably inherited consumption, which had been fatal to many of his brothers and sisters, and which was destined, at a later period, to consign to an early grave his son and heir. But the careful and never-ceasing attention of those by whom he was surrounded prevailed against the insiduous enemy, and after a time he was taken from Dublin to the country house of his maternal grandfather, Mr. Patrick Nagle, at Castletown Roche. It is the unexpected that happens, and when, in after years, the little community at Castletown Roche heard the wondrous stories of the intellectual giant, whom they had been entertaining unawares, it was the proud boast of the Village Schoolmaster, whose name was O'Halloran, that he gave Edmund Burke his first Latin Grammar.

After leaving Castletown Roche, he stayed with his parents in Dublin for about a year, and was then sent, with his two brothers, Garrett and Richard, to a classical academy at Ballitore, in the County of Kildare, kept by Mr. Abraham Shackleton.

At school, he was fond of reading, and, by diligent application, he acquired a store of knowledge. He rather liked to be left alone with his books; but he was cheerful and affectionate, and always willing to communicate what he knew, or to assist others. His brother, Richard, after one of Edmund's oratorical outbursts in the House of Commons, exclaimed :—" I have been wondering " how Ned has contrived to monopolize all the talents of the family; " but then again I remember, *when we were at play, he was* " *always at work.*"

As a proof of the early maturity of his mind, we find that before he left Ballitore, he had been able to discern the terrible consequences to Ireland of the religious prejudices of both the Catholics and the Protestants. It may be, that in consequence of the advantages he possessed, of being afforded an insight into the private lives of representative families of the rival religionists, he became alive to the folly of religious fanaticism.

Subsequently he entered Trinity College, Dublin, his admission to which is dated the 14th April, 1743. He took his B.A. degree in the early part of 1748, and, in 1751, he obtained his M.A. degree. He was presented with the honorary degree of LL.D. in 1791.

Opinions differ as to whether he gave much proof of superiority at the University. His studies took a very wide and, perhaps, a rather discursive range; but it is clear that, whatever may have been the mode of application or the effect produced, he left the University thoroughly equipped for the battles in which he was destined to take part; his mind afterwards proved a veritable store-house of knowledge, and he was ever ready with classical and other quotations. He was among the foremost members of the Historical Society of the University, and his historical researches proved in after life to be not the least useful part of his equipment. Many years afterwards Macleod asked Johnson of dictionary fame, " What is the particular excellence of " Burke's eloquence ?" Johnson replied, " Copiousness and " fertility of allusion ; a power of diversifying his matter by " placing it in various relations. Burke has great information " and great command of language."

His partiality for the stage commenced at a very early period. He and a number of his fellow students at Trinity College were banded together for the purpose of resisting an attempt by a number of persons to destroy the Dublin Theatre, then managed by Thomas Sheridan, the father of the celebrated Richard Brinsley Sheridan.

In the year 1747 a literary club was established in Dublin. Burke took a very great interest in it, and was one of its most constant frequenters.

Burke, senior, had determined that his son should go to the English Bar, and Edmund's name was duly enrolled at the Middle Temple. He arrived in London in the early part of 1750. In a characteristic letter, written soon after his arrival in London, there are to be found passages which, although much overdrawn, clearly indicate the bent of his mind, " As to the state of " learning in this City (London) you know I have not been long " enough in it to form a proper judgment of that subject. I " don't think, however, there is as much respect paid to a man of " letters on this side of the water as you imagine. I don't find " that genius the 'rath primrose, which forsaken, dies,' is " patronized by any of the nobility, so that writers of the first " talents are left to the capricious patronage of the public. " Notwithstanding discouragement, literature is cultivated in a " high degree. Poetry raises her enchanting voice to heaven. " History arrests the wings of Time in his flight to the gulf of " oblivion. Philosophy, the queen of arts and the daughter of " heaven, is daily extending her intellectual empire. Fancy sports " on airy wings like a meteor on the bosom of a summer cloud : " and even Metaphysics spins her cobwebs and catches some flies."

In the year 1754 we find him very often in the company of the leading actors of the day. His friendship with David Garrick commenced about this period, and it continued down to the date of the great actor's death. Garrick's letters were sometimes addressed to "Carissimo mio Edmundo." On more than one occasion Garrick showed by substantial practical help the interest he took in him.

Macklin another famous actor, who had acquired his early laurels in Bristol, was one of Burke's intimates. Macklin had retired from the stage in the latter part of 1753. He afterwards kept a tavern and coffee house in the Piazzi, Covent Garden, and he there established a debating society or "School of Oratory"; he also gave lessons in elocution. The house became the rendezvous of authors, players, barristers, students, and the society loungers of the period. At this debating society Burke made his first oration in public, and there is very little doubt that he gained much knowledge of the elocutionary art and of oratorical action by his connection with Macklin and other actors; and he was not slow to admit that he owed much to his visits to Garrick's Theatre. Macklin's debating society collapsed after a brief existence of four months, and its decease was attributed to the shafts of ridicule hurled at it by Foote and other kindred spirits, and by personal enemies of the unfortunate Macklin, who was declared a bankrupt in 1755. Macklin's history is full of vicissitudes and adventures, and in some respects his career was as strange as that of Cibber. There is a local story concerning him. During the time he was playing at the Jacob's Wells Theatre (the predecessor of the present Theatre Royal, King Street) he made the acquaintance of a young lady whom he had arranged to visit in a clandestine manner at her father's house after he had finished his performances at the theatre. By some accident, the unlucky actor in going into the room, the window of which had been left open by the young lady, managed to overset a large china jar, which made a great noise and alarmed the household and he was compelled to beat a hasty retreat from the abode of his lady love. Macklin's friends published two plays written by him by a subscription which amounted to £1,500, and this amount was invested in the purchase of an annuity of £200 for himself and £75 for his wife in case she survived him. He also obtained damages against certain of his enemies and traducers. He returned to the stage when past 80, and lived to the extraordinary age of 107 years, which must have made the annuity other than a profitable transaction to those who had engaged to pay it. He died on the 11th of July 1797, just two days after the death of Burke. He has been described as the Nestor of the English Stage.

Burke's theatrical acquaintances included the celebrated Margaret, otherwise known as Peg Woffington, whose symmetrical beauty and fascinating manners had made willing captives of many of the greatest men of the day. Her house was the meeting place of men of the highest rank; and having regard to her great knowledge of the world, her accomplishments, sparkling wit and vivacity, it is not surprising that her society was eagerly sought after. At a time when the discussion of French literature was the ephemeral topic in the literary circles of the English Metropolis it was no small advantage that she knew France well; was acquainted with its literature: and spoke its language fluently. There was an attractive charm in her manner which called for universal acknowledgment. Of her it was well said that she would have been perfect had she been virtuous. She was extremely partial to Burke, and at some of her charming receptions he made many acquaintances, and he enjoyed to the full all the benefits which are to be derived from a woman who has the power and is desirous to use it on behalf of one for whom she has conceived a liking. That her partiality for him gave rise to scandal goes without saying, but he was absolutely indifferent to the attacks of the scandal-mongers.

In the year 1755 he was offered an appointment in one of the provinces of America, but, owing to his father's objection, he declined to accept it.

In the early part of 1756 he published the " Vindication of "Natural Society," otherwise designated " A view of the miseries "and evils arising to mankind from every species of civil society, in a letter to Lord ———, by a late noble lord." This work was a satire in the vein of the publications of Lord Bolingbroke, but it was such a close imitation of Bolingbroke's style that even astute and wide awake critics were taken in. When it leaked out that Burke was the author, the public did not see that it was a satirical publication, and eventually he thought it desirable to explain its real character. Many people, however, regarded it as a serious publication. At that period some English writers had been affected by the views of French writers who had advocated equality, the abolition of religion and of the marriage tie, etc. A friend, some time after the publication, asked Johnson if he thought it would hurt him (Burke). Johnson replied " No sir, not much. It may perhaps be mentioned at an "election." Later on, in the same year, he established his reputation as a writer by publishing his well known work— " A Philosophical Inquiry into the origin of our ideas of the " Sublime and Beautiful."

Burke's frame was never robust, and his application to literary work, combined perhaps with the absence of an opportunity to indulge in relaxation, had been gradually undermining his physical powers, and at this period he found it necessary to undergo a temporary retirement,

Burke visited Bristol and Bath to recruit his health. Some references to his visits to these two places will be found later on.

It is generally believed that a work which was published in 1757, " An Account of the European Settlements in America," in two volumes, octavo, was the united production, or represented the united ideas, of Edmund Burke, his brother Richard, and their kinsman and friend William Burke. No one who wishes to trace the connection of Edmund Burke with the history of the American Colonies, a connection which was destined to bring him to Bristol as a candidate for the representation of the city in Parliament, can possibly avoid mention of this publication, because it affords evidence, if any were needed, that the affairs of the American Colonies, and the rightful position of the colonies to the mother country had been the subjects of deep thought to him; that his interest in these matters had been awakened and his opinions thereon formed at an early period of his literary career. There is no doubt that in the construction of the above work the master mind was that of Edmund Burke.

The Abbé Raynel incorporated the greater portion of this history in his own elaborate work on the Indies.

Although he had, in the year 1755, with a view to save his father from anxiety, given up the idea of going to America, there can be little doubt that the interest he took in the Colonies had prompted in him a great desire to visit them. In a letter, bearing date the 10th of August, 1757, addressed to an old friend at Ballitore, we find that he contemplated "shortly "please God, to be in America." But his wishes were never realized, and it would appear that there was always some obstacle to prevent the gratification of his desire. As a matter of fact, and notwithstanding statements to the contrary, Edmund Burke never visited America.

In the same year (1757) a new edition of the Essay on the Sublime and Beautiful was issued, and to this edition he added the chapter on "Taste.' Before this he had finally given up the profession of the law, and had determined to devote himself to literature. Many years afterwards, *when he had placed himself in the political arena*, Goldsmith wrote a mock epitaph as follows:—

> Here lies our good Edmund, whose genius was such,
> We scarcely can praise it, or blame it too much;
> Who born for the universe, narrowed his mind,
> And to *party* gave up what was meant for mankind.

Putting aside many minor events in his literary career, we will now pass to his connection with the Annual Register, published by Dodsley, a celebrated printer and publisher of the period, the first volume of which appeared in June, 1759. Dodsley was one of Burke's earliest patrons and friends, and, in after years, he was the publisher of most of his important speeches, many of which rapidly ran through several editions. The connection of Burke with the Annual Register necessitated frequent attendances in the gallery of the House of Commons, from which visits he necessarily gained much experience, and the association of his name with the publication helped to bring him before the notice of the political world.

In the year 1761, Lord Charlemont, a warm admirer of Burke, recommended him to Mr. Wm. Gerard Hamilton, who had been appointed Chief Secretary to Lord Halifax, Lord-Lieutenant of Ireland, and he was engaged to take the somewhat anomalous position of "part friend and part secretary."

In 1763 he received a pension of £300 per year on the Irish list through the influence of Hamilton, but, in consequence of the latter's claims upon his services which were considered by him to be, and certainly were, incompatible with independence and freedom of action, the pension was assigned to Hamilton's attorney in April, 1764. Burke used some very expressive language as to Hamilton's conduct towards him.

It was in February 1764, that the celebrated Literary Club was formed at the Turk's Head, Garrard Street, Soho. The first members were Sir Joshua Reynolds, Dr. Samuel Johnson, Edmund Burke, Dr Nugent, Topham Beauclerc, Bennett Langton. Oliver Goldsmith, Ant. Chamier, and Sir John Hawkins. Subsequently, David Garrick was a frequenter of the Club, the meetings of which were held every Monday, at 7 in the evening.

We have now to record the commencement of the Parliamentary career of Burke. In July 1765, he was appointed private secretary to Charles second Marquis of Rockingham, who had just entered office at the head of a section of the Whig party. Directly the appointment became known, the Duke of Newcastle called on the Marquis, and intimated that he was about to appoint as his secretary a Jesuit, *who had received his education at St. Omer's*, and that, in reality, Burke was an Irish Papist named O'Bourke. To the everlasting honour of the Marquis be it said that he would not accept the word of the Duke, and immediately sent for Burke, who, of course, gave a denial to the slander. Burke's friendship for the Marquis was cemented, by the kind way in which he expressed his acceptance of the denial. Many suggestions have been made as to the motive for the Duke of Newcastle's attempt to nip Burke's Parliamentary career in the bud, but the most probable explanation is that Peg Woffington at one of her receptions, introduced Burke to the Duke, and extracted a promise that he would interest himself on behalf of her protégé; and that in consequence of the Duke having failed to keep his promise, or having failed to take any notice of Burke, the latter had made some attack on the Duke which had caused his resentment. The rumour that he was a Jesuit, and educated at St. Omer's, was frequently re-published, and when, in 1774, he was a candidate to represent Bristol in Parliament, a statement to the same effect was industriously circulated. This was one of the many petty attacks he had to endure, by way of penalty, for possessing talents superior to the common herd of men. Through the interest of Lord Verney, he was elected M.P. for Wendover, in the County of Bucks, one of several pocket-boroughs in the hands of the Verney family. The session opened on the 17th of December, 1765, but it was almost immediately prorogued, and the business did not commence until the 14th of January, 1766. The Stamp Act passed in the previous session had caused great alarm and discontent in the American Colonies. A long course of unwise restrictions and arbitrary conduct had caused a slumbering feeling of discontent, which was gradually being fanned into activity by attempts on the part of the Parliament, or rather of the King, to impose upon the colonists measures which they deemed obnoxious. The Stamp Act was objected to on the ground that it was an attempt to tax the colonists by a Parliament in which they were not represented, and it was argued, that if the principle of taxation without representation was not then opposed, there was no knowing to what extent the Imperial Parliament might proceed. In New York the obnoxious Statute was printed with a skull and cross bones, *instead of the Royal Arms*, and hawked about the streets by the title of " England's folly and America's ruin." At Boston the flags were hoisted half mast high, and the church bells tolled a funeral knell. At Philadelphia the people spiked the guns on the ramparts. It was in connection with the state of the American Colonies that Burke made his maiden address in the

House of Commons. His speech was cleverly framed, his arguments in favour of the repeal of the Stamp Act being well chosen, and he sat down at the close amidst the applause of both sides of the House. He was followed by Mr. Pitt (afterwards Earl of Chatham), who, in the course of his speech, highly praised his ingenuity and eloquence, congratulated him on his success, and complimented the members of the Government on the acquisition they had made. No aspirant for Parliamentary fame could have wished for more than such a compliment, and Burke's reputation in the House was from that time accepted without question.

The Rockingham Ministry lasted only one year and twenty days, but it succeeded in abrogating the unpopular Stamp Act. It was believed by many that the king had dismissed them because they were not very desirous to push forward a proposal for a grant to the king's younger brother; but it seems clear, that, apart from the king's displeasure, assuming that it had an existence, the Ministry, or in fact any Ministry, could not be kept going without the active support of Pitt. The Bristol merchants had petitioned for the repeal of the Stamp Act, and, after its repeal in 1766, they forwarded an address of thanks to Lord Rockingham.

Burke drew up and published a concise account of the doings of the late Ministry during its brief existence. It was designated "A short Account of a late short Administration." It was republished, in extenso, in the Bristol newspapers at the time he was a candidate for the Parliamentary representation of the city in 1774.

In July, 1766, a new Ministry was formed by Pitt, who, to the astonishment of all parties, offered to take the office of Privy Seal, which necessitated his removal to the Upper House. Lord Chesterfield expressed surprise that Pitt should have elected "to go into that Hospital of Incurables, the House of "Lords," adding that "nothing but proof positive could make "one believe it, but so it is." The King created Pitt Viscount Pynsent and Earl of Chatham.

Overtures were made to Burke soon after the change of Administration, and again in the next year, to attach himself to the new Ministry, but he steadily declined, preferring to remain true to his friend and patron, the Marquis of Rockingham,

The newly elected peer acted in a very strange manner, that can only be explained by a failure of his great mental powers; he kept away from Parliament; he refused to see his colleagues; and the entire management of business was left to subordinate Ministers. The repeal of the Stamp Act had temporarily disarmed the opposition of the Colonists, and a spirit of content was gradually taking the place of the former feeling. when, to the astonishment of the country, the new Ministry, not long after its formation, was found to be actively engaged in promoting legislation reversing the policy of "the late short "Administration." Duties were imposed on teas and other imports, and the New York Assembly was prohibited from any legislation until it had given its submission to the Quartering Act of 1765.

During the session of 1767 Burke particularly distinguished himself in a vigorous speech against a proposal to prevent the importation of Irish wool into certain ports in England, and the Bill was thrown out. This was not the first time he had endeavoured to render assistance to his native country, and it may be appropriate to here mention that it was in this year (1767) that the freedom of the City of Dublin was conferred upon him "in consideration of his distinguished abilities, so "frequently exerted for the advantage of this kingdom" (Ireland).

In 1768, the imperial troops were sent to Boston to enforce the Act by which the new taxes had been imposed. A general election took place this year. Burke was re-elected for the borough of Wendover on the 16th of March, 1768. The new Parliament was summoned to meet on the 10th May, and when it assembled, attention was immediately drawn to the position of the notorious John Wilkes. The circumstances which led to the retirement of Wilkes to Paris and his outlawry—in connection with the publication of the North Briton and the Essay on Woman—occurred before Burke entered Parliament. Wilkes had not only returned from France but had secured his election as M.P. for Middlesex. On the day fixed for the opening of Parliament—the 10th of May—the mob which had assembled near the King's Bench Prison, in which Wilkes had been incarcerated, fully expected that he would be allowed to leave the prison in order to enable him to take his seat in Parliament, and finding this expectation disappointed a serious riot was the result, some persons being shot dead and others wounded by the military in St. George's Fields. The proceedings added to the unpopularity of the King. During the next Session the Earl of Chatham withdrew from the Government, and he was succeeded in the office of Privy Seal by the Earl of Bristol. Burke was heard to advantage in the House of Commons in a speech made in support of a demand for an inquiry into what had been described as "the Massacre in St. George's Fields," and also on the debate on the motion to expel Wilkes from the House. Burke proved to be an eloquent champion of the rights of the freeholders of Middlesex. In this Parliament there were majorities in both houses in favour of the King's policy towards the Colonies, and the Lords recommended, in an address to the King, that the colonists who had disobeyed the law should be brought over to England to be tried. The House of Commons by a large majority agreed to concur in the Lord's recommendations. Burke "characterised all the preceding measures of "Government as rash, raw, undigested measures which had "inflamed America from one end of the country to the other." He said "if you have not a party among 2,000,000 of people, "*you must either change your plan of government, or renounce* "*the Colonies for ever. If the people are uniform, and steady,* "*and united, you never can punish them.*" On the 9th of May, 1769 the Parliament was prorogued. The news from the Colonies clearly demonstrated that the colonists were determined to resist, to the utmost of their power, the impositions of a Parliament in which they were not represented. The King was equally determined to make no concessions. Burke foresaw that the rupture would end in a collision. It was in this year that the letters of Junius first appeared, and Burke was for a time almost unanimously pointed out as the author. He subsequently thought it advisable to give the rumour an explicit denial.

In 1770, he published a pamphlet on the "present discontents," which was a powerful attempt to bring discredit upon the Government policy. This work has always been regarded as a master piece in political literature.

The Act which authorised the arrest of American colonists for the purpose of being brought to the Mother Country for trial, was denounced by Washington, who, declaring that it was an attack on freedom, asserted that a resort to arms in defence of freedom was justifiable, but that arms should be the dernier resort.

In the year 1771, Burke was appointed agent in England for the State of New York, an appointment which was conferred upon him in consequence of his abilities and his special aptitude for dealing with questions affecting the State. It has been considered that the acceptance of this office, to which certain emoluments were attached, somewhat diminished the force and power of the great orator's efforts to induce people to adopt his views on the American difficulties. It should however be remembered that his opinions had been formed years before, and that it was about the most natural selection that the New Yorkers could have made. At a critical period they wanted an agent, and their attention was almost necessarily fixed on Burke as the best man for the position. No person who thoroughly understood his nature could accept the suggestion that the emoluments attached to the office would influence his course of conduct in Parliament. The brilliant men of his set—which included Sir Joshua Reynolds, Johnson, Garrick, Hume, his brother Richard and others—to whom he was so well known, would have repelled with scorn the small-minded people who were foolish enough to think that he was capable of meanly swerving from his principles on such a momentous question.

In addition to certain other events which portended the revolt of the colonists, it soon became known that the Bostonians had boarded three ships laden with tea, and that they had thrown the goods into the sea.

[The inhabitants of Bristol were soon made aware of any hostile demonstrations on the part of the colonists. Descriptions of the seizure of the East India Company's tea " by a number of " men, *having the appearance of Indians,*" were published in the Bristol newspapers.]

On the 7th March, 1774, the King officially acquainted the Houses of Parliament with the facts. The Government then brought in a Bill known as "The Boston Port Bill," which aimed at the annihilation of the port of Boston, and a warm debate arose thereon, which was renewed when they brought in proposals for an alteration of the Charter relating to the Province of Massachusetts. Burke opposed both Bills. On the 19th April, 1774, he delivered the celebrated speech on American taxation, which might, with truth, be designated as one of the finest of his oratorical exhibitions in the House of Commons. He had been preceded in the debate by Mr. Charles Wolfran Cornwall, one of the Lords of the Treasury, who had made a vehement speech on the Ministerial side; consequently, Burke's speech being, to a considerable extent modelled to serve as a reply to Cornwall, was not altogether a studied effort. His ideas were beautifully expressed and exquisitely accentuated. All the finer elements of his mind were brought into action. During the progress of the speech the assembly was kept almost spell-bound, and it is related that Lord Townshend said, "Good God! What a man this is! How " could he acquire such transcendent power?" A distinguished American colonist, who was in the gallery of the House, said

aloud, "You have got a most wonderful man here; he under-
"stands more of America than all the rest of your House put
"together." His arguments were directed throughout to the
position of the King and Government with regard to the tax on
tea—the other taxes to which the Americans had taken exception
having been repealed. Towards the end of his speech he said,
"Again, and again, revert to your old principles. Seek peace
"and ensue it. Leave America, if she has taxable matter in
"her, to tax herself. I am not going into the distinction of
"rights, nor attempting to mark their boundaries. I do not
"enter into those metaphysical distinctions. I hate the very
"sound of them. Leave the Americans as they anciently stood,
"and these distinctions, born of our unhappy contest, will die
"along with it. They, and us, and their and our ancestors, have
"been happy under that system. Let the memory of all actions
"in contradiction to that good old mode, on both sides, be
"extinguished for ever. Be content to bind America by laws of
"trade; you have always done it. Let this be your reason for
"binding their trade. Do not burden them with taxes; you
"were not used to do so from the beginning. Let this be your
"reason for not taxing. These are the arguments of states and
"kingdoms. Leave the rest to the schools; for there only they
"may be discussed with safety. But if, intemperately, unwisely,
"fatally, you sophisticate and poison the very source of govern-
"ment, by urging subtle deductions and consequences odious to
"those you govern *from the unlimited and illimitable nature*
"*of supreme sovereignty, you will teach them by these means to*
"*call that sovereignty itself in question.* When you drive him
"hard, the boar will surely turn upon the hunters. If that
"sovereignty and their freedom cannot be reconciled, which will
"they take? They will cast your sovereignty in your face.

. . . .

"I look on the imperial rights of Great Britain, and the
"privileges which the colonists ought to enjoy under these
"rights, to be just the most reconcilable things in the world.

"The Parliament of Great Britain sits at the head of her extensive empire in two capacities: one as the local legislature of this island, providing for all things at home, immediately, and by no other instrument than the executive powers. The other, and, I think, her nobler capacity, is what I call her imperial character; in which, as from the throne of heaven, she superintends all the several inferior legislatures, and guides and controls them all without annihilating any. As all these provincial legislatures are only co-ordinate to each other, they ought all to be subordinate to her; else they can neither preserve mutual peace, nor hope for mutual justice, nor effectually afford mutual assistance.

.   .   .

"I have shewn that you threw everything into confusion when you made the Stamp Act; and that you restored everything to peace and order when you repealed it. I have shewn that the revival of the system of taxation has produced the very worst effects; and that the partial repeal has produced not partial good, but universal evil. Let these considerations, founded on facts, not one of which can be denied, bring us back to your reason by the road of your experience." Burke's eloquent appeal was made in vain, as the majority of the members of the House were servile supporters of the King's policy. The speech, printed by Dodsley [96 p.p., 8vo.] some time after, soon passed through several editions, and was extensively circulated in Bristol.

Then came the grave Canadian questions, which were well calculated to cause dismay. Fortunately, however, concessions were made. In connection with the Canada Bill, Burke's knowledge again proved of great service. A difficulty arose as to the boundary line between Canada and the New York State, the defining of which might have imperilled the passing of the Bill. Burke, with several other members rushed upstairs into a private room, and with the aid of a number of maps, he drew the line of demarcation which was subsequently agreed to. An enthusiastic biographer has contended that he saved Canada by his promptitude.

On the 22nd of June, 1774, the Canada Bill received the Royal Assent, and the same day the King prorogued the Parliament.

Burke's position at this time is very accurately described in the Right Hon. John Morley's work on Burke, pp. 72-3, " Burke "was now rewarded by the discovery that his labours had "earned for him recognition and gratitude beyond the narrow "limits of a rather exclusive party. He had before this, "*attracted the attention of the mercantile public.* The Company "of Merchants trading to Africa voted him their thanks. The "Committee of Trade at Manchester formally returned him their "grateful acknowledgments for the active part that he had taken "in the business of the Jamaica free ports. In two Parliaments, "Burke had been elected for Wendover free of expense. Lord "Verney's circumstances were now so embarrassed, that he was "obliged to part with the four seats at his disposal to men who "could pay for them. Burke's constancy of spirit was "momentarily overclouded. . . . Lord Rockingham "offered his influence on behalf of Burke at Malton, one of the "family boroughs in Yorkshire."

. . . .

Some of Burke's speeches and letters, made or written during the time he represented Bristol, from 1774 till 1780, are of more than ordinary interest and deserve more than passing attention, because they contain, not only valuable additions to the national literature, but constitutional maxims which have been quoted, from time to time, by many of the greatest British statesmen.

Burke's Connection with Bristol.

THE Parliament at the time it was prorogued on the 22nd of June, 1774, had nearly a year to complete its septennial term, and it may be supposed that after the prorogation rumours of a dissolution would occasionally be heard. In Bristol it was generally believed that the king (George III.) would shortly dissolve Parliament and issue writs for a general election, and it was whispered from time to time that there was a probability that whenever the election took place, the sitting members—the Right Honourable Viscount Clare, an Irish peer, the patron of Goldsmith, a member of the Privy Council, and high in the king's favour, and Matthew Brickdale, a retired local woollen draper, formerly in business in High Street, a member of the Bristol Corporation, and locally a man of importance, with influential local connexions—both of whom had proved themselves to be obsequious supporters of the king's policy towards the American Colonies—would be opposed. It was pretty well known that a candidate had been found in the person of Mr. Henry Cruger, Junior, a very well known and very influential Bristol merchant, an American by birth—a native of New York—and, at the time, largely interested in the American trade. He had married the daughter of Mr. Samuel Peach, a wealthy linen draper of Bristol (the founder of the Peach family of Tockington), and had many friends in the city, owing partly to his popularity and partly to his connexion with Mr. Peach, and he had been, since 1766, a member of the Corporation. Mr. Peach had accumulated a large fortune partly derived from investments in the slave traffic and West India produce. He afterwards became associated with a Bristol bank.

The vast interests of many of the commercial houses in Bristol in the trade carried on with the American Colonies, had been seriously affected through the actions of the king and his Ministers, and there existed a strong feeling in the city—owing, to a considerable extent, to patriotic sentiments of sympathy with the colonists, but to be attributed to a larger extent to motives not wholly unselfish or entirely disinterested—in favour of a policy of conciliation. A reference to the state of trade in Bristol at the period is to be found in Latimer's Annals, pp. 614-15. It is there stated that "the effect of the quarrel, long "before the actual outbreak of hostilities, was painfully felt in "many branches of business. . . . . . . It appears that a "single firm in the city employed 400 hands in making serges for "America, and that the manufacture came wholly to an end. "Another house was accustomed to purchase every spring, for "export across the Atlantic, 3,000 pieces of stuff, but the "quantity fell in 1774 to 200 pieces, and afterwards to nothing. "Until the quarrel arose, the tobacco-pipe makers of Bristol— "a numerous body—each sent 500 or 600 boxes of pipes to the "Colonies" (Latimer's Annals). These examples are merely given to show the effect of the difficulties with the American colonists upon certain trades in Bristol. The great commercial houses had already found their trade partially, if not completely, paralysed, in consequence of the non-receipt of remittances to meet bills long overdue, and it was fast becoming clear that there would shortly be a cessation of commercial intercourse.

The inhabitants of Annapolis and Baltimore by way of protest against one of the Acts passed by the Parliament of Great Britain, had agreed to stop importations from or exportations to Great Britain and the West Indies.

It had become known that a meeting of the delegates from the different counties in Virginia had been summoned if not actually held for the purpose of considering the advisability of abstaining from importing any goods &c., from Great Britain after the 1st day of November following; and that unless American grievances were redressed before the 10th day of August, 1775, they would not, after that date, export tobacco or any other article to Great Britain. The Bristol traders were large importers* of tobacco, cotton, rice, rum, sugar, molasses, coffee, iron, hemp, hides, skins, tallow, oil,† tar, pitch, indigo, turpentine, mahogany, oak, lignum vitæ, ebony, walnut, cedar, cypress, logwood, deals, pipe, hogshead and barrel staves, masts, fustick, cordage, pimento, flax and flax seed, linen yarn, ginger, fruits, and the minor products of the American colonies and the West Indies; there were frequent sailings from Bristol to New York, Boston and Philadelphia, to North and South Carolina, Virginia, Annapolis, Chester Town, and Baltimore in Maryland, Portsmouth, Providence, Salem and Marblehead in New England, Newfoundland, Quebec, Honduras Bay, and to the West India Islands; and there were many persons and firms in the City interested in the carrying trade, which comprised both cargoes and passengers. Under the latter head it may be mentioned that a considerable number of emigrants to the Colonies from time to time sailed from Bristol. Obviously, therefore, either in the event of reprisals by the colonists, or in case of the outbreak of hostilities, the men of Bristol would be amongst the first to suffer and amongst those who would suffer most.

It would be difficult to calculate the amount which the wealthy residents of Bristol had at stake. Many of the sugar and tobacco plantations were owned by Bristol people, who were also interested to a large extent in other plantations by reason of advances made on mortgage to the owners. The wide-spread interest may be guessed at from information contained in notes made by Mr. John Latimer, as to the "company of merchants, "trading to Africa." This great trading monopoly was practically established for supplying African Negroes for the work connected with the plantations of the American Colonies and the American Islands (the West Indies). The negroes were generally obtained

---
* A very limited quantity of flour, wheat, &c., came to Great Britain at this period.
† The importation of tar, pitch, indigo, &c., from the Colonies was on a considerable scale owing to the grants of premiums and bounties.

in exchange for goods sent from England to Africa, and immense profits were frequently made. Bristol had at one period as great as, if not a greater share in the traffic in slaves than, any other city in the Kingdom. The company of merchants trading to Africa was managed "by nine persons, three of whom were "elected by the members in London, Bristol, and Liverpool "respectively," (Latimer's Annals). In the year 1753, there were in Bristol *157 members of the company*, in London 135 members, and in Liverpool 101 members. In the year 1755, the membership was represented as follows:—Bristol 237 members, London 147, and Liverpool 89. In a list issued in 1759, we find that *there were in Bristol 242 members*, in London 144, and in Liverpool 87. Even Quakers indulged in investments in the slave traffic, and the lists include the names of some of those pious and good people, who, by the way, in the neighbourhood of Bristol, were not averse to receive tithes, but the purchases were made in the names of agents. Of the members of the African Company in 1759, a considerable number who still had an interest in the traffic were surviving in 1774, and were still residents in Bristol. When hostilities commenced, the following list by no means representing the whole of the large traders, or those who were actually engaged in carrying on business between Bristol and various places in America or the West Indies, will give some idea of the mercantile houses of importance in Bristol:—Samuel Bailsford (Carolina), the Brights (West Indies), Richard Champion (America), Jeremiah Coghlan (Newfoundland), Lancelot Cowper (America), Thomas Daniel (West Indies), Mark Davis (West Indies), Samuel Delpratt (West Indies), Farrell and Jones (Virginia), Richard and Thomas Farr (Virginia), Farr, Pardoe and Hanbury (Virginia), Joseph Glovier (Virginia), John Gordon and Robert Gordon (West Indies), Thomas Hayes (America), Henry Lippincott & Co. (Virginia), Robert Lovell (West Indies), Wm. Miles (West Indies), Cruger and Mallard (America) Stephenson Randolph and Cheston (America), John Noble (Newfoundland), Perry and Hayes (America), George Pow,

(Guinea), Samuel Span (West Indies), Nathaniel Wraxall (America), Pennington & Co. (America), and Watts and Maskelyne. There were also considerable interests at stake in Bristol in connection with sugar-refinery establishments which included Ames, Ireland & Co., Harris and Rice, Battersby, Hull & Co., Brice & Co., Daubeny & Co., Flinn and Palmer, Keene, Allis and Thomas, John Merlott, Munckley & Co., Peach and Henderson, John Sandy & Co., Wright & Co., Nehemiah Champion, John Banister. A very large number of citizens found employment as sugar-bakers. The trade with Africa, America and the West Indies kept the shipbuilders yards and the cooperages, in which were employed a large number of hands, in a flourishing condition, and immense quantities of staves and headings for the various kinds of casks were imported from America.

Bristol had always stood pre-eminent in commercial intercourse with the American Colonies and the West Indies, and the trade had been slowly, but firmly, built up during a long course of years. The pioneer of the colonisation of America, Sebastian Cabot, sailed from Bristol, and it has been claimed that men from Bristol planted the first English flag upon the Continent of America. The connection of Bristol with some of the Colonies dated back to the time of their colonisation, the first settlers in many places having been largely, if not wholly, composed of Bristol men. In the early part of the seventeenth century, King James granted a patent to the "Company of Adventurers and Planters of the cities of London and Bristol," to establish a settlement in Newfoundland, and the trade with Newfoundland* was a great source of profit to Bristol traders. Northern Virginia and portions of Massachusetts were colonised, to a large extent by Bristol men. It is recorded that, in the year 1625, certain Bristol merchants had an agent in the Paraquid Country, and received grants of portions of land from the Council of New England. The Bristol merchants were amongst the earliest to take advantage of the colonisation of Barbadoes, and other islands in the West

---

* At the period just preceding the outbreak of hostilities with the American Colonies, the lamps used in Great Britain involved immense supplies of oil, extracted from fishes, and the Bristol merchants had, to a large extent, a monopoly of this trade.

Indies. In Bristol malefactors were offered their lives, provided they would proceed to the plantations and work as slaves. The demand for labour tempted the aldermen of Bristol to frighten persons who had committed trifling offences to save themselves from conviction, by agreeing to go to the plantations. " When "any pilferers or petty rogues were brought before them (the " Bristol aldermen) they threatened them with hanging, and then " some officers, who attended, earnestly advised the ignorant, " intimidated creatures to beg for transportation." When Judge Jeffries delivered his celebrated charge at Bristol, in 1685, he referred to this matter, and to the kidnapping (*i.e.*, stealing children), which was also resorted to by Bristol men for the purpose of keeping up a supply of labourers in the Colonies.

The judge said, "this city, it seems, claims the privilege of " hanging and drawing amongst themselves. . . . . "I find they can agree for their interest, or if there be but a kid "in the case, for I hear the trade of kidnapping is of much request "in this city. They can discharge a felon or a traitor, provided "they will go to Mr. Alderman's plantation, at the West Indies." The Mayor was fined £1,000, and six aldermen were bound in recognisances " to appear to answer an indictment at the King's " Bench for kidnapping." At this period a considerable number of persons were engaged as " common man-stealers," for the purpose of stealing and selling men into slavery in the plantations.

At a later date men and boys were frequently induced by false representations to sign indentures by which they were bound to labour in the plantations for a certain number of years as " servants," but they soon discovered that they had actually agreed to be placed in the same position as the slaves during the period of servitude.

The magistrates, who were themselves interested in the supply of labour, upheld the validity of these agreements and no redress could be obtained. These "indentured servants were sometimes sold by auction, and brought generally £15 currency in market." It was stated in 1774 that at the end of their term of service "they only get a suit of clothes, an hoe, an axe, and a bill." In some of the colonies, however, the "indentured servants" were entitled, *after the expiration of the servitude*, to a grant of a certain number of acres.

In the early days it was considered the correct thing for one of the partners of a Bristol commercial house to reside in one or other of the Colonies or Islands, and on his return to Bristol another partner would take his place. Sometimes persons connected with the Bristol houses simply acted as agents abroad, and made their money by commissions on the transactions both on the imports and exports. The money invested on mortgages of the plantations was not unfrequently lent on the condition that the lenders should take the whole of the produce on certain terms, thus enabling them to secure both profits and commissions. In this way the Bristol men practically secured to a great extent a monopoly of the trade. Early in the eighteenth century Isaac Hobhouse and Onesiphorus Tyndall, who were partners in the slave trade, had as Jamaica agents Messrs. Tyndall, Assheton, Jones & Co., the first being a relative of the Bristol merchant, and the last a nephew of Hobhouse.

Noblet Ruddock, elected Common Councillor 1718, and Sheriff 1725, subsequently settled in the West Indies, doubtless acting as agent for some Bristol house. In consequence of his absence he was removed from the Corporation, May 28, 1734 The principal importers of tobacco were Mr. Chamberlain, Mr. Farrell, Mr. Innys, all having resided in Virginia, and they were followed by Lidderdale, Harmer and Farrell, who had also resided there. By these such large quantities of tobacco were imported that the agents of the French contractors were frequently compelled to supply themselves in Bristol. The principal traders to Carolina included Mr. Alderman Jefferis and others, who had resided there. As to sugar, that article formerly was chiefly imported in Guinea ships (of which 40 sail belonged to the port of Bristol), and the sugar received frequently represented the value in exchange for negroes carried to the islands in Bristol ships. About the year 1720, Harington Gibbs, who had resided many years in Jamaica, contracted acquaintance with the representatives of the families of Beckford, Pennant (afterwards Lord Penrhyn), Morant, and others, returned from thence, and became their agent in Bristol for the sale of sugar. Harington Gibbs was elected a member of the Corporation, August 11, 1720. After his decease Mr. Atkins, who had then lately returned from Jamaica, continued that business, and extended it to a great degree. Mr. Atkins was succeeded by his nephew, John Curtis, who had also resided in Jamaica. Curtis was elected a member of the Corporation in 1749. On his death in 1768, the business was divided between his executors.

About the year 1726, Mr. William Gordon returned from Jamaica, and opened the business which was afterwards carried on by his nephew, Alderman Robert Gordon, who was elected a member of the Corporation in 1756.

About the year 1740, Mr. Mark Davis, after residing many years in Jamaica, returned from thence, and founded the business which was afterwards continued by his son and partner.

About the year 1750, Mr. Henry Bright, who had resided in St. Kitts and Jamaica, returned from the latter and opened the extensive trade which was afterwards continued by his family, one of whom also resided in Jamaica. Mr. Bright became a member of the Corporation in 1753.

About the year 1755, Mr. William Miles returned from Jamaica, after having resided there for many years. He was elected a Common Councillor in 1766. He was the father of P. J. Miles, M.P. for Bristol, 1835, and grandfather of P. W. S. Miles, M.P. for Bristol 1837-52. He died March 12, 1803.

In connection with the trade between Bristol and Barbadoes, Mr. Daniel and his successors went to reside there and opened out a large business; also with Nevis. The extent of the slave traffic may be vaguely realized by a glance at the state of the Island of Antigua, in the year 1774. From a return made in that year, we find that the *white inhabitants of all ages and sexes were 2,500,* and the enslaved Negroes 37,808. Immense supplies of Negroes were needed to carry on the work of the plantations. It has been estimated that out of a total of 60,000 Negroes *taken in one year,* the Bristol vessels were concerned in one-half of this traffic in human flesh.

. . . .

In order to grasp the situation of the political parties in Bristol at this period it is necessary to go back to the first election of Lord Clare as member for the City. Prior to the general election of 1754 the Tories had held the representation of the City for a long time. Mr. (sometimes styled the Hon.) Robert Nugent (afterwards Lord Clare), one of the Lords of the Treasury in the Whig Administration of which the Duke of Newcastle was Prime Minister, was at that period a promising member of the Whig party in the House of Commons. He was elected one of the members for St. Mawes (alias Mawditt) Borough Cornwall, at the general election in 1741, and re-elected at the general election in 1747. The Rev. Josiah Tucker, Dean of Gloucester and Rector of St. Stephen's in Bristol, wrote that St. Mawes was a pocket borough belonging to Mr. Nugent, and that almost every house in the borough was his property. It is clear that prior to the general election of 1754, when he was first elected for Bristol, the Whigs of the City had been in frequent communication with the member for St. Mawes, whom they regarded as a man of more than average ability, and there is very little doubt that he was a man of influence in the House of Commons. When the Bristol Whigs desired to petition Parliament in favour of or against proposals for legislature they sent their petition to the member for St. Mawes. The London agents of the Bristol Whigs frequently applied for and were directed to be guided and governed by his advice. When the general election of 1754 was pending, the Bristol Whigs applied to Mr. Nugent for his consent to champion their cause at the hustings—in other words they wished him to represent them in Parliament. (By the way, it should be mentioned that he was again returned as member for

St. Mawes on the 19th of April, 1754). Their proposal was accompanied with an offer to pay him a large sum of money towards the election expenses, which offer he did not hesitate to reject "with some degree of indignation!" The Bristol Whigs were very unhappy when they found they had offended him, and, as another candidate "equal to him in abilities" could not be found, they had no alternative but to submit to his own terms "*or to continue in subjection to the same party who had* "*so long oppressed them*"; they, therefore, resolved to send a deputation of the principal Merchants to London "to apologize "to him for their former proposal, and to offer him carte-blanche "for the future." His consent was ultimately obtained. An attempt had been previously made to prevent a contest, but it came to nothing. Preserved in the Jefferies' collection of books, MSS., &c., lately purchased by the Corporation, is a sheet of paper containing the names of the representatives of the Union (Whig) Club and the White Lion (Tory) Club who were appointed to negociate.

"Coalition members chosen to promote a general harmony "between the citizens—

" John Clements, Esq., Mayor.	Mr. Jos. Percivall.
" John Towgood, Esq.	Mr. Wm. Barrow.
" Mr. Michael Atkins.	Mr. John Brickdale, junr.
" Morgan Smith, Esq.	Mr. Jos. Lewis.
" Mr. Chas. Devonshire.	Mr. Edwd. Gwatkin.
" Henry Swymmer, Esq.	Jarrit Smith, Esq.
	Mr John Freeman.
" Union Club, 1753.	White Lion Club, 1753."

This paper, having regard to future events in connection with the representation of the City, is somewhat important. After a general election and a bye-election had been fought a compromise or compact was arrived at, which, as will be seen hereafter, had a bearing on the election of 1774.

All negotiations for a settlement on the basis of the allotment of a member to each of the two political parties having failed, the election commenced in Bristol on the 17th of April 1754, and the polling continued until the 30th of April. The candidates were Sir John Philipps, Bart., and Richard Beckford, Esq., a very rich member of an immensely rich and influential family, who was in the West Indies at the time for the Tories ; and Robert Nugent, Esq., was the Whig or Government champion. It is very essential to bear these facts in mind, not only by reason of their having an important bearing on a compact as to the representation of Bristol in Parliament, made by the Tories and the Whigs at a subsequent election, but also because many persons, including the late Lord Brabourne, who wrote about this election, have judged the politics of Nugent from his connection later on with the Tories, or rather with the supporters of the King in his attitude towards the American Colonists, and have erroneously stated that Nugent was the Tory candidate at the Bristol contest in 1754, and that Philipps and Beckford were Whigs. The result of the election was the return of Nugent (a Whig) and Beckford (a Tory). There is reason to believe that this election cost the Whigs not less than £20,000, probably paid to a large extent out of the party chest, notwithstanding the indignation of the worthy Mr. Nugent as to the proposal to pay a certain sum towards his expenses. The Tories also must have spent an enormous sum. Nugent, having been elected for two places, elected to represent Bristol and the seat at St. Mawes was thereupon declared vacant. Beckford died in January, 1756, and an election of a member to fill the vacancy took place in the following March. *The Whigs*, or a considerable section of the party, contrary to something amounting to an unwritten understanding which had been come to between some of the leading Tories and some of the leading Whigs just after the general election of 1754, to the effect that each party should, in future, nominate one candidate only, resolved to fight, and they selected the Hon. John Spencer (afterwards Earl Spencer) to be their candidate against Mr. (afterwards Sir) Jarrit Smith, a local attorney, the Tory candidate. The Tories won. Dean Tucker stated that "*it was* "*well known that Mr. Nugent disapproved and discountenanced*" this contest. Nugent was of opinion that, as the election could only be contested at an enormous expense, and, with a doubtful result, it would be better to enter into a compromise. This election " led to a solemn agreement between the agents of both "parties, that the candidate to be named by one, should be "supported by the other *during three successive Parliaments,* " which compact was universally acquiesced in and acknowledged "by five unanimous elections and re-elections of Mr. Nugent, "named by the Whigs, and by two elections, one of Sir Jarrit "Smith, and the other of Mr. Brickdale, named by the Tories." On the 26th of December, 1759, Nugent was returned unopposed, in pursuance of the compact, *at a bye-election*, which was necessitated by his having accepted an office under the Crown. (He had been appointed to the office of Joint Vice-Treasurer of Ireland.) At the *general election* of 1761 Nugent (Whig) and Smith (Tory) were returned unopposed in accordance with the compact, which, according to a local paper, was said to " have "delivered the city from a very oppressive weight it used to "labour under on such occasions."

[It must not be assumed that the members were returned free of expense. By the custom of Bristol the freemen of Bristol received the "polling money" which at a non-contested election became the subject of agreement between the agents of the parties. It varied from 7s. 6d. to 4s. In addition, the worthy freemen considered their rights infringed if they were not indulged with a procession in which the various trades, accompanied with bands of music, took part, the expenses of which were borne by the candidates. Public-houses were opened in each ward by both parties which were known as "open houses" for the supply of refreshments. Flags, bearing the party colours, were attached to the houses, which at non-contested elections were only "opened" for the day or part of a day; but at a contested election they remained "open houses" as long as the poll continued open.] On the 16th of December 1766, Nugent (now Lord Clare, in the Irish Peerage) was returned unopposed at a bye-election on his acceptance of an office under the crown (the office was that of First Lord of Trade), and at the *general election* in March 1768, he and Matthew Brickdale, *who was nominated by the Tories* in the place of Sir Jarrit Smith, who had retired, *were returned unopposed in pursuance of the compact.* At this election, Mr. Richard Combe, a local Tory, made an attempt to break the compact by offering himself as a candidate, but he retired on the eve of the nomination day, having found that most, if not all. the leaders of the two parties would vote for Nugent and Bricklade. In the Jefferies' collection at the Bristol Museum Library there exists an original letter from Mr. Erle-Drax, M.P., addressed to "Wm. Gore, Esq., at Bourton, near Bristol" (Mr. Gore was an ancestor of the Gore-Langton family), in which a reference is made to the contemplated revolt of the Tories: —

DEAR SIR,

Having heard that two gentlemen have declared themselves candidates for the City of Bristol, asking for single votes, each for himself, I hope you will excuse my earnestness to serve Lord Clare, when I beg the favour of you to continue your kindness to his lordship's interest at Bristol, who means nothing but such a conduct as every man of every party must approve of. Should either of those gentlemen succeed in obtaining many single votes, you must be senceable (*sic*) how detrimental it would be to Lord Clare.

I am, dear sir, your most obedient and obliged humble servant,

London, Feb. 2nd, 1766. THOS. ERLE DRAX.

Drax's interference is explained by the fact that he was brother-in-law to Lord Clare, who had married the widowed Countess of Berkeley, née Drax. In the month of February Combe, who resided in College Green, issued an address and commenced a canvass. Directly Lord Clare arrived from London a coalition committee was formed, and houses were opened for the supply of refreshments in the various wards. Clare and Brickdale were conducted to the hustings by the Mayor, and a considerable number of leading citizens of both sides. The "chairing" procession was a grand one, the bearers of the chairs and the vast concourse of persons who took part in the procession, wearing yellow and blue rosettes to signify the coalition. " Houses were opened for "the reception of the friends of all parties, and, in the evening, "there was a dinner, which was attended by the leading men of "both sides; at which Mr. William Weare presided." Combe was very angry with the citizens, and threatened to leave the city. Lord Clare was re-elected at a bye-election on the 27th of June, 1768, without opposition, on his acceptance of an additional office under the Crown. The office was that of joint Vice-Treasurer of Ireland, which he had previously held. Lord Clare was in high favour with the King. The Election skits of the period contain many hits against him as an office holder, although they are apparently directed in general terms against "place-men and pensioners.") It will be observed that "*the compact as to the representation of the City in Parliament* having been entered into *for three Parliaments*, and two general elections having taken place, viz., 1761 and 1768, it was still binding for one more Parliament, and in the ordinary course of things *it would have bound the leaders of the two political parties to again return Lord Clare and Matthew Brickdale*. Lord Clare had, however, by his own acts, put an end to the compact. He was no longer a Whig; but, on the contrary, was one of the most obsequious supporters of the King's policy towards the American Colonies. As a reward for his apostasy, he was the recipient of many favours at the King's hands; and it may readily be guessed that there had been a growing feeling of discontent among his former supporters in Bristol.

That the King's temper and mode of conduct towards the Colonists should be watched with anxiety by the men of Bristol is not a matter for wonder; the appearance on the political horizon looked as gloomy as it was possible to imagine; the means of existence of the Bristol traders were likely to be cut off, consequently their fears, as is usual with men when they are surrounded by unpleasant forebodings, were probably somewhat magnified. In the year 1769 the symptoms of discontent at the conduct of Lord Clare and Mr. Brickdale, the representatives of the city in Parliament, were publicly shown at a meeting held at the Guildhall, which had been convened by certain members of the Whig party. The prime movers—the initiators of the gathering—were Messrs. Richard Champion and Joseph Harford, two comparatively young Bristol merchants—both of them Quakers—and both interested in the China manufactory then being carried on in Castle Green. As the result of the meeting it was apparent that a considerable number of Bristol men had come to the conclusion that it was necessary to take steps to alter the generally accepted view of the right of a member of Parliament to act and to vote in accordance with his mature judgment, and to substitute a system of representation by which the electors should "have "their opinions represented, not guided, by members of their "choice." [By-the-way it is indeed strange that the irony of fate should decree that later on Edmund Burke, the chosen candidate of the originators of the meeting referred to, in the very first speech delivered by him after his election as M.P. for Bristol should have taken great pains to uphold the right of a member to vote independently of the wishes of his constituents.] A petition, signed by about 1,500 Freeholders and Freemen resident in Bristol, and embodying their views, was forwarded to the city members. No reply was received from Brickdale, and it seems probable that Lord Clare's reply was meant to be a joint one. It is evident, judging from the tone of the reply, and of Lord Clare's subsequent conduct, that he had failed to realize the full extent of the discontent which his votes had caused to a large number of his constituents. Meanwhile Champion and Harford and a few active friends, including Henry Cruger (afterwards M.P. for the city), and Cruger's father-in-law (Samuel Peach), were quietly engaged in undermining the influence of Lord Clare and Brickdale with their constituents.

Richard Champion, whose name will ever live as the manufacturer of the celebrated Bristol china—" the true porcelain," as it was then termed—was born on the 6th November, 1743,—he married Judith Lloyd—his brothers-in-law Caleb and John Lloyd were settled in South Carolina with which province Champion traded, and a ship belonging to him was named the "Lloyd." John Lloyd, one of Champion's brothers-in-law a son of Caleb Lloyd of Bristol, was a member of the Assembly of South Carolina having been elected as the representative of Charlestown (now called Charleston); and on the 19th of August, 1769, he wrote to Champion to the effect that "our importations will be discontinued till the Revenue "and Admiralty Court Acts are absolutely repealed;" in the same letter he gives a curious example of what the Colonists were capable of doing:—" Last week, a member of the Assembly "(*i.e.* the Carolina Assembly) who lived at 100 miles distance, came "to town, dressed in a fustian coat, dimity jacket, thread "stockings, shirts, &c., raised and manufactured on his own "plantation, leather breeches tanned there and made by his own "slaves, and a beaver hat made by his neighbour." The Bristol men were kept au courant with the proceedings of the disaffected Colonists and it is not at all improbable—judging from the frequency of their communications—that they were in a better position than the King and his Ministers for forming a sound judgment as to the effect of the King's policy towards the Colonies. After the 1774 election Richard Champion was Burke's constant and confidential correspondent. Champion was in receipt of the latest and most accurate information as to American affairs, not only from his relatives, the Lloyds, in South Carolina, but from his friend, Robert Morris, of Philadelphia, one of the signers of the Declaration of Independence, who financed the young government all through the war; and the valuable information thus obtained was placed at the service of Edmund Burke, and was added to the amount of knowledge on American affairs possessed by him   John Lloyd of Charlestown turned up at the

1774 election, and recorded his vote as a Freeman of Bristol for Cruger and Burke.

John Lloyd was admitted a Freeman (probably immediately upon his arrival from America), during the progress of the poll and the entry of his admission in the book of Burgesses, (No. 15. p. 134), dated the 12th October 1774, states that he was a son of Caleb Lloyd, deceased; his grandfather, Caleb Lloyd, was admitted a Freeman on the 5th of October, 1700, and his father, described as "Caleb Lloyd, junr., son and apprentice of Caleb Lloyd," was admitted on the 20th Dec., 1732. There are several interesting entries in the books of burgesses relating to this family. The Lloyds and the Champions had been long connected by marriage. In 1731, Sampson Lloyd, whose great grand uncle Thomas Lloyd joined William Penn in the colonisation of Pennsylvania and was Deputy Governor and President of the Colony from 1684 till 1693, married a daughter of Nehemiah Champion, a Bristol merchant. It is easy, therefore, to realize the interest taken by Richard Champion in the affairs of the American Colonists. Joseph Harford was also connected with the Lloyd family by marriage, and "Harford Lloyd," a Quaker, was admitted a Freeman of Bristol on the 12th of November, 1735.

Amongst some beautiful specimens of china manufactured by Champion for Joseph Harford, a superb flower plaque was embellished with a coat of arms showing the alliance of the Harford and Lloyd families—Sable two bends argent; on a canton azure a bend or, impaling, sable a chevron between three fleur-de-lis argent. Crest, out of a coronet issuing fire flames proper, a griffin's head or between two wings azure, fire issuing from the mouth, (vide Owen's "Two centuries of Ceramic Art in Bristol," p. 91).

[Joseph Harford was an active politician. He was an iron merchant, and resided in St. James's Barton. Harford and Champion were two of the original founders of the Bristol Library Society (1772).

Joseph Harford subsequently became connected with the Bristol Corporation; was made a common councillor on the 21st of August, 1779; served the office of Sheriff 1779-80, 1785-6 and 1791-2; was elected Mayor in 1794 but declined to serve; and was made Alderman on the 12th of June 1797. He died October 11th, 1802.]

Having regard to the extent of the Bristol interests involved in the dispute between the Mother Country and her Colonies, it is not surprising that someone thought of Edmund Burke, in connection with the representation of the City in Parliament.

In the following copy of a letter, from the Rev. Dr. Wilson to Edmund Burke, will be found some pertinent allusions to the state of affairs. This letter is very important, because it contains the first recorded mention of Edmund Burke's name in connection with the representation of Bristol in Parliament:—

HOTWELLS,
Bristol, *June 28th, 1774.*

DEAR SIR,

In the course of three months residence at this place, for the benefit of my health, I have had frequent opportunities of conversing with a few friends at Bristol, merchants of fortune and character, and warm well-wishers to the liberties and constitution of this once free nation. I frequently took an opportunity of talking about the next general election, and the necessity of having members of ability and integrity to represent the second City in the Kingdom; and I found a proper juncture *to mention your name* as having so ably stood forth in opposition to many odious measures carried on, *especially the affairs of America*, in the event of which *they are so nearly interested.* And I am desired by two or three, who will keep the secret, to write to you immediately, *under the seal of secrecy, and in great confidence,* to know whether, if they find themselves strong enough, you will be ready to serve them, if they put you up as a Candidate to represent them. Those gentlemen, I apprehend, will furnish you with a proper colleague of their own town, who has a very great influence, and a large family connexion, and a man of spirit and understanding in commercial affairs, and is expected every day to arrive from New York, where he has been to settle a large and outstanding debt, which he has happily succeeded in. The Quebec affair has given an amazing turn within these three weeks to the tame dispositions of the Quakers and Dissenters, who before that time were fast asleep, but this has roused them, which makes it a more favourable juncture to carry our point than it ever was before.

When you have seriously considered this important affair, you will please to communicate your sentiments to me in a letter, to be communicated only to the two or three friends who are in the secret, and it shall be kept private; and, I dare say, *you will depend upon my secrecy, and honour and zeal in this affair.*

> I go from this place to-morrow to Bath, where I shall only stay long enough to receive a letter from you; and then, if it meets with your approbation, I shall step over with it to Bristol, and meet with the friends I have hinted to you, and the result of which you shall immediately know.
>
> I need not, I hope, tell you what a pleasure I shall have in being instrumental in serving my poor distressed country, and a person at the same time, *who stands foremost in the rank of unbiassed patriots.*
>
> I am, Dear Sir,
> your faithful friend and humble servant,
> THOS. WILSON.

There is very little doubt that the Rev. Dr. Wilson, who was a son of the Bishop of Sodor and Man, sometimes met Edmund Burke, who was one of Wilson's old friends, at Bath. The reverend gentleman was well known in Bath, and the gossips of that city told some queer stories of him in relation to Catherine Macaulay, the historian, he having fallen in love with that lady when long past the beauty of her prime. His amorous advances were not reciprocated, and the lady married a young man *about twenty-one years of age.* This divine, who was the Rector of St. Stephen's, Walbrook, London, placed himself in a ridiculous position in connection with his adored Catherine. He placed a white marble statue of her, *within the altar-rails of his church,* in which she was represented in the character of "History" with a pen in her right hand, and with her left arm leaning on some volumes of her historical work, and when, in the latter end of 1778, his "goddess," then of the ripe age of 47, espoused " a stout, brawny Scotchman " (the brother of a celebrated quack, Dr. Graham), the statue was quickly removed, and the parishioners of St. Stephen's, Walbrook, were never again allowed the privilege of worshipping at the shrine erected for their special benefit by their Rector. As early as 1753 Burke had been a visitor to the City of Bath, when he made the acquaintance and the life-long friendship of Alderman Thomas Atwood, who was Mayor there in 1752-3; these friendly relations were maintained with Atwood's son, Thomas, who was Mayor in 1760, and again in 1769. The elder Atwood had realised a fortune in business and in speculations, and, after his death, his son built himself a residence on a lovely natural terraced site at Turley, near Bradford-on-Avon, and it was at this beautiful retreat that Burke frequently visited his friend.

In all probability Burke had visited Bath before 1753, for we find that he was at Bristol with a view to the restoration of his health in 1751, and again in 1752, and that he derived great benefit from his visits. He probably stayed at the Hotwells, then a very fashionable resort, and took the waters, which at that period were considered beneficial for numerous complaints.

In the year 1745 Dr. George Randolph had written on the medicinal virtues of the Bristol Hotwell water in a little work, which he dedicated to Dr. Wilmot, the King's Physician. The publication had materially assisted in adding to the reputation of the waters. In 1756 Burke again visited Bristol and Bath, these places at that period being frequented in common by invalids. It was a matter of ordinary occurrence for persons to stay at one of the two places for a short period in order to have the benefit of the waters and then to proceed to the other by way of change. In Dr. Wilson's letters we find him wandering between these two fashionable health-resorts.

It was in this year (1756) that Burke, when at Bath, consulted Dr. Christopher Nugent (who resided at Circus House) as to his health, and on this occasion he met Miss Nugent, to whom he was married the following year. The marriage was a happy one. Burke always spoke and wrote of his wife with the most tender love and respect. Dr. Nugent, who was a man of learning and great professional reputation, removed to London, and was elected a member of the famous Gerrard-Street Club. Frequent mention is made of him in connection with Burke, Johnson, Goldsmith, Bennett Langton, Beauclerc, &c.

Burke, no doubt, was endeared to Bath, not only by reason of the great benefit he had derived from the thermal Waters, but also by the personal associations connected with the city. After the famous Bristol election of 1774, Burke, on his way home, visited his old friend Atwood at his residence at Turley.

Dr. Wilson's mention of the expected arrival from New York of a proposed "colleague" had reference to Mr. Henry Cruger, whose name had been previously whispered as a probable candidate.

On Sunday, the 3rd of July, 1774, Mr. Cruger arrived in Bristol from New York, after an absence of fourteen months in America. [There is very little doubt that Mr. Cruger, with a prescience of what might at any time happen, had deemed it advisable to visit America with a view to adjust certain business transactions of considerable importance in which he was interested.]

The Bristol Gazette. of Wednesday the 6th of July, contained a paragraph which put it beyond doubt that Cruger's friends were determined to nominate him at the next general election.

On Saturday, the 9th of July, 1774, the Crugerites had recourse to an electioneering dodge in order to throw discredit on Brickdale, in a letter addressed as follows :—

> To the Printer of *Felix Farley's Journal.*
>
> As we are now on the eve of a General Election, and as it is the inclination of many in this city to change one of our late members, it is earnestly wished that the gentlemen who are concerned in this business, will pay the most serious attention to the peace and welfare of the city of Bristol. Such a conduct is more especially necessary at this time. The great stagnation of trade, and multiplied distress of the lower class of citizens, must make every lover of his country dread the return of those fatal disturbances and commotions, which we experienced upon a former occasion, and which were productive of such feuds and animosities, as will ever be destructive of the good order of society, and the well-being of a city dependent upon trade and commerce. We cannot, however, forbear expressing our warmest wishes that such members may be returned as shall contribute to the commercial interests and ably support the dignity of this great city. The many important services done by Lord Clare to the city in general, and to a great abundance of individuals amongst us, have made so deep an impression, that every grateful heart must unite in supporting so respectable a representative. Upon this occasion we cannot but congratulate our fellow citizens on the late arrival of a gentleman from America, whose liberality of sentiment, extensive connections in trade, and knowledge of the commercial interests of the city, flatter our most sanguine expectations. It has, therefore, been with the utmost pleasure that we hear it is intended to nominate Henry Cruger, Esq., as one of our candidates.
>
> That he may be well supported, and that the toast which now runs through the city of *Clare* and *Cruger* may be realised, is the united wish of
>
> THOUSANDS.

The *Bristol Journal*, of Saturday, the 9th of July, contained the following anonymous contribution :—

> To the Printer.
>
> As the paragraph in W. Pine's paper (the *Gazette*) of Wednesday last, seems calculated to inflame the city, I beg you will insert the following card, which will oblige many of your constant readers :—
>
> A CARD.
>
> A very great number of the principal traders of the city, present their compliments to the friends of Henry Cruger, Esq. (lately arrived from a tour through the American Colonies), and beg leave to assure them, that it is far from being the general wish that he may be one of our representatives in the next Parliament—being as yet well satisfied with our present members—and having felt too severely the ill effects of contested elections, we esteem the peace of the city too much to countenance a clamour as ridiculous as it is ill-founded.

This was followed by a reply, in which it was asked—" What " kind of traders those are, who have the assurance to declare " that we are well satisfied with our present members ? "

The Rev. Dr. Wilson, in another letter to Burke, dated " Bath, " July 11, 1774," informed him that Mr Cruger, who had just arrived from New York, was " intended as a candidate at " the ensuing election, and supported by the gentlemen who " desired me to write you, *I make no question of his carrying* " *it*. He called upon me last night on his way to London, and I " have asked him to wait upon you, and you may confide in his " secrecy, honour, and integrity, and he has a regard for you, as a " true friend of liberty," &c.

[NOTE.—The letters for Burke were official communications to him as Agent for the State of New York.]

Cruger waited upon Burke at Beaconsfield, and it is believed that the latter was led to believe that he would receive assistance from Cruger in the event of his deciding to come forward as a candidate ; and there is very little doubt that Cruger approved of the suggestion that Burke should become a candidate. Later on, however, it will be seen that Cruger's friends and supporters did not, at first, approve of the selection of Burke as the second candidate.

On the 29th of July, 1774, a letter was published with the signature, " A plain common tradesman," in which the writer described a conversation, real or imaginary, between two gentlemen, as to the coming election. According to the writer he was passing the Exchange and overheard one of the two say, " Possibly, in the capacity of merchant, Mr. Cruger might be " serviceable to the City, but (the writer goes on to say) the " speaker added, *with an impertinence peculiar to his character,* " but my connections are with the gentlemen, and we are " determined to counteract and oppose the designs of the " middling class of people and the vagabond tradesmen. With " such epithets (continues the writer) as ' vagabond tradesmen,' " ' scum of the earth,' ' low mechanics,' and a variety of others " equally respectable, the Freemen of the City must expect to be " honoured by *such* gentlemen." It is quite possible that some conversation of the kind had been used by Brickdale or one of his friends, and had been made the subject of local gossip, and probably circulated in an exaggerated form, because this publication was followed by another pointing out the absurdity of persons who receive their income from trade or as the result of trading trying to make their neighbours believe that they are other than traders. [If rumours are correct there are many specimens of this contemptible class still to be found.] " In this " town (the writer said) the distinction of *gentlemen* in opposition " to *tradesmen* is absurd. There are some few who through a " concurrence of fortunate events have acquired a considerable " share of riches ; forgetting what they once were, and, swelling " with a vain consequence, they assume the name without " possessing one essential qualification of gentlemen. Their " circle is happily but small, and they are well known ; it is " such men, and such men only, who bestow so plenteously their " liberal epithets on the more industrious and laborious part of " the community."

The first intimation of the impending dissolution was announced in an address issued by Lord Clare.

[COPY ADDRESS.]

To the Gentlemen, Clergy, Freeholders and Freemen of the
City of Bristol.

GENTLEMEN,
It is probable that the present Parliament will soon be dissolved; and, as I have had the honor to be one of your representatives in three successive Parliaments, the continuance of that honor is the highest and dearest object of my ambition.

I, therefore, earnestly intreat the favor of your votes and interest at the approaching election, and am,
Gentlemen,
Your most faithful friend and obliged, humble servant,
CRAGGS CLARE.

Truro, Sept. 26th, 1774.

On the 30th of September, 1774, the King dissolved Parliament, and the whole kingdom was suddenly aroused by the sounds of party strife; special messengers on horseback and in chaises were quickly in motion, and soon the news of the dissolution was spread from one end of the kingdom to the other. It is related that in the course of one day no less than sixty or seventy messengers passed through a particular turnpike.

The following addresses were issued by Matthew Brickdale and Henry Cruger, on the 30th of September, before the news of the actual dissolution had reached Bristol:—

To the Gentlemen, Clergy, Freeholders and Freemen of the
City of Bristol.

GENTLEMEN AND FELLOW CITIZENS,
Conscious that I have in no instance swerved from my duty and attachment to you and the public; and animated with every sense of gratitude for the honour you so unanimously conferred on me at the last General Election of members to represent this, my native City, in Parliament, and I again presume, from the great and generous encouragement I have received, to offer myself a Candidate for the same honourable station in the ensuing one, and to solicit the favour of your votes and interest. Should your kind suffrages replace me in your service, I shall continue to act with the same zeal, honesty and independence, as have hitherto regulated my conduct.

I am, with unfeigned esteem and respect,
Gentlemen,
Your most faithful and devoted, humble servant,
MATTHEW BRICKDALE.

Clifton, Sept. 30th, 1774.

To the Gentlemen, Clergy, Freeholders, and Freemen of the
City of Bristol.

GENTLEMEN AND FELLOW CITIZENS,
Various reports having been circulated respecting my intention to stand a Candidate for the high honor of representing this City in

Parliament; and as some of these reports have been disingenuously promoted with an evident view to prejudice me in your opinion, I think it incumbent on me to assure you that the many promises of assistance and support which have been made to me for several years past, and the numerous and respectable applications of my friends within these last two or three months, have determined me to offer you my service; and *should I be honored with a nomination at a General Meeting*, I will most certainly stand a Poll to the last man.

I am conscious how unequal my abilities are to so distinguished a station; but I will venture to hope, that by spirit and assiduity, fidelity and integrity, I shall render myself not altogether unworthy of your confidence and approbation—the first object of my ambition, and the highest reward to which I aspire.

I am, with great respect,
Gentlemen,
Your faithful and obedient servant,

September 30, 1774.　　　　　　　　　　　　　　HENRY CRUGER.

The Bristol Journal of Saturday, the 1st of October, contains the following paragraph:—

> We take this early opportunity to acquaint our readers, that by an express arrived in this city *yesterday*, we are credibly informed that His Majesty in Council *has dissolved the Parliament*, and that *writs are issued* for returning a new Parliament within forty days.

Felix Farley's Journal of the same date, announced that:—

> A Member of Parliament who left London yesterday morning at 1 o'clock, and arrived here yesterday afternoon, positively asserts that the Parliament was to be dissolved that day, and that he received his intelligence from the most undoubted authority—yet the London papers of Thursday morning are quite silent on the matter, not giving even the least hint of the kind.

On the same day Mr. Cruger issued another address to the Electors:—

> To the Gentlemen, Clergy, Freeholders and Freemen of the City of Bristol.
>
> GENTLEMEN AND FELLOW CITIZENS,
>
> When I published my address to you yesterday, I had no idea of so sudden a dissolution of the Parliament. I am now, therefore, under the necessity of soliciting your suffrages in this abrupt manner.
>
> The early day which I presume will be fixed for the Election, will, I fear, put it out of my power to be as general in my personal application as I wished and intended. Should I be deprived of this pleasure, the peculiar circumstances of the present period, will, I hope, be a sufficient apology. Strongly attached to the principles of our glorious constitution, if I have the honour to be returned one of your representatives, it shall be my invariable study to support and defend our civil and religious rights, to promote your particular interests, to extend the commerce of this great city, with which I am so essentially connected, and by a manly and independent conduct, to approve myself on all occasions.
>
> Gentlemen,
Your faithful and obedient servant,

Oct. 1, 1774.　　　　　　　　　　　　　　　　HENRY CRUGER.

Some of the country news-writers were very indignant that the date of the dissolution had not been made known to them beforehand; and there were complaints in the newspapers of the want of courtesy in not giving them any information before it reached the general public. By virtue of the King's proclamation, the writs for the election were to bear teste on Saturday, the 1st of October: the elections were to take place within forty days, and the writs were to be returnable on Tuesday, the 29th of November following.

On Tuesday, the 4th of October, the friends of Mr. Brickdale were summoned to meet at 1 p.m., at the Tailors' Hall, Broad Street. The notices convening the meeting were sent out early in the morning. It was an open secret that the Whigs were about to hold a meeting to select a candidate or candidates. Henry Cruger's name was in everybodys mouth, and as it was sometimes *coupled with that of Burke*, nobody seemed to know exactly what was going to happen.. It was only certain that Cruger was not only willing but desirous to become a candidate.

You must sometimes go from home to hear the news, and the following extract from a letter, sent by a Bristol correspondent to a London Journal, published this day (Tuesday, the 4th of October) contained some important information:—" We are in a " state of confusion and uproar, the Patriots, with the Almighty " Mob, are determined to turn out the old members. They have " sent to Mr. Burke to beg he will come down and join Mr. " Cruger. However the friends of the present members are in " good spirits ; they offer bets of £500 that Mr. Cruger does not " come in."

Tne friends of Lord Clare held a meeting at the Merchants' Hall, and as his Lordship was absent, it was decided that *an address to the electors* should be published. There is very little doubt that Lord Clare had been kept uninformed of the state of discontent which his conduct had occasioned to the Citizens, and that it was difficult to make him understand the exact position of affairs.

The following brief report of the meeting of Lord Clare's supporters was printed :—

Bristol. *October 4, 1774.*

At a very numerous and most respectable meeting of Magistrates, Clergy, Merchants, principal traders, Freeholders and Freemen of the City of Bristol, held this day at the Merchants' Hall—It was unanimously agreed and resolved upon to support the interest of the Right Hon. Lord Viscount Clare at the approaching election of members to represent this City in the ensuing Parliament.

[LORD CLARE'S ADDRESS.]

To the Gentlemen, Clergy, Freeholders, and Freemen of the City of Bristol.

GENTLEMEN,

I throw myself upon that favour and indulgence with which you have long and often honoured me, to excuse my late appearance amongst you. I have been detained by unavoidable accidents ; and upon my arrival this day, I was too much fatigued to seize the first opportunity of returning you in person my grateful thanks for the encouragement and support with which you honoured me in my absence, and to entreat a further continuance of them.

I shall endeavour to-morrow, at the Exchange, to acquit myself of this duty in the best manner that the present state of my health and the shortness of the time allow to.

Gentlemen,
Your ever faithful and affectionate Servant,
CRAGGS CLARE.

Bristol, Wednesday, *October 5, 1774.*

On Wednesday the fifth of October, " a general meeting of the citizens," [it was a meeting of the Whig party,] was held at the Assembly Room in Prince Street for the purpose of considering the representation of the City in Parliament. Mr. Samuel Peach presided, and on the nomination of Mr. Thomas Lediard, seconded by Mr. John Wallis, Mr. Henry Cruger was adopted as a candidate without a dissenting voice. Mr. Cruger was in the building and was waiting to play his part in the little comedy that was then being acted. At the proper moment he was brought into the room and placed upon a table and this is what he said to the good people who had assembled to hear him:—

GENTLEMEN AND FELLOW CITIZENS,

With much deference and respect I presume to offer myself a candidate for this City, at the ensuing election. The countenance and support I have so universally met with, encourages me to hope the address I have now the honour of making, will not be unfavourably received. The nature and dignity of the trust I am now soliciting strikes me very forcibly. The only merit I claim, gentlemen, is a consciousness that I am a friend to trade and the constitutional liberties of this country. With these principles I now offer my services to you, they are too firmly rooted in my heart for time, or circumstances ever to alter.

Honor'd as I am with your support, it will be my uniform ambition to merit the continuance of your approbation. No station, no private interest shall make me ever forget the duties I owe to the Citizens of Bristol.

The candidate having got off the table, Mr. Joseph Harford at once got on it, and begged leave to propose Edmund Burke, Esq., as the second candidate, and the proposal was seconded by Mr. Richard Champion.

Cries of "Cruger only," rent the air, and Mr. Cruger was at last persuaded that it would be better "to paddle his own canoe," so he declared that he would stand alone.

The proposal to nominate Mr. Burke was then withdrawn. Another scene in this election comedy had been arranged to be acted. The candidate "was conducted through Queen Square, "along the Back, and up High Street, to the Council House, "where Mr. Peach introduced him to the Mayor and Aldermen, "and informed them that at a *very* numerous and respectable "meeting at the Assembly Room, Mr. Cruger had been "unanimously nominated. They then proceeded to the "Exchange, attended by a prodigious concourse of the Electors, "where Mr. Cruger delivered an address nearly of the import "with that he spoke at the Assembly Room. After which he "was conducted back to the Assembly Coffee Room, and the "people retired."

The provincial correspondent of the *London Chronicle*, sent an account of the proceedings to that influential journal, and he stated that the meeting had "inspired the whole city with a "general joy." This journal also contained an announcement that, "at a meeting of the Freeholders and Freemen of Bristol "residing in London, at the Swan-with-Two-Necks, in Carter "Lane, Doctors' Commons, it was unanimously agreed to support "Henry Cruger, Esq., a very eminent merchant of that city, who "offers himself as a candidate to serve them in Parliament."

The Swan-with-Two-Necks was one of the houses patronised by the agents of the Bristol Whigs, and it was there and at another public-house, the Queens, in Newgate-Street, that they made arrangements for despatching the out-voters to Bristol.

On the same day the following address was issued by Mr. Cruger :—

> To the Gentlemen, Clergy, Freeholders and Freemen of the City of Bristol.
>
> GENTLEMEN,
> I cannot sufficiently express my obligations for your zealous and unanimous support of my nomination this day at a General Meeting, at the Assembly Room. Permit me to intreat the continuance of your countenance and support, as well as the favour of your votes on the day of election; and believe me always to be, with the sincerest gratitude and regard,
> Gentlemen,
> Your most obedient, humble servant,
>
> HENRY CRUGER.
>
> Park Street, Wednesday, 3 o'clock.

Messrs. Champion and Harford, or one of them, had previously communicated with Edmund Burke, to whom a special messenger had been despatched with a letter, which brought him to Bath, and it had been arranged that he should stay there until the result of the meeting was known. It should seem from this that Messrs. Harford and Champion had made sure that the meeting would accept the joint nomination, and that Burke would be selected. Immediately after the meeting Messrs. Champion and Harford went over to Bath, and announced the result to Burke, who was doubtless very much disappointed, as he was anxious to represent Bristol, which, at that time, was in importance second only to London. A seat had been found for him by Lord Rockingham, who had offered to bring him into Parliament as one of the members for Malton, in Yorkshire, a pocket borough under the control of his Lordship.

The two following broadsides were issued by Mr. Cruger :—

> To the Gentlemen, Clergy, Freeholders and Freemen of the City of Bristol.
>
> GENTLEMEN,
> Should I be so happy as to be chosen one of your representatives in the ensuing Parliament, I hereby declare that I will, on all occasions, vote for shortening the duration of Parliament, *and limiting the number of placemen and pensioners* in the House of Commons.
> I am, Gentlemen,
> Your most obedient, humble servant,
> HENRY CRUGER.
>
> Park Street, Oct. 7th.

> Bristol, October 7th, 1774.
> Mr. Cruger will esteem himself under additional obligations to his friends who have votes, and also to his well-wishers, who have none, to use every effort in their power to preserve the peace of the City by all means; thereby to support their own dignity and the freedom of election.

On Friday the 7th October the election commenced, when Lord Clare and Mr. Matthew Brickdale were put in nomination by the Tories, and Mr. Henry Cruger by the Whigs. Prior to this, both sides had been working day and night in tracing out men who were entitled to be made freemen by virtue of their having served their apprenticeships to freemen, or were the sons of freemen, or had married the daughters or the widows of freemen. From the date of the issue of the writ (the 1st of October) to the date of the nomination, (the 7th of October) more than 1100 freemen were admitted for the express purpose of voting, and during the progress of the poll over 900 additional men were admitted; in fact, altogether about 2080 new votes were created.

[Some details will be met with later on as to the admission of freemen prior to the Reform Act]. At no previous election had there been so much activity and determination shown. There existed scarcely any unanimity between the friends of the two Tories. It is almost certain that Brickdale's agents were employed to ferret out the new voters in the interest of their employer, and without any regard to the interest of Lord Clare. Each of the two Tory candidates had a separate committee and a separate meeting place. Brickdale's friends were certainly very active. The adherents of Lord Clare were supine. There had arisen in the minds of some of Brickdale's friends a vague dread that there was a possibility that the Whigs had determined to carry Cruger, and therefore they appeared lukewarm with regard to the candidature of Lord Clare. His lordship certainly had a number of supporters, but by far the larger number might be described as political rather than personal friends; on the other hand Brickdale was an old resident, a member of the Corporation, and had a number of relatives and personal friends who were anxious on personal grounds that he should retain his seat. Brickdale's friends doubtless argued amongst themselves that as it was almost certain that one or other of the Tories would be outvoted, it was their duty to stand by their friend and fellow citizen. There are reasons for believing that a compromise was suggested on the basis that Lord Clare should nominate Mr. Brickdale for St. Mawes, and that a coalition should be formed with the Crugerites, but Lord Clare was in doubt (and properly so) as to whether it was possible to carry out the arrangement which, in the event of a second Whig candidate being brought forward, might have resulted in his being left without a seat in Parliament.

The poll began at 2 o'clock, and ended at 3. It became apparent to Lord Clare that the relationship between himself and the Brickdale party was not of a very cordial nature. By arrangement the poll closed early: the numbers recorded were:—For Lord Clare, 12; for Cruger, 11; and for Brickdale, 10. One of the voters for Brickdale, being a newly made freeman, was successfully objected to on the ground that he was not of age. Brickdale's friends were working hard for him, and a local newspaper reports that they continued firm and sanguine in his interest, "which animates " him to proceed to the poll with spirit and resolution, though the " opposition seems so formidable." Lord Clare soon came to the conclusion that he would be sacrificed after nearly twenty years' service, and he retired in other than a pleasant mood to Bath, having given an intimation that he declined the contest. It appears from a paragraph in the *London Chronicle* that his Lordship had made sure of his election—that he had been too sure—that his friends had been " supine and negligent, and when " the day of election came, seemed to be in confusion. . , . " that if he came in *it must be by Mr. Cruger's friends giving* " *him the preference.* This sensibly hurt his Lordship, who " expected to be unanimously chosen, and he declared he would " not come in under the wings of Mr. Cruger." Dean Tucker wrote that " Lord Clare found out that he was considered by " many of his old friends only as their second object."

The news of Lord Clare's resignation came to the knowledge of Messrs. Champion and Harford very late in the evening (Friday.) A meeting of some of Burke's supporters was immediately held, and after a long discussion it was resolved to do nothing until the views of Mr. Peach (Mr. Cruger's father-in-law) had been ascertained. Thereupon it was decided to leave Messrs. Champion and Harford to interview him, and as the matter was so urgent they went at night to Mr. Peach's house at Tockington, near Almondsbury, and on their arrival thither very early the next morning (Saturday), roused him from sleep. Mr. Peach gave a favourable consideration to the proposal, and promised to give his second vote to Burke. The deputation then returned to Bristol.

It was pretty generally known that Lord Clare had resigned, and when the Sheriffs opened the poll in the morning— at nine o'clock—his resignation was officially declared. Messrs. Champion, Harford and others now saw that there was an opportunity to nominate Edmund Burke. It would not mean the breaking of any compact; and it was soon ascertained that the Crugerites would afford help, subject nevertheless to the condition that their own candidate's success would not be imperilled. Mr. Cruger refused to act jointly with the Burke party, but it was well known that he sympathized with the proposal, and a large number of his friends had agreed to give their second vote to Burke. But as the Crugerites refused to join with the committee formed for the purpose of securing

Burke's election, it became apparent that the Whigs would have to encounter two sets of election expenses. It was a great undertaking for Burke's friends, but they determined to run all risks. A large number of the supporters of Edmund Burke assembled at the hustings. He was duly proposed by Richard Champion. The Brickdale party objected to the nomination on the ground that it was illegal to nominate a candidate after the poll had begun, and it was claimed on behalf of Brickdale that as Lord Clare had resigned the poll had closed. On behalf of Mr. Brickdale, Messrs. Baker and Lippincott raised a protest, and they expressed a desire to see Burke, and to ascertain his qualification. But these objectors could not or would not see the absurdity of their position. On Saturday morning when the poll opened, and Lord Clare's resignation was announced, the figures stood:—For Lord Clare, 12; for Cruger, 11; and for Brickdale, 10; therefore, if the poll was finished, Lord Clare and Cruger had been returned. The friends of Mr. Burke intimated that they had taken legal advice, and that, in the circumstances, the nomination was good. A number of voters, amongst whom were Joseph Harford, John Champion, and William Franks (the last named was connected with the china manufactory in Castle Green), *tendered their votes for Burke*, but the Sheriffs intimated, at the close of a very lengthy discussion by the legal representatives of the respective candidates, that they would adjourn the poll until Monday morning, and that in the meantime they would obtain the best legal advice. The polling was practically suspended owing to the length of the discussion. Brickdale's friends insisted on giving a sufficient number of votes to place him in a majority, and Cruger's friends were allowed to poll a few votes. At the close of the day, the numbers stood thus:—Brickdale, 25; Cruger, 16: and Lord Clare, 12. After the tendering of the votes for Burke, it was agreed that the subsequent proceedings were not in any way to prejudice his position. It was understood that the Sheriffs would take the advice of Mr. John Dunning, M.P.,

Barrister, and Recorder of Bristol, and the Town Clerk (Sir Abraham Isaac Elton, Bart.) The poll was then adjourned until Monday morning.

The following addresses were issued this day, without signatures, but dated Bristol, October 8, 1774 :—

(FIRST ADDRESS.)

A poll has been this morning demanded in favour of Edmund Burke and Henry Cruger, Esqrs., to represent this city. The Sheriffs, my countrymen, have refused to take your voices. The present instant, big with importance, strongly demands us to assert our right in the Freedom of Election, thus flagrantly violated.

(SECOND ADDRESS.)

Lord Clare having declined the poll, your votes and interest are requested for Edmund Burke, Esq., as one of our representatives in the ensuing Parliament.

His distinguished abilities, well-known integrity, and steadfast adherence to the interest of the Constitution, during a series of years in Parliament, are sufficient to recommend him to the regard of every friend to civil and religious liberty.

(THIRD ADDRESS.)

As a report has been propagated that Mr. Burke cannot legally stand the poll on account of his not having been nominated at its commencement; his friends assure the public that they are furnished with sufficient precedents to prove the legality of the Measure; *and that he will be at the Poll on Monday*, to assert the just rights of the Freemen to give their votes for the object of their choice, notwithstanding a treacherous combination to deprive them of their Birth-right, and to transfer the representation of this opulent city as a private bargain.

[NOTE.—The deputation had started for London, and it was evidently believed that he would return with them in time to be present at the opening of the Poll on Monday.]

These addresses were followed by two broadsides respectively signed, " A Freeholder," and " Senex."

To the Friends of Mr. Cruger, and to every Independent Elector of the City of Bristol.

GENTLEMEN,

As Mr. Burke is now a candidate for this City, I would recommend to you a retrospective view of the prevailing considerations that led you to support Mr. Cruger; and see whether they are not of equal weight, when applied to Mr. Burke.

From the almost universal neglect of your late members both of the cause of their country, and of your own *instructions* and applications unto them, you were induced to look out for others, whom you had reason to believe would not betray the great trust you might commit unto them; and Mr. Cruger offering himself, and *promising* to serve you in an *obedient* manner, gained your confidence and support. I have great reason to believe the sincerity of his pretensions, and that he will serve you to the utmost of his power. And I have equal reason to believe *that Mr. Burke will do the same.* He is a gentleman of tried constitutional principles; he has supported the cause of his country many years in Parliament; and his character and abilities are known throughout the nation.

Therefore, my fellow Citizens, I call upon you at this important juncture, to be unanimous, for those two gentlemen who will support your rights and liberties—do all in their power to remove the present load of grievances you labour under—obediently and faithfully attend to your *instructions**—and execute them in the best manner they are capable of doing. And as to their capacity they have a prior claim to your suffrages; their integrity and upright pretensions cannot be doubted; and would you wish to be faithfully and honourably represented, make *Cruger* and *Burke* the men of your choice.

A FREEHOLDER.

To the Gentlemen, Clergy, &c.

GENTLEMEN,

The noble principle of preserving the peace and harmony of this City which has induced Lord Clare to resign, should now clearly point out to you the line of your conduct; and the people, who continue to disturb the tranquility of the City, will now appear in their proper colours. Will nothing but popular clamour and continued contest please? As you have thus most ungratefully abandoned and drove away one of your members, who has unceasingly advanced your interests as a commercial City; and been always ready to serve individuals,—cease to pursue with unremitting rancour the other, who has never deserved it at your hands—whose conduct in Parliament has been irreproachable—who has most diligently attended his duty there,—and whose independency and honest principles (for which he will be supported to the last man) you may certainly rely on for his future conduct.

A superior fortune in these corrupt times is a necessary qualification, and one chief security to you for the independency of a member in Parliament, considering the high bribes and offices of profit a Minister has in his power to bestow, to seduce the needy member, *and even to strike the Orator dumb.* Whether your new expected Candidate is so qualified, I shall leave to your own cool enquiry and determination.

SENEX.

Bristol, Oct. 8, 1774.

[COPY REPLY TO SENEX.]

† To the old woman, who, last Saturday night, supported herself on her pillow, and with much fatigue and vexation signed her proper name Senex.

Madam,—You will doubtless think it a piece of impertinence, if not cruelty that I, who am a young fellow in active life, should dare approach you in so rude a manner as to disturb your repose, by a reply to your peaceful and harmonious address to my fellow citizens, but as the ladies, particularly the writing one, are delighted when they find themselves taken notice of by the men, I still flatter myself with the hopes of a pardon, though perhaps my honest roughness may put you to more pain, I sincerely pity the infirmities of *old age*, and am certain to be *bedridden* must be a most pitiable condition.—Pray, madam, what is your disorder?

---

* A misrepresentation so far as it purports to refer to Edmund Burke.
† Some little time elapsed between the dates of the correspondence or publications which followed the publication signed "Senex," but it has been considered advisable to here insert the reply, counter-reply, &c.

If I judge right, it must be somewhat of a nervous hysteric, or splenetic kind; and, if so, the loss of your *dear fugitive Lord* must be a most afflictive circumstance; this must likewise be heightened by the chagrining sound of *Cruger and Burke for ever!* continually repeated under your windows, by the boys in the street.

Fie upon them,—little varlets! they deserve to be well slashed for disturbing the peace of the City.—But what I most fear is, that your grief has somewhat impaired your intellect. How!—I beg pardon, Madam, I thought not to offend. But really, upon my attending to some passages in your address, I apprehend the proper meaning of various words is totally reversed, and that you often mistake one word for another.

You set out with observing the noble principle that induced Lord Clare to resign; which you say was that of preserving the peace and harmony of the City. Not to mention any doubt whether Lord Clare has, or ever had any truly noble principles; I shall say with some degree of confidence, that preserving the peace of the City was the last motive in his lordship's thoughts if it at all occurred to him. No, my good dame, the true reason was, to shun the dishonour of which he saw immediately impending over his devoted head, to avoid the mortification of being rejected by an infinite number of free and unanimous voices. Had peace been his motive, he would have thrown in the Olive branch twenty four hours sooner, but his not totally declining a contest, induced him and his party, to think they might at least secure the interest of his colleague. This was thought a most curious and effectual—an excellent piece of jockeyship—*somewhat similar to an instantaneous dissolution of Parliament.* But my fellow citizens may be assured that their rights in the freedom of election, shall not at this time be violated.

I need not, Madam, repeat to you the motives which have induced those who once gave his lordship their suffrages, now to withhold them, and, as you term it, abandon him; I dare say your attendants have already made you acquainted with them, as they are very notoriously known; be assured, however, that his lordship errs, in imputing it to the supine inactivity of some, or the infatuated conduct of others. Depend upon it the Citizens of Bristol, whatever they formerly may have done, will not again repose their confidence, their liberties and property *with a man whom experience has taught them they ought not to trust.* The general *cool reception,* together with the animated but decent reprehensions he has now met with from the most sensible and discerning part of his constituents, are likely, indeed, to be for ever remembered by his Lordship, but will work no change in him. No,—it is now too late in the evening for Lord Clare to think of a revolution in principle—early initiated in that religion, and in those sentiments so favourable to despotism, it is no wonder if his Lordship should carry with him through life, the rooted poison of our glorious Constitution.

So much for Lord Clare. He is gone (may peace be with him, though I much doubt it), and I think I may congratulate my fellow citizens that we are once well rid of him.

Now for a smack at *my little Matty,**—I know, Madam, he is your favourite. I could,--yes, I could make him feel the lash,—but fear not, Madam, -I intend him no harm. Though he has served an apprenticeship, Matty is not yet master of his trade. Dubious and timid, he seems not yet to have formed his plan of political conduct. His judgment, and principles, are still in embryo. Neither a true patriot, nor a complete courtier. Neither a man of spirit, nor a dastard. Possessed not of sufficient fortitude boldly to oppose the torrent of venality, nor daring to accept a bribe to betray his trust, his virtue seems lost in mediocrity; and the most conspicuous part of his merit as a statesman, appears to be a distrust of his own abilities.—Yes, Matty, indeed, has one sneaking virtue—he is an economist, and governs well his own

* Matthew Brickdale.

household. One virtue, did I say? He has many; to speak the general dictates of my heart, I sincerely believe Mr. Brickdale to be a good and honest man, benevolent, inoffensive, a good citizen, a good subject, and, in short, a gentleman. But I really think his virtues would appear much more brilliant *in the character of a private gentleman*, than a member of the British Senate.

Is it possible, then, that we can pursue such a man, with "uncommon rancour?" Forbid it, heaven! Why, Madam, what do you make of us? I fear you have lately looked upon the *black part* of humanity—but old folks are often cross and ill-natured, and think all the world like themselves. Pardon me—I mean not to offend.

Though I cannot agree with you that Mr. Brickdale's conduct in Parliament has been irreproachable, yet I believe he has few enemies, and many well wishers; and out of the many thousands, whose reason alone would induce them to vote against a member of Parliament, I don't believe there are ten whose rancorous hearts would injure the man. As for myself, I own I don't intend to give him my vote (though some connections with his family, and even interest would urge me to it), but, perhaps, no one is a more sincere well wisher of his happiness. I love Mr. Brickdale—but I love my country better.

Mr. Cruger is now a popular man—I shall vote for him, not because he is so, but because I think his being one of our representatives will be of superior service, not only to the city but to the State. I have not the least doubt, but that, before seven years are past, we shall all have reason to acknowledge him a shining ornament to both. The same I say of Mr. Burke;—this gentleman, indeed, is already universally acknowledged to be so; his abilities as a commoner, his integrity, his general rectitude of conduct, are not only well known, but shine with a distinguished lustre.

Reason now, "will clearly point out to us the line " of our conduct," and a dispassionate person would scarcely believe there could be a single objection against these men, who we have cause to think are not only sincere but zealous lovers of the Constitution of our country.

To be serious (for I find, in spite of a ludicrous beginning, I cannot help growing serious), whoever has made himself in any way acquainted with the nature of the British Government, well knows that this cannot subsist one moment after the destruction of public liberty; whoever freely and candidly reviews the late conduct of the Ministry, and considers what illegal and contemptible measures and artifices have from time to time been made use of, in order to obtain a balance of power in favour of the Crown, must unavoidably be alarmed at the encroachments continually advancing on the liberty and power of the people; and whoever compares the principles of our Constitution, as established at the Revolution, with the conduct of the Ministry, will easily observe on which side the scale is ready to preponderate. Whenever this falls—the crush will be very great indeed!

If facts are thus, it follows, that the primary motive which ought to actuate the breast of every freeman, in his choice of a member, is the establishment of an honest House of Commons (I mean a majority of honest men, for it is in vain we wish the whole were so.) And whoever is not thus far a friend to his country, is a traitor to it, and to his King.

Wretched, indeed, is the situation of those poor men, who have wives and families to maintain by laborious industry, whose reason and conscience urge them to vote for the man of probity; yet are deterred from the object of their choice by the imperious commands or threatening of their arbitrary superiors! They will be honest if they dared to be so. But surely the hotter vengeance is reserved for the tyrant!

What is it, then, that this Senex, or anyone else, tells us about the peace and tranquility of the city, at a time when convulsions shake the State? Why are we told of gratitude and ingratitude, and serving the interests of individuals?—These are all secondary considerations, and must ever give place to the great object I have mentioned.—Dear as are my connections in life—dear as my native city is to me, I had rather weep over it, reduced to ashes, *than see it contribute to the downfall of my country.*

JUVENIS.

"Senex" replied to "Juvenis" in a long address from which the following extracts have been made:—

Your preamble sets forth a production low as satiric, and contemptible as illiberal. Possessed of a fancied talent to amuse, you have advanced from your splenetic haunts, and under an assumed signature, declared publicly that your proper one would have been Shylock. Your attack upon the noble principle, which induced Lord Clare to decline, has no other basis than your ungenerous surmise, or the rancour of party so cruelly to subvert the intentions of his lordship and to blacken that as a crime which is deserving the applause of his most inveterate enemies. This unnatural return of evil for good can only spring from principles like yours. And I now call upon you to make good your assertion, when, with a far greater degree of confidence than truth you impudently dare say, "such was his lordship's motive." Your truly noble doubt, whether Lord Clare was ever possessed of any truly noble principle, proves your ample possession of that you are so unwilling, even in the most trifling degree, to allow his lordship: But I pity your unmanly manner of doing things for even an enemy may be generous. I would wish to know the being I am addressing, therefore good sir. pardon me if I ask a few questions.

Are you not some disappointed man, who, time past had your hopes frustrated of a seat in Queen Square? Or one for whom his lordship has, by his interest, amply provided, but by his resignation cut off from the pleasing expectation of acquiring by him, one more lucrative, more dignified? Or are you some hireling scribe ever ready to destroy the reputation of those you have not virtue to copy after? What or whoever thou art, I wish you that peace which now supports his lordship, under the unkind return this City has tendered him for his faithful services and should, be glad to congratulate you on your return to virtue, and your having shook off your demoniac disposition. Your humanity, in sparing from the lash the man you acknowledge to esteem, is as truly generous as Mr.———after being entrusted with the secrets of his friend, then exhibiting them for the public entertainment. All the merit you claim thereby shall be freely told, without deduction of interest, for fame shall record your unparalleled and truly noble principle, that you could ever condesend to spare the man the last of public censure whom you acknowledged possessed of every required virtue in private life.

"Juvenis" prepared and published a further reply, from which it is only necessary to give a few extracts:—

Public virtue is not yet extinct; nor is patriotism the mere phantom it has been industriously represented. That it is not so, is chiefly owing to the freedom of the press, which is now the chief bulwark of English liberty.

The terror of corrupt statesmen, and scourge of tyrants, has been the principal, perhaps the only effectual means of preserving the constitution from the attacks of lawless powers. Through this channel are circulated the transactions of a whole nation. Grievances are made known—public misconduct is censured and public virtue applauded. We are deeply interested in knowing, and we have the right to censure the conduct of our ministers. It is our privilege not only to elect, but to advise, instruct and minutely to inquire into the parliamentary conduct of our representatives; and, if this be found to be unconstitutional, or trifling, we are constrained, by the duty we owe to our country, freely and openly to reprehend and exclude from our future favours, such blameable or unprofitable servants. We intrust them with our liberties and property; we delegate to them our power of acting and controlling in the senate, and they are responsible to us for their behaviour there.

We have little to do with the private vices or virtues of any man. It is mean and illiberal to expose the private feelings of a minister to public censure, as mankind are not likely to be benefitted by exhibitions of vice. But their parliamentary conduct and political principles cannot be too publicly known, nor too freely animadverted upon. This, indeed, is the only real control that we have over our representatives, and every independent elector would do well in making use of his liberty upon these occasions. Free strictures upon public conduct are generally of service both to the candidates and electors. Many truths, highly necessary to be known, are frequently brought into light in the midst of contest; many invidious falsehoods spring from the womb of malice, but these soon drop to the ground, and a discerning eye will easily distinguish one from the other. The facts told to Senex, indeed, were well known before, but it was necessary to repeat them.

We shall soon see too, what effect all this *sad disturbance* will produce on the citizens.—Little minds may perhaps retain a tincture of malice, but men of more liberal sentiment will be cordially united!

We must now leave these two disputants and again return to the actual proceedings of Saturday the 8th of October. A rather important broadside, of which a copy is appended, was issued:—

> The friends of Lord Clare and of the City, are justly alarmed at the step his lordship has taken, and who still wish for a continuation of his long and faithful services, are earnestly desired to give their votes for him at opening of the Poll on Monday next; as nothing that is past can be a legal bar to any votes that may be offered in his favour, or to his lordship's acceptance of a seat in Parliament for this City, and should the citizens be inclined (as it is known great numbers are) to do themselves the justice of replacing him in it.
> Saturday, Oct. 8, 1774.

You must read between the lines of this innocent looking publication for the true meaning. It was issued by the disappointed Brickdale section of the Tory party, and they in fact would have had the Crugerites believe that if they persisted in Burke's candidature, the men who had jockeyed Lord Clare, in the full and certain hope that Brickdale would be returned as a matter of course, were prepared to take his lordship on again, *nolens volens*. But the Whigs knew their position, and they also knew that they had sufficient money at their disposal to prevent their chances of taking the two seats being spoilt.

Where the enormous sum that was spent came from cannot now be ascertained, unless, indeed, by chance some MS. notes or original accounts should at any time hereafter be discovered. The Whigs only required the formal decision of Edmund Burke to enable them to say "We've got the men and we've got the "money too."

Sunday, the 9th of October, was a busy day for the friends of the candidates; and the Sheriffs must have had a busy time, but as the result of taking the best advice they could obtain, it became generally known that the nomination of Burke would be accepted. In the course of the day a Bill was issued, dated October 9, 1774 (Sunday), and signed "DETECTOR," "All found out! All found out! A bargain and Sale! By "Clare to Brickdale! The Gentlemen, Clergy, Freeholders, and "Freemen of Bristol, are hereby acquainted that a most "infamous Sale and Bargain have been made, in order to deprive "them of the right of voting, and to obtrude Mr. Brickdale as one "of the Representatives of the City. The case I am told is thus, "On Friday last Lord Clare, in company with another gentleman "went to an eminent Counsellor near the Hotwells, in order to "ask his opinion; whether, if he appeared as a candidate and "polled a tally and then declined, if any other person could be "nominated after the poll began? The Counsellor answered "No. Lord Clare acted in conformity to that opinion and "declined. *How much you are sold for*, has not yet been "discovered, but it is supposed that the sum cannot be incon- "siderable. Mr Brickdale was so confident of being returned on "Saturday morning, according to his bargain with Lord Clare, "that he absolutely had *ordered his chair* of his upholsterers." [This refers to the richly decorated chair in which a successful candidate was carried through the principal streets, accompanied by a procession, a function then known as chairing.]

On the following Monday, the 10th of October, "Detector's" Squib was replied to as follows:—

"A scandalous paper signed 'Detector,' being distributed about "in order to prejudice Mr. Brickdale in the good opinion of his "fellow citizens, asserting that a bargain had been made between "Lord Clare and him, in order to deprive the Freemen of their "votes: No such bargain has been made, nor ever was intended "to be made and, as a further satisfaction, John Damer, Esq., the "only Counsellor at or near the Hotwells, a particular friend of "Mr. Burke's, and the person supposed to be alluded to, is ready "to declare that he never spoke to Lord Clare on the occasion." "Detector" replied that his authority was Mr George Daubeny, who had "acknowledged it to be so in a public coffee house in "this city," but it would seem to have been like the tale of the Three Black Crows, for Mr Daubeny, when appealed to intimated that what he had originally said was, "That *it looked* very like a bargain."

When the Sheriffs arrived at the Hustings on Monday morning, they were asked to declare Mr. Burke a candidate, but their answer was, "We are ready to receive a poll for any man." Mr. Burke's friends again nominated him. Mr. Daubeny protested, and, at his request, his protest was duly recorded. Mr. Harford then tendered his vote as a freeholder, and it was recorded by the Sheriffs. Then a Mr. Rice badgered the unfortunate Sheriffs. When he came to record his vote, he asked who were the candidates. The records were read over to him, but he pressed the Sheriffs to declare the names of the candidates, and they then and there declared that Lord Clare, Matthew Brickdale, and Henry Cruger, Esqres., were nominated candidates on the first day of the poll, and that Edmund Burke, Esq., was nominated on the second day. Burke received to-day, the first day of his poll, 71 votes; Cruger polled 95 votes, making a total of 111; Brickdale polled 46 votes, making a total of 71, Lord Clare's total of 12 votes polled on the opening day of the poll was not added to. It will be seen that Burke's friends had polled a sufficient number to put him on a level with Brickdale.

A deputation from the City had previously set off post haste to London, to bring back Edmund Burke with them, but on their arrival in London they found he had started for Malton in Yorkshire, in order to be present on the day of election, which had been fixed for the 11th of October. The deputation saw Mr. Richard Burke, the candidate's brother, and obtained an assurance that the nomination would be acceptable. The result of the visit is clearly set out in the two published addresses, which speak for themselves.

> October 10th, 1774,
>
> The Committee of Mr. Burke's friends beg leave to acquaint the gentlemen, clergy, freeholders and Freemen of the City of Bristol, that Mr. Burke's brother is arrived express from London, with an account of a messenger being despatched for Mr. Edmund Burke, who had set off for Yorkshire on Friday last *on unavoidable business.* Ignorant as he then was of the events which induced his friends to comply with his earnest request, to offer him as a candidate to the consideration of the Electors of this City, whenever a favourable opportunity should happen; the Committee *and his family* earnestly entreat, that this unfortunate absence, *in no sort to be justly blamed in him*, may not prejudice him in the eyes of the electors, or damp the ardour of his friends. He will certainly pay his respects to them and solicit their favours in person *on Thursday next* at farthest.

> October 10th, 1774,
>
> The gentlemen who went to Mr. Edmund Burke, found he was not in London, but were assured that he had given authority to his brother Mr. R. Burke, *to inform any gentlemen who might come from Bristol, that he should esteem it as the highest honor to represent this City in Parliament.* Mr. R. Burke *came to this City last night,* in order to repeat that assurance to the friends of Mr. Edmund Burk's here, *but having indispensable business elsewhere,* was obliged to depart again. Mr. Burke's friends are resolved to continue the poll as that gentleman's absence cannot be the least obstacle to his being chosen. Richard Beckford Esq., was elected to represent this City in Parliament, when he was in the West Indies, and John Spencer Esq., stood a candidate with our late worthy member Sir Jarrit Smith, Bart., although absent.
>
> *A messenger is despatched for Mr. Burke,* and he will most certainly be here on Thursday next at furthest, to assert and vindicate our rights of election.
>
> [NOTE.—This refers to the election of 1754, when Lord Clare, then Robert Nugent, and Beckford were elected after a contest.]

A Bristol correspondent of the *London Chronicle* wrote to that journal as follows:—

> Mr. Edmund Burke has been nominated by some gentlemen after the Poll began, and having many friends, from the respectableness of his character, *and the friends of Mr. Cruger leaning hard this way,* though they do not care absolutely to join him, it is very likely he will be preferred to Mr. Brickdale, the third candidate.

The following address was sent by Lord Clare to the electors:—

To the Gentlemen, Clergy, Freeholders and Freemen of the City of Bristol.

Altho' the supine inactivity of some, and the infatuated conduct of others, left me unassisted and deserted by many who called themselves my friends, I owe to justice, honor, and gratitude, this public declaration, that many respectable bodies of men, and very many individuals remained faithful to their professions, constant in their friendships, and grateful for the endeavours of an old servant, who, tho' no longer the chosen Representative, shall ever remain the warm and zealous friend of Bristol.

Bath, October 10, 1774. CRAGGS CLARE.

Thus ended Lord Clare's connection with the City, he had been one of its members for a little over twenty years, having been first elected in May, 1754 (see *ante* p. 11). To him had been intrusted, from time to time, the nomination of every place and employment in the disposal of the Government, within the City of Bristol. His influence had always been used on behalf of the interests of the City, and he had on several occasions successfully opposed attempts made to give undue preference to the port of London.

Amongst other measures affecting the City which came before Parliament, two important Bills, viz.: The Act for rebuilding Bristol Bridge, and The Act for establishing a nightly watch, were piloted through Parliament by his lordship, and subsequently became law. He also rendered assistance in connection with several schemes of street improvement in Bristol, and for cleansing, lighting, and new paving the streets. It was stated at the time that he was the largest private subscriber to the cost of constructing the new street, now known as Clare Street, after his name.

His Lordship at once made his way to Cornwall, and was duly elected for his pocket borough—St. Mawes (*alias* Mawditt). The seat had been held in the previous parliament by Edmund Nugent, a relative of his Lordship. Later on, he was created Earl Nugent, in the kingdom of Ireland. He retired from parliamentary life in 1784, and died on the 13th August, 1788.

On Tuesday, the 11th of October, at the close of the poll, the following totals were recorded:—Cruger, 344; Burke, 235; Brickdale, 181; Clare, 13.

In the course of the day a skit was circulated, of which the following is a copy :—

> To the Freeholders and Freemen of the City of Bristol.
>
> * Dr. Ryan, colleague to Dr. Rigge, thinks you so mad that he has declined, and recommended Dr. Munro, who has had long experience in Bedlam. An *Express* is sent for him, and when he arrives, he makes no doubt they will *jointly* remove your *complaints*.
>
> CRAW-THUMPER.
>
> October 11. 1774.

In order that the Whigs might not lose votes, an address was issued advising them to vote for Cruger and Burke.

> [COPY ADDRESS.]
>
> To such of the Electors as intend to give a Single Vote for Henry Cruger, Esq.
>
> GENTLEMEN,
>
> No man can more applaud your steady friendship to your worthy candidate, Henry Cruger, Esq., than we do. The zeal of his friends has already secured success to his election *beyond a possibility of doubt*. You will have, after giving him one vote, another left. Do not waste it.
>
> To throw away the power of serving your country is as much as a breach of duty, as to use that power ill. Ask yourselves this plain question. Which do you think the most proper man to represent you, Mr. Burke or Mr. Brickdale? Consider seriously. The times are full of danger. Much will depend on the abilities and knowledge of your members. Do you think Mr. Brickdale as able to do you service in Parliament as Mr. Burke? Consider them well, and yon will plainly see, that by refusing your second votes to Mr. Burke, you do in effect give them to Mr. Brickdale, and you are accountable to your country for any misfortune which may at this dangerous and alarming time, be the consequence of your depriving the nation of so able and honest a member of Parliament as Mr. Burke has always shewn himself; and making a member *of such an inactive and useless man, as you know from past experience Mr. Brickdale has been.*
>
> Many steadfast Friends of Mr. Cruger, who will Give their Second Vote for Mr Burke.
>
> Tuesday, October 11, 1774.

The poll for Wednesday, the 12th, recorded the following totals up to the close of the poll :—

Cruger.	Burke.	Brickdale.	Clare.
549	403	303	17

In consequence of the state of the poll, it was thought advisable to circulate a handbill, in order to bring home to the minds of the voters that every man was entitled to vote for two candidates.

---

* Dr. Ryan was a well known medical man residing in Charles Street, St. James. Dr. Rigge practised and resided at the Hotwells. Dr. Munro was probably a specialist in disorders of the brain.

[COPY.]
To the Citizens of Bristol.

The method of voting seems not to be understood. Every vote you give single for Mr. Cruger is a great injury to Mr. Burke, and a very essential service to Mr. Brickdale; whereas if you vote for Cruger and Burke, you will vote two for one of them to one for Mr. Brickdale.

The citizens must remember that every man has two votes, for two different men, and if he gives a single vote for Mr. Cruger, he loses his other vote, which, given to Mr. Burke, would help him considerably. All those, therefore, who are independent and lovers of liberty, will vote for

CRUGER AND BURKE.

On the morning of Thursday, the 13th, the following address appeared:—

To the Independent Freemen.

Do not be deceived by the friends of Mr. Brickdale. You are each entitled to vote for two different men, therefore, let every Freeman split his votes for

CRUGER AND BURKE.
NO PLUMPERS.

In the course of the day an address appeared containing some statements which were reiterated later on, when, as will be seen hereafter, they were fully answered by Mr. Burke's friends:—

To the Citizens of Bristol.

GENTLEMEN,

Are you acquainted with Mr. Burke? Do you know that he is the agent and instrument of the Rockingham party? Do you know he has written a book recommending the principles of that party? That they amount to this—That this party will make the King easy as to his Revenue and expenses, and redress some trifling grievances. In consideration of which, that they will kindly take the Government of this kingdom on themselves. That they will invest themselves with the peoples rights, who shall be free in their power, but no otherwise, for that they shall have virtue and ability enough for you all. That you shall have no other security, no resource but in them, and in particular, that the ancient Constitution by short Parliaments shall never be restored. This very man, who is so unaccountably, so mistakingly popular among you, doubtless through inattention or ignorance of his principles; this very man, I say, has pledged himself in print, as the opposer of short Parliaments, and consequently is the enemy of a free and well-balanced Constitution.

He has great and shining qualities you say, so much the worse for you, if he is the enemy of a popular interest, without a due portion of which there can be no freedom. Would you run upon a sword which bears a point and an edge against you, merely because it shines with uncommon lustre?

CAUTION.

October 13, 1774.

In the afternoon Mr. Burke arrived in a post-chaise, having left Malton, in Yorkshire, on Tuesday evening. He arrived in Bristol about half-past two, having accomplished a journey of 270 miles in 44½ hours.

He drove direct to the Mayor's house, but, as the Mayor was not at home, he proceeded to the Guildhall, where he ascended the hustings, and, having saluted the sheriffs, the two candidates and the electors, he reposed himself for a little while. He afterwards addressed the assembled crowd as follows :—

GENTLEMEN,

I am come hither to solicit in person that favor which my friends have hitherto endeavoured to procure for me, by the most obliging and, to me, the most honorable exertions.

I have so high an opinion of the great trust which you have to confer on this occasion, and, by long experience, so just a diffidence in my abilities, to fill it in a manner adequate even to my own ideas that I never should have ventured of myself to intrude into that awful situation, But, since I am called upon by the desire of several respectable fellow-citizens, as I have done at other times, I give up my fears to their wishes. Whatever my other deficiencies my be, I do not know what it is to be wanting to my friends.

I am not fond of attempting to raise public expectation by great promises. At this time, there is much cause to consider, and very little to presume. We seem to be approaching to a great crisis in our affairs, which calls for the whole wisdom of the wisest among us, without being able to assure ourselves that any wisdom can preserve us from many and great inconveniences. You know I speak of our unhappy contest with America. *I confess it is a matter on which I look down as from a precipice.* It is difficult in itself, and it is rendered more intricate by a great variety of plans of conduct. I do not mean to enter into them. I will not suspect a want of good intention in framing them. But however pure the inventions of the authors may have been, we all know that the event has been unfortunate. The means of recovering our affairs are not obvious. So many questions of commerce, of finance, of constitution, and of policy, are involved in this American deliberation, that I dare engage for nothing, but that I shall give it, without any predilection to former opinions, or any sinister bias whatever, the most honest and impartial consideration of which I am capable, The public has a full right to it, *and this great City,* a main pillar in the commercial interest of Great Britain, *must totter on its base by the slighest mistake* with regard to our American measures.

Thus much, however, I think it not amiss to lay before you. That I am not, I hope, apt to take up, or lay down my opinion lightly. I have held, and ever shall maintain, to the best of my power, unimpaired and undiminished, the just, wise and necessary constitutional superiority of Great Britain. This is necessary for America as well as for us. I never mean to depart from it. Whatever may be lost by it, I avow it. The forfeiture even of your favor, if by such a declaration I could forfeit it, though the first object of my ambition, never will make me disguise my sentiments on this subject— But,—I have ever had a clear opinion, and have ever held a constant correspondent conduct, that this superiority is consistent with all the liberties a sober and spirited American ought to desire. I never mean to put any colonist, or any human creature, in a situation not becoming a freeman. To reconcile British superiority with American liberty shall be my great object as far as my little faculties can extend. I am far from thinking that both, even yet, may not be preserved.

When I first devoted myself to the public service, I considered how I should render myself fit for it; and this I did by endeavouring to discover what it was that gave this country the rank it holds in the world. I found that our prosperity and dignity arose principally, if not solely, from two sources, our constitution and commerce. Both these I have spared no study to understand, and no endeavour to support. The distinguishing part of our constitution is liberty. To preserve that liberty inviolate, seems the particular duty and proper trust of a member of the House of Commons. But the liberty, the only liberty I mean, is a liberty connected with order; that only exists along with order and virtue, but which cannot exist at all without them. It inheres in good and steady government as in its substance and vital principle.

The other source of our power is commerce, of which you are so large a part, and which cannot exist, no more than your liberty, without a connection with many virtues. It has ever been a very particular, and a very favourite object of my study in its principles, and in its details. I think many here are acquainted with the truth of what I say. This I know, that I have ever had my house open, and my poor services ready for traders and manufacturers of every denomination. My favourite ambition is to have those services acknowledged. I now appear before you to make trial, whether my earnest endeavours have been so wholly oppressed by the weakness of my abilities, as to be rendered insignificant in the eyes of a great trading city; or whether you choose to give a weight to humble abilities, for the sake of the honest exertions with which they are accompanied. This is my trial to-day. My industry is not on trial. Of my industry I am sure, as far as my constitution of mind and body admitted.

When I was invited by many respectable merchants, freeholders, and freemen of this city, to offer them my services, I had just received the honour of an election at another place, at a very great distance from this, I immediately opened the matter to those of my worthy constituents who were with me, and they unanimously advised me not to decline it. They told me that they had elected me with a view to the public service; and as great questions relative to our commerce and Colonies were imminent, that in such matters I might derive authority and support from the representation of this great commercial city; they desired me to set off without delay, very well persuaded that I never could forget my obligations to them, or to my friends, for the choice they had made of me. From that time to this instant I have not slept; and if I should have the honour of being freely chosen by you, I hope I shall be as far from slumbering or sleeping when your service requires me to be awake, as I have been in coming to offer myself as a candidate for your favor.

[The end of Edmund Burke's speech on his arrival in Bristol.]

The candidate's address was then issued:—

To the Gentlemen, Clergy, Freeholders, and Freemen of the City of Bristol.

GENTLEMEN,

I have been called upon by a numerous and respectable part of your body to offer you my services as your representative in Parliament. I should not have presumed to make you that offer without such an invitation. The motive has probably been my public conduct.

E

My friends perceived in it a great deal of good intention; and they were so generous as to look upon the rest with a very partial indulgence. In conformity to their wishes, I now request the favour of your votes and interest; and if I should have the honour of becoming one of the objects of your choice, you may be assured that my future conduct in Parliament, encouraged by that flattering mark of your approbation, will continue exactly the same in principle, and certainly not less active in exertion.

The welfare of commerce, in which the most essential interests of this great city in particular, and of the kingdom in general are involved, will be the principal object of my attention. I feel the whole importance of the trust which you may confer upon me, and I shall, therefore, ever feel the warmest affection, respect, and gratitude towards those who shall think me not totally unworthy of it.

I have the honour to be, Gentlemen,
Your most obedient, obliged, and humble Servant,

EDMUND BURKE.

Bristol, October 13.

Up to the close of the poll on the 13th, the numbers were:—

Cruger.	Burke.	Brickdale.	Clare.
780	583	431	21

The following broadsides now appeared:—

To the Corporation, Merchants, Freeholders, and Freemen of the City of Bristol.

GENTLEMEN,

It is notorious that the present long duration of Parliament has taken from you all constitutional check and control over your members, except the very trifling one of a septennial election. Is it not, therefore, incumbent on you to chose your representative from among your own citizens resident among you, that your praise or censure, which in some case they must need, may serve as a control on their actions. You have nothing else left for it. You must make them answerable to you in their characters, and in the peace and quiet of their minds. Will Mr. Burke be answerable to you? Will he reside among you? He is answerable another way to the Rockingham party, with whom he is too closely connected to regard your demands. Ask him if he will pledge himself to vote for short Parliaments? If he declines the most express and solemn engagements on this head, what right will you have to censure him hereafter? Citizens be cautious, be zealous for liberty, but be not the dupes of your own zeal.

TEST.

October 14, 1774.

[Copy Address issued by Brickdale's Committee.]

The friends of Mr. Brickdale return their most grateful thanks to the Right Worshipful the Mayor, those other members of the Corporation, and the Rev. and learned Clergy, who favoured him this day with their votes; they are extremely concerned that the very orderly and respectable manner in which they proceeded to the hustings should occasion their being insulted in the most gross and insolent manner by those who professed themselves to be friends of those candidates who found their pretensions to the suffrages of the electors of the city of Bristol on professions of their attachment to the cause of liberty, government, order, and due subordination, constitute the basis on which our civil and religious liberties are founded.

Those who publicly and grossly insulted the Magistracy and Clergy of the city of Bristol, when they were about to exercise the most invaluable franchises of Englishmen, can never be considered by any thinking mind as friends to the civil or religious liberties of its citizens.

October 14, 1774.

[The following answer to the above Address was issued :—]

A friend of Mr. Burke's presents his compliments to those complaining friends of Mr. Brickdale who penned the advertisement in last Saturday's papers, asserting that insults were offered to the Magistracy and Clergy, begs they would be more explicit on that head, as he neither saw nor can hear of anything that could possibly deserve the application of that term, respecting either the Clergy or those two or three Magistrates who accompanied them. He must, therefore, unless better informed, treat it as a false assertion.

The objection made by a gentleman of the law to the Clergy's right of voting, though now so much inveighed against to serve a turn, Mr. Brickdale's friends are desired to recollect, did not originate from that quarter, but has been the sentiment of many, and expressed on various occasions, and especially by Mr. Brickdale's father in 1754, who insisted largely on this very point, a matter which, after all, seems rather to have been granted by courtesy to those reverend gentlemen, than to result from any principle of law.

On Friday the 14th, and the following day a few amusing squibs were let off :—

To Mr. Alderman Mugleworth.

SIR,

You are desir'd to assign a reason to the public for your very extraordinary conduct in going into a Public-house in your ward and telling the Landlord, because he would not promise to vote as you would have him for Mr. Brickdale, "That 'twas very well, you knew what you had to do."—You could mean nothing by these words, but that you would prevent his having a fresh license, when he wants it.—Are you not ashamed of such conduct!—Such mean, dirty work for any man—particularly an Alderman to be concern'd in? You dare not deny a syllable here asserted—Gentlemen of fortune superior to your own—and *of equal rank everywhere but in this city*, in which you wear a gown, that you disgrace, are ready to prove the fact against you at any time—and if you have confidence enough to dare call upon the Author of this with your name, he will produce the person, who shall tell you to your face everything here said against you.

Until you assign a reason for such behaviour, you can only be look'd upon as *a disgrace to Magistracy, to Manhood, and to this City.*

Exchange Coffee House,   STINGO.
Oct. 14, 1774.

The insolence of that scribbler Stingo is unbearable, *to have the audacity to attack an Alderman* of this city in such a scandalous manner.—Has he not an *absolute* right *over the Publicans in his own Ward*, to dictate to them as his superior judgment shall direct? Therefore be it known to you Stingo, that he will be absolute, and unless the refractory Publicans comply, not a single tap shall be allowed to run within the limits of his Ward, and if he hears any more from your scurrilous pen you may expect the reward you so justly deserve, that of your *being rivetted in the stocks*, or to have your flagellations in the mansions of Bridewell. Resentment has filled his breast.

Bristol, Oct. 15, 1774.   BY-STANDER.

Bristol, October 15, 1774.

No stingo will be given away in Alderman Mugleworth's Ward to any of the Freemen, unless they promise to vote for Mr. Bricklade.
By order,
MUGLEWORTH AND LIBERTY FOR EVER.

To the Bristol Electors.

GENTLEMEN,

The old adage, that "many an ass is made a Justice of the Peace," was never more glaringly exemplified than in the person of Mr. Alderman Feather, also Justice Shallow—a man who has never been remarkable for anything but stupidity and attachment to slavish principles. A man of neither sentiment nor expression—a mere echo of what he hears from others; an over bearing partial abuser of power —and so very silly as to commence a prosecution, Woodcock-like, against a poor fellow upon the Game Act, because forsooth a couple of woodcocks were found upon him—were it not better that this old boy did, as in former days, retire to his summer-house, and as he wisely terms it, "Read, read his book, *and nobody* is never the wiser," rather than shame the Magisterial character by exposing his folly, and alarm the peaceable inhabitants of his Ward by his uncouth braying. Happy were it for the public, if in chusing magistrates, a proper regard were always paid to their abilities. An able bad man, it is true, is more formidable than a weak one—but then few men of understanding are easily betrayed into acts of gross dishonour; *such as terrifying by threats, and influencing voters at a (pretended) free election.* For common sense will always tell him who possesses it, that considering the test the voter is liable to, such a flagrant breach of all order, decency and justice, especially in a Magistrate, must brand him with eternal infamy; which nothing but "that party-coloured creature called knave and fool," would bear the thought of being exposed to. And yet such is undeniably *the practice of the above Just Ass of Peace*, a contemptible tool of power who sticks at nothing to gain his purpose; a mere phantom of Magistracy, shrugging up his shoulders in all the grimace of self-applause, like Hudibras (in the picture) just going to sally forth. How dirty must that cause be, that can want such wretched men, and such scandalous means to support it? How enslaved are those subjects, how miserable those citizens *who are to feel all the severity and malice of a magistrate*, unless they will be tamely hectored into a servile and infamous prostitution of faith, and basely surrender the freedom of their votes to a shameless Alderman (Happy Bristol! he stands individually). Even just as miserable as those Englishmen whose members of Parliament can obtain for them no justice, no protection of shipping; no exemption from quartered soldiers, &c., &c., &c. (if ye believe the bugbears of the friends of slavery), but by the favor of those very tools of power, whom 'tis the special duty of our delegates to guard us against. This, it seems, is the perpetual cant of the pitiful operator before mentioned. But 'tis hoped that the common sense of freemen will see through the design of such futile stuff. There is no doubt but even the worst and most selfish of all Governments will take care to protect that trade, from the safety of which their own resources are derived. As to favors done for Custom House officers, &c., such a numerous body of dependents will always attract sufficient regard. And as for soldiers, it is weak to imagine any city in danger of being unequally pestered with them, and an exemption from our own quota, would be unreasonable to desire, and dishonourable to grant. Regard not, therefore, fellow citizens, the threats of the weak, nor the insinuations of the deceiver. Be true to the name of Englishman, struggle for that freedom without which no good, public or private, can be lasting; and ever *prefer in your choice the man who appears the farthest from Court connection.* BRITON.

As a set-off to the conduct of Alderman Mugleworth towards the publicans of his ward (St. Michael's), *Felix Farley's Journal* of Oct. 8, 1774, recorded a concession to the publicans by the Mayor :—

> On Wednesday last Samuel Peach, Esq., at the head of a very respectable and numerous body of Merchants, returned our Chief Magistrate, Charles Hotchkin, Esq., their thanks in the Council House, *for his great impartiality in permitting the publicans in his ward to vote at the present election, as they think proper.*

The following skit refers to a device common to both parties for obtaining by purchase dead freemen's copies and hiring persons to personate the deceased freemen :—

> Huzza!   Defunct Freemen for Ever!   Huzza!
> Wanted immediately, a few hundred dead freemen's copies, and a number of respectable journeymen, at half-a-guinea each, to represent the defunct at the poll.
> Apply to Doodle-doo,* or to the Hibernian Demosthenes,† at the Three Queens, in St. Thomas Street.

Early on Saturday morning, the 15th of October, the friends of Brickdale issued the following broadside :—

October, 15.
State of the Poll Last Night.

	F.	S.	M.	T.	W.	T.	F.		Total.
Mr. Cruger	11	5	95	233	205	231	183	...	963
Mr. Burke	0	0	71	164	168	180	157	...	740
Mr. Brickdale	10	15	46	110	122	128	141	...	572
Lord Clare	12	0	0	1	4	4	47	...	68

True, Mr. Cruger and Mr. Burke have a great majority over Mr. Brickdale, and what then! Two tallies to one is twenty to ten; C and B and B and C are playing into one anothers hands. But Mr. Brickdale's friends need not be alarmed. Mr. Brickdale will poll on, *and speak when some folks are silent.*

---
* Crnger.   † Burke.

The following lines appeared in a local journal the same day :—

Cruger, Burke and Liberty for Ever!
On the present contest between Mr. Brickdale and Mr. Burke.

Brickdale and Burke, O, how they sound!
A penny, and a thousand pound!
A cock boat and a Man of War!
An atom and a radiant star!

CONTRAST.

A local journal (dated 15th October) published the following paragraph :—

We have never seen a contested election in this city conducted with so little disturbance. notwithstanding the poll is very strenuously carried on by all the candidates. Lord Clare, indeed, had declined, but some of his friends insisting on it, the books are still kept open.

Immediately upon his Lordship's declining, Mr. Edmund Burke, whose integrities and abilities are well known, was nominated, and a poll demanded for him, in consequence of which he came to town on *Thursday*, having travelled upwards of 200 miles in less than two days. The numbers on the poll last night were :—

For Henry Cruger, Esq.	962
" Edmund Burke	739
" Matthew Brickdale	572
" Lord Clare	66

[These totals were not quite correct. The numbers previously given, viz. :—Cruger, 963 ; Burke, 740 ; Brickdale, 572 ; and Clare, 68, were the correct totals.]

[The following broadside was also issued :—]

Mr. Burke,

Your abilities make, and ought to make you responsible. The line you have taken in politics is taken by choice, and not by chance, and perfectly conformable to your ideas of things. We may lament, but must not blame. The freedom of sentiment which we wish to preserve to ourselves, we must not deny to others. Yet we cannot but wonder that born in a middling rank of life, you should have imbibed sentiments so adversarious to general freedom. If we could suppose them to be derived from your late connections, we should pay you, I am afraid, but an ill compliment. We wish that your distinguished abilities were employed in supporting the falling interest of the people, which at present demands support. But as you seem far gone in another interest, already much too powerful, you cannot be surprised, if we do not wish to put arms in your hands for our own destruction. You say, the motive of your invitation hither was probably drawn from your public conduct, and you say in conformity to this suggestion, that your future conduct will continue exactly the same in principle. It is fairly and handsomely said, though, perhaps, somewhat proudly ; it is at least what the gentlemen, who invited you hither, honestly deserve. But do you really think that they knew exactly what your public conduct has been ? They have heard that you make excellent speeches, and oppose the Ministers, and I am afraid that is all they know. or have heard. Do the Quakers think you know that you were a violent opposer of that religious liberty, which the Dissenters in general have of late petitioned for? I blame not you; but I pity them who are making such strange mistakes. Do you think that the friends of general liberty, who seem to join you with Mr. Cruger, were acquainted that you were the enemy of short Parliaments? You may be assured, they were not, or the sentiments which recommended Mr. Cruger would have excluded you. And yet you tell them that you suppose your public conduct has obtained their favor, and you promise perseverance in the same principle. A declaration proper enough, perhaps, for you to utter, but dreadfully mortifying, let me tell you, for them to hear. In short, it is plain that ye have greatly mistaken one another, and the best thing that can now be done, is to make explanations and apologies on all sides and part; but not without every testimony of sorrow and concern on their part, that they have given you so much unnecessary trouble.

Oct. 15, 1774.
BRISTOL.

On Saturday, the 15th, the poll closed as follows :—

Cruger.	Burke.	Brickdale.	Clare.
1164	904	693	79

On Monday, the 17th, considerable additions were made to Cruger's total, and at the end of the day's poll the figures stood :—

Cruger.	Burke.	Brickdale.	Clare.
1408	1098	814	83

The friends of Burke now issued a copy of the pamphlet written by him shortly after the collapse of the short-lived Rockingham Ministry :—

A Word in Season.

On the change of Administration, by the dismission of Lord Rockingham and his friends from the King's service, the following concise history of their actions and conduct was published. It never has been yet contradicted, or the truth of it disputed. Let Mr. Brickdale's friends determine whose cause they have most effectually served, that of Mr. Brickdale or Mr. Burke, by informing the electors of Bristol how intimately Mr. Burke was concerned in such measures, and how firm and inviolable he has preserved his attachment *to the principles from which they flowed*, and his friendship to the persons of those who carried them into execution.

[COPY PAMPHLET.]

"A Short Account of a Short Administration.

"The late Administration came into employment under the mediation of the Duke of Cumberland, on the 10th day of July, 1765, having lasted just one year and twenty days.

In that space of time—

The distractions of the British Empire were composed by the repeal of the American Stamp Act.

But the Constitutional superiority of Great Britain was preserved by the Act for Securing the Dependence of the Colonies.

Private houses were relieved from the jurisdiction of the Excise, by the repeal of the Cyder Tax.

The personal liberty of the subject was confirmed by the resolution against general Warrants.

The lawful secrets of business and friendship were rendered inviolable by the resolution for condemning the seizure of papers.

The trade of America was set free from injudicious and ruinous impositions—its Revenue was improved and settled upon a rational foundation—its commerce extended with foreign countries; while all the advantages were secured to Great Britain, by the Act for repealing certain duties, and encouraging, regulating, and securing the trade of the Kingdom, and the British Dominions in America.

Materials were provided and insured to our manufactures—the sale of these manufactures was increased—the African trade preserved and extended—the principles of the Act of Navigation pursued, and the plan improved—and the trade for bullion rendered free, secure, and permanent, by the Act for opening certain ports in Dominica and Jamaica.

The Administration was the first which proposed and encouraged public meetings and free consultations of merchants from all parts of the Kingdom, by which means the truest lights have been received; great benefits have been already derived to manufacture and commerce; and the most extensive prospects are opened for further improvement.

Under them, the interests of our northern and southern colonies, before that time jarring and dissonant, were understood, compared, adjusted, and perfectly reconciled. The passions and animosities of the colonies, by judicious and lenient measures, were allayed and composed, and the foundation laid for a lasting agreement amongst them.

Whilst that administration provided for the liberty and commerce of their country, as the true basis of its power, they consulted its interests, they asserted its honor abroad, with temper and with firmness; by making an advantageous treaty of commerce with Russia; by obtaining a liquidation of the Canada bills, to the satisfaction of the proprietors; by reviewing and raising from its ashes the negotiation for the Manilla ransom, which had been extinguished and abandoned by their predecessors.

They treated their Sovereign with decency, with reverence. They discountenanced, and it was hoped, for ever abolished the dangerous and unconstitutional practice of removing military officers for their votes in Parliament. They firmly adhered to those friends of liberty, who had run all hazards in its cause, and provided for them in preference to every other claim.

With the Earl of Bute they had no personal connection, no correspondence of Councils. They neither courted him nor persecuted him. They practised no corruption, nor were they ever suspected of it. They sold no offices. They obtained no reversions, or pensions, either coming in or going out, for themselves, their families, or their dependents.

In the prosecution of their measures they were traversed by an opposition of a new and singular character; *an opposition of placemen and pensioners.*

They were supported by the confidence of the nation. And having held their offices under many difficulties and discouragements, they left them at the express command, as they accepted them at the earnest request of their Royal Master.

These are plain facts, of a clear and public nature; neither extended by elaborate reasoning, or heightened by the colouring of eloquence. They are the services of a single year.

The removal of that Administration from power is not to them premature; since they were in office long enough to accomplish many plans of public utility, and, by their perseverance and resolution, rendered the way smooth and easy to their successors; having left their King and their country in a much better condition than they found them. By the temper they manifest, they seem to have no other risk than that their successors may do the public as real and as faithful service as they have done."

Bristol, Oct. 18, 1774.

This publication was answered by a writer, who signed himself, "A Word to the Wise."

MR. WORD IN SEASON,

A short account of a short Administration that was dissolved in its own weakness:—

By reprinting this, I suppose, you want to arrogate to Mr. Burke the whole management of Lord Rockingham's Administration. Modest enough I must confess, if they were entitled to any merit, but let us examine their pretensions.

1st.—You say they repealed the American Stamp Duty. I grant it, but at the same time insist by their timidity they are chargeable with all the disturbances that have happened since, and may hereafter. If that Act had been altered a little and enforced, all would have been quiet in America now.

2nd.—They passed an Act for securing the Dependence of the Colonies on the Mother Country. That is, they first cowardly declined the combat, and afterwards exulted in declaring themselves masters. Risum teneatis, amici?

3rd.—You assert the Cyder Tax was repealed. You should have said altered.

4th.—They made a resolution against General Warrants.

5th.—Another resolution for condemning the seizure of papers.

These two resolutions signified no more than if they had been made by Drunken Porters. The Courts of Law removed these grievances by Juries. In short, I am tired with refuting so many absurdities placed to their account, and shall conclude with admitting, that Mr. Bnrke opposed the late Quebec Bill. This Bill, as to religion, grants the inhabitants no more, *than they are entitled to by the Capitulation*, when they surrendered. With regard to their laws, they enjoy no more privileges than the inhabitants of Minorca. But I am at a loss to account for Mr. Burke's strenuously attacking Popery at a distance, when all the world know that he married, and took unto his bosom a Roman Catholic! Is this a proof of Mr. Burke's boasted consistency?

A WORD TO THE WISE.

[This reply was probably penned by Dean Tucker; it bears unmistakable marks of his style.]

On Tuesday, the 18th, at the close of the poll, it was found that Cruger and Burke had again put on a spurt, as will be seen by the totals :—

Cruger.	Burke.	Brickdale.	Clare.
1734	1358	968	86

Mr. Cruger's committee still continued very active—slips of paper in the following form were circulated :—

Bristol, Oct. 19, 1778.

> As the poll is far advanced, the friends of Mr. Cruger are earnestly requested to be early in their attendance at St. George's Chapel,* in the Guildhall, to-morrow, and the following days.

State of the Poll this day.

Cruger.	Burke.	Brickdale.	Clare.
2012	1581	1133	100

At the close of the poll on the 20th October, the figures were :—

Cruger.	Burke.	Brickdale.	Clare.
2303	1787	1304	120

This day was issued a very scurrilous broadsheet :

QUERIES ADDRESSED TO MR. BURKE.

> 1.—Was he not a student at St. Omer's, and is not the history of the tête-a-tête, or memoirs of the Hibernian Demosthenes and Miss S————r, in the "Town and Country Magazine" for February, 1774, true?
>
> 2.—If he is a staunch Protestant, how came he to marry Dr. Nugent's daughter, who was and is a Roman Catholic; and why did he send his only son to France for his education? What could he learn there in preference to England but the tenets of the Church of Rome?
>
> 3.—Has he not now a pension of £800 a year from Lord Rockingham, and whether he has any other support than this and his agency for New York?
>
> 4.—Must not he in consequence of the third query be always dependent on the Rockingham party and North America, and, of course, in direct opposition to Government; and by what interest can he be serviceable to this city in procuring convoys for our merchantmen in time of war, &c , or in preventing Dragoons and foot soldiers being quartered upon us, to the oppression of the Publicans, and destruction of the morals of the people?
>
> When he has answered these queries, he shall hear further from
> MODESTUS.
> Oct. 20, 1774.

---

* The hustings were erected and the poll taken by the Sheriffs in St. George's Chapel, in the old Guildhall.

[Very soon after Burke's marriage to the daughter of Dr. Nugent, some of the malicious and ill-conditioned fanatics, propagated and systematically kept alive a report that he and his wife were Papists, and were secretly working to prejudice the Protestant religion. The father of Jane Burke was an Irish Roman Catholic, but her mother was a Presbyterian, and it is believed that the daughter (Mrs. Burke) was brought up as a Presbyterian by her mother in consequence of an agreement made upon her marriage with Dr. Nugent. It is certain that her father, who was a liberal-minded man of the world, never attempted to influence his daughter's religious education, and from the date of her marriage to Edmund Burke till her death she was and continued to be a Protestant.]

The following broadside was immediately issued by way of answer to the questions put by "Bristol," and "Modestus." It is not at all improbable that the answer was Burke's own production or dictated by him :—

ANSWER TO A SET OF SCANDALOUS QUERIES.

Mr. Brickdale's agents, by the methods they employ to ensure his ill success, contrive at the same time to take away all pity from his misfortunes. They join the most odious baseness to the lowest folly. Not satisfied with our contempt, they are candidates for our hatred and indignation.

What a figure do they make in their false and groundless charges of Mr. Burke's being a Roman Catholic, who have formerly supported, and are now themselves supported by Lord Clare, who is admitted to have been of that persuasion a considerable part of his life? Whether their consistency in voting for Lord Clare, or their gratitude for the votes they got on his account, is the most shining part of their character they must adjust with Lord Clare, with one another, and with the public.

Not being able to attack any part of Mr. Burke's public conduct, which has been as blameless as it is illustrious, they amuse us, as if we were idiots, with idle and false stories *of his amours, of his family, his fortune, his wife and his children.* The lie in the dress of one day is no sooner demolished, than it appears in another the next; but it appears only to die, and to be disgraced with all the former, and with their contemptible authors. Baffled in the direct narrative of falsehoods and follies, they new model the same thing in queries and insinuations.

You ask whether the tête-a-tête be true. We answer that this tête-a-tête, with all its anecdotes of amours with people who never existed, in places which Mr. Burke never saw, is false and ridiculous, and without the least foundation from the beginning to the end; your managers have not a spark of ingenuity in their malice. They are obliged to steal from the lowest libels, and are liars without the credit of invention.

To their other indecent and senseless query about Mr. Burke's motives to marriage, we answer that we never inquired into them, or into the pedigree of Mr. Burke's wife. It is no sort of concern of ours. We have heard that she is a woman adorned with every virtue, and worthy of the husband whose happiness she makes. *None but such wretches as Mr. Brickdale's runners* could use the name of a respectable matron in election squibs, or endeavour to create uneasiness in the heart of families.

As to the query about the education of Mr. Burke's son; it is exactly like the rest. We hear that this son is a young gentleman of the greatest hopes; that he was first bred at the school of an eminent dissenter; thence transplanted to Westminster School, and now a member of Christ Church College in Oxford; and that whilst he was a short time (fifteen months) in France, he was accompanied by a respectable and learned Clergyman of the Established Church, son of another eminent Clergyman who has a dignity in it.

The insinuation in your query of Mr Burke's having a pension from Lord Rockingham or any other person, is infamously false and utterly groundless. His private fortune has hitherto enabled him to act with independence, that has shamed the proudest fortune in the Kingdom.

To the demand whether if you elect Mr. Burke, your trade will be convoyed in time of war; or how quartering of troops can be prevented—We put another query to them.—Silly as you are, can you be so consumately foolish as to threaten us, to be dragooned and deprived of our trade, if we don't elect Mr. Brickdale? Is this their idea of free election? Do they threaten to starve and dragoon us as they have done at Boston? I hope a Mother City will shew as much virtue as a Colony. But do not believe that a powerful oration in the House will not do more to intimidate Mr. Brickdale's Ministerial friends from such Measures, than poor Mr. Brickdale, who dares not speak against them if he could, *and cannot if he dared.*

After all, their utmost efforts cannot keep Mr. Burke out of the House of Commons; he is in it. The only question before you is this. Is it worth while for the Citizens of Bristol to attach to their immediate service such a man as Mr. Burke, even tho' Mr. Brickdale should be obliged to sleep in the pure air of Clifton, instead of snoring in the unwholesome air of St. Stephen's Chapel.

CIVIS;

The local poet now thought it was time to unburden himself :—

FREE REPRESENTATION.

IN King Lucius's reign,
   Did the patriots obtain
A free, popular representation,
The three states of the realm
Wisely ordered the helm,
And Parliament righted the nation.

These gave ready supplies
(No historian denies)
On each real emergent occasion ;
They contrived wholesome laws,
And despatched with applause
The weighty concerns of the nation

No defaulter accounts
For enormous amounts,
Expended in servile donation ;
On the house he depends,
Who his knav'ry defends,
And he's safe in abusing the nation.

Who then in their senses,
On futile pretences,
Venal members would keep in their station?
Or what are those men
Who return such again,
Whom they know to be selling the nation?

No premiers, mean-while
Did the senate defile,
Till by treacherous insinuation
A scandalous practice,
(Notorious the fact is)
Took place to the hurt of the nation.

Now with bribes, and douceurs,
The favorite procures
Two to one by a cool estimation !
Such an odds in the house
Their constituents to chouse
To betray and to plunder the nation.

"Sorry weeds grow apace,"
The perfidious race
So increas'd, that free representation
By a fatal decay,
Quite dwindled away,
And the premier enslav'd a free nation.

To the colonies he hies
To extort new supplies
By oppressive, unjust innovation ;
Boston's not to be pardon'd
For being so harden'd
In asserting the rights of the nation.

Dirty boroughs may sell,
Their birthright for a spell
While we hold them in just detestation ;
Who votes *for a placeman*
We count him a base man
For such are the pest of the nation.

When our members turn tail,
And their pockets avail,
By compounding with administration,
Then we who have chose 'em,
Will straightway depose 'em,
And for honester men search the nation.

We trust *Cruger* and Burke
Will stand true to the work
Of regainiug free representation,
That approv'd in the cause
Of our Freedom and Laws,
They will merit the thanks of the nation.

On the 22nd of October, additional addresses were issued.

[COPY.]
THOUGHTS ON THE PRESENT CONTESTED ELECTION.

It is obvious to every unprejudiced mind, that the present contested election has been replete with absurdity and contradiction.

The line of conduct pursued by Lord Clare, has astonished the public, and astounded his most intimate friends ; his Lordship appears to have sacrificed his favourite view to the mere impulse of a proud heart, - else what could have induced his Lordship (remarkable for perseverance) to abandon so very precipitately all thoughts of success ? Had the noble Lord been possessed of sufficient patience to have waited the issue of a few days, in all human probability he would have been secure of his election.

The unexpected retreat of Lord Clare introduced a new scene of affairs; many of the friends of the popular Candidate, not contented with obtaining their wishes in favor of one man, could not forbear attempting the introduction of a second.

The distinguished character and abilities of Mr. Burke afforded them sufficient reason to hope that his being returned, would compensate for the loss the citizens sustained in the resignation of Lord Clare.—The more strenuous part of the electors who pleased themselves upon adhering to a particular party conceived the introduction of Mr. Burke at this juncture, as a manifest intrusion ;—consequently interested themselves warmly in the opposition.

As to party it exists but in the name.—Those respectable bodies originally formed to preserve a proper balance of influence in this City, *are now confusedly intermixed with dissenters of every denomination ;* and it is much *to be* doubted *if ever the citizens* of Bristol *recover their* primeval independence. *The security of Mr. Cruger renders the contest between the other candidates more violent,* in consequence of which, those who before professed attachment to Mr. Cruger now solicit in favor of Mr. Brickdale—such the prevailing impropriety, such the degeneracy of the citizens of Bristol.   CRITO.

Bristol, October 22, 1774.

TO MR. BURKE.

Your runners are upon the fret, they have almost lost their cause. They make use of Billingsgate language because they think themselves in safety, but they ruin your interest instead of serving you. I have been longer acquainted with you than any of them. It is only since your intimacy with Lord R———m, that you have been able to keep a table of your own—you lived before with your father-in-law Dr. Nugent. Where was your independency then? That you received £800 a year from the Rockinghams "is a fact that may be softened, but cannot be denied," it may be settled upon you for life and out of their power, but it still deserves the name of a pension. Where have you a foot of property (in fee simple) in any part of the three kingdoms?—They say, you only called at St. Omers in your way to Paris—it may be so, but how came you to stay there so long? Was it to study *Nature* or Philosophy? Don't provoke me to discover a secret. As to religion, if I may believe your own words, you have none, for, 'tis a common expression of yours "*That you "neither read God's books, nor the Devil's* books,"—meaning the Bible and Cards—an excellent recommendation to your *devout Bristol friends*— Your powers as a Rhetorician are great—as a sound reasoner but indifferent. You are the mouth of the Rockingham party—they, by a combination, want to establish an Aristocratic Government, to keep the King in leading strings, and dragoon the people. For the truth of this assertion I appeal to your own book. Such principles, let me tell you, *are more fit for venal boroughs* than *Commercial Cities.* About seven years ago you went to offer your services at Lancaster; having but few acquaintances, you laid a wager, with an intention to lose, that you might have an apology for inviting the principal gentlemen and merchants to partake of it. Did you learn this *low cunning* at the college of Dublin or St. Omers?

MODESTUS.

In Bonnor and Middleton's *Bristol Journal* of the 22nd of October, the following electioneering items appear:—

A correspondent remarking upon the impropriety of Mr. Burke's not being a Candidate—observes that the three old Candidates might have agreed amongst themselves to poll each a tally, afterwards to retire to a Tavern, and by the chance of the dice determine who should be the losing Candidate.—Query, if the Electors of Bristol are to be disposed of by way of raffle?

A Card.—Can a Freeman be arrested, and committed during the time of election? An answer to the printer, or in Mr. Pine's Gazette will oblige.

HUMANUS.

Lost, supposed to go away with Lord Clare, the justice, honor and gratitude, and common sense of a great part of the Citizens of Bristol. Whoever can bring them back to where they are most wanted, shall receive of Mr. B———'s Committee, a cockade for their trouble.

The friends of Cruger issued a manifesto, of which the following is a copy :—

Bristol, October 22, 1774.

As the poll is very far advanced, the friends of Mr. Cruger are earnestly requested to be early in their attendance at St. George's Chapel, in the Guildhall, this morning.

State of the Poll Last Night :—

C.	2547
B.	1948
B.	1516
Lord Clare	149

A similar manifesto was circulated by the friends of Mr. Burke.

The following appeal was circulated by Mr. Brickdale's runners :

Bristol, October 22, 1774.

Mr. Brickdale presents his compliments to such of his friends as have not already polled, and requests the favour of their early attendance at Tailors' Hall, this and the following days.

State of the Poll :—

	Brickdale.	Cruger.	Burke.	Clare.
Thursday	1304	2303	1787	120
Friday	212	244	161	29

A chance now occurred for a local poet to publish a few verses :—

REASON AGAINST RAILING.

A SONG.

I.

WHEN the tools of a party to slander descend,
And by Billingsgate reason a bad cause defend,
By their prudent example repeatedly press'd on
We might drag out the slaves t'other side of the question.
Derry Down, Down, Down, Derry Down.

II.

The most abject of them, who for slavery plead,
Uncandid, ungenerous in word and in deed,
Never stating the case either fairly or fully ;
From Councillor Codhead to Walter the Bully.
Derry Down, &c.

III.

But the aids of scurrility those will disdain,
Who the cause of their country sincerely maintain
To the votary's of falsehood they leave the foul play
Who are bart'ring the rights of the people away.
Derry Down, &c.

IV.

They tell us " Lord Clare has done much for the city,
" And thus to desert him, by Jove, it were pity,
" Damn'd hard, he has helped us at many dead " Lifts,"
And forgot that he blinded the people with Gifts.
Derry Down, &c.

V.

We are told that his colleague will bribery scorn,
"That he'll stand for his country,—a Citizen "born,"
But I fear the great Duty his Talent exceeds;
For a niggardly soul is unfit for great deeds.
            Derry Down, &c.

VI.

We have heard it asserted "The struggle were "vain,
"To recover our freedom, or rights to regain,"
But whatever a servile Declaimer may prate;
True Britons will never despair of the state.
            Derry Down, &c.

VII.

"Fie, beware what ye do—nor disturb the "town's quiet,
"Who complains of abuses, are guilty of riot;"
Thus the Heart of these Englishmen come to that pass is,
That instead of brave Lions, they're more like tame Asses,
            Derry Down, &c.

VIII.

Now let no man cajole ye with crafty delusion,
Of disturbing the peace or creating confusion;
Purge the house, and replace it with good men and true,
And the good of the people will be their sole view.
            Derry Down, &c.

IX.

While the national trust is committed to knaves,
We dream but of freedom—the humblest of slaves;
Search the cause to the bottom, resolve to procure
A free Parliament—That's the infallible cure.
            Derry Down, &c.

X.

Never give up the point—to your country be staunch,
Drive dishonour and fraud from the house root and branch,
And in the pursuit of so glorious a work,
Be each Parliament Hero like Cruger and Burke.
            Derry Down, Down, Down, Derry Down.

The local poet was followed by one of Burke's supporters:—

To the Citizens of Bristol,—

The contradictory and self-destroying charges brought against Mr. Burke, might be well left to their own absurdity for refutation. A manly, sober and steady conduct generally produces such accusations, but these always defeat their own purposes. A good man and a great poet said long since, that

    Tories call him Whig—and Whigs a Tory.

A proof that he went to the extremes of neither. A further refutation of these charges may seem unnecessary; but if called for it will be found in the private life and conduct of Mr. Burke,—in his actions and in his writings. From his earliest infancy, educated by the care of a father, a member of the Established Church (whose profession was incompatible with the Roman Catholic Religion), in the most public places of Protestant education, schools, and University (at the latter of which he took his degree) from thence removed to the Temple, where he pursued his studies for five years; afterwards nine years in Parliament *where no Roman Catholic can sit*, and now actually again a member of Parliament for Malton. Notwithstanding which, whilst he solicits, not for a seat in Parliament, *but the honor of representing Bristol*, he is by the candid friends of Mr. Brickdale, *called a Roman Catholic.*

Conduct in Parliament cannot be concealed, though a few people may be imposed on, and misled by an artful and disingenuous misrepresentation of it. For nine years he has been the strenuous defender in the House of Commons of the Established Church—for nine years, he has pleaded for the just and wise toleration due to conscientious dissenters of all denominations—for nine years he has defended the rights, the privileges and the liberties of the people, regardless of the displeasure or enmity of Ministry—for nine years he has supported Law, order and steady and effectual government, at the risk of losing the favour of inconsiderate popular men. In his writings the same spirit of Civil and religious liberty, of good order and government breathe throughout. His conduct has been public in the face of the world; judge by that. His writings are in print, and in the hands of most people; read them and judge. Judge not by malicious hints, sly insinuations and dark suggestions. His life and actions will bear the broadest day; they are in a glare of light. Judge for yourselves, ye sensible and spirited electors; and let us confer the great honour of representing us in Parliament upon him, who thro' so long and so laborious a service, has defended and adorned the cause of

CIVIL AND RELIGIOUS LIBERTY.

The *Bristol Journal* of October 22, 1774, contained the following important publications :—

To THE PRINTER,—

The various and contradictory reports circulated by Mr. Burke's opponents concerning his political and religious principles, need only to be set in contrast to invalidate each other :—

Mr. Burke is said to be,

1st—A Roman Catholic, educated at St. Omers.
2ndly—Unfavourable to religious liberty.
3rdly—A dissenter, or at least partial to the dissenters, and an enemy to the Church on this account.

Can anything surpass the absurdity of *these opposite charges from the same quarter*; their *self-contradiction* seems to render any further remark unnecessary—however, I would, through the channel of your paper, convey a few observations relative thereto; in which I shall adhere to the order above stated.

To the 1st, Mr. Burke is descended from Protestant ancestors, was educated in the Church of England, sent from thence to the University of Dublin, where he took a degree; from thence to the Temple; from thence was called to Parliament :—never was at St. Omers during his minority, nor since, but passing through on a tour to Paris.

The University degrees and the seat in Parliament *require solemn engagements on admission*, utterly incompatible not only with a profession of Popery, but with a secret attachment to it. Mr. Burke's conduct in Parliament has evinced a regard to the preservation of the just rights of the Established Church; particularly on occasion of the petitioning clergy; *to which the Lord Bishop of Bristol cannot but bear witness;* and on occasion of the Bill for establishing Popery in Canada, which he strenuously opposed. Judge then, which is most liable to the charge of favouring Popery, he who opposes the establishment, or he who concurs in promoting it.

2ndly—The writer of a paper arrogantly signed Bristol; amidst many other insinuations equally false, asks this question—Do the Quakers know that Mr. Burke is an enemy to religious liberty? He attempts not to advance a single fact to support this insinuation; he knew he could not. How mean and detestable is this inuendo! The only thing this writer could have a reference to, was Mr. Burke's opposing the petitioning clergy, but not on principles adverse to religious liberty, of which (as will under the next head be more explicitly spoken of) he has been on all occasions a zealous and steadfast advocate—but while he earnestly wished to allow unlimited toleration to all who dissented from the Established Church, he could not think it reasonable at the request of those gentlemen, to hazard the experiment of innovation with respect to the Church itself—concluding probably with Lord North, that the article of public peace was at least as sacred as any of the thirty-nine—not that but every judicious man, who has attended to the subject, must think with the Bishop of Bristol and Dean Tucker (not to mention many others of the established clergy) that an alteration might be made to great advantage, at a suitable season, when the minds of the people are properly disposed to candor and reflection; though, after all, he wishes to refer to the gentlemen whose province it is, the task of discussing theological dogmas.

3rdly—Mr. Burke is also charged with the opposite extreme, of leaning too much to the Dissenters, and wishing to subvert the Established Church in their favor. If this charge be true, it is utterly inconsistent with the former; yet both have originated (as may be proved) from the same quarter. Mr. Burke, from a steadfast regard to the just rights of conscience, strenuously seconded the application of the Dissenters for the repeal of the penal laws; laws enacted at a time when the minds of men were not sufficiently enlightened to discern their impropriety—and which those, who plead against their abolition, at the same time confess ought not to be carried into execution. For what purpose then retained? If these laws are just they ought to be executed, if unjust repealed. If thus to think and speak be disaffection to the Established Church, some of the most respectable names in her communion are liable to the aspersions; and while Burnet, Hoadley, Locke, Tillotson, Chillingworth, &c., with many eminent and truly respectable characters now living are in the list, Mr. Burke need not blush to be found in such company. But what kind of compliment do those pay the Established Church *who suppose it cannot subsist in safety but on the ruins of the rights of conscience.*

The query being particularly addressed to the Quakers, is intended to insinuate, that they are the only, or at least the chief abettors of Mr. Burke; but the writer is conscious, that the cause, they with others are engaged in, is the cause of every friend of civil and religious liberty, whether Churchmen or Dissenters, as such it is considered and patronised accordingly by the most respectable of each denomination; maugre the opposition of those who are friends of arbitrary power and oppressive principles.

Thus much for religion;—next for Politics.

We are told Mr. Burke is for advancing the power of the crown, beyond its due bounds, and abridging the liberties of the people. So the true blues at length stand forth as jealous and vigilant defenders of the liberties of the people. We congratulate you, gentlemen, on the change, but the joy we should otherwise conceive is for the present allayed with some doubts; as we wish to see this profession confirmed by a correspondent conduct which alone can assure us of its sincerity. But while your past declarations and conduct are recent in memory, we must be somewhat apprehensive of your returning to what you have been used to call "the "good old cause." But to proceed—What is alleged in support of this charge? Why truly that Mr. Burke is averse to short Parliaments, this is taken from a late publication, entitled, Thoughts on the cause of the present discontents; wherein amidst a variety of observations on the present state of the nation, he has said, " That the introducing triennial " Parliaments is a matter of great and serious deliberation, not to be " hastily or rashly determined—that on candid consideration of the " matter, he feared it would increase the power of the crown." Of the same opinion Lord Chatham declared himself in Parliament. And would these candid opponents infer, that either of those gentlemen were for advancing the power of the Crown; because they objected to a measure which they thought must be attended with that very effect. With regard to triennial Parliaments, the friends of liberty and the constitution appear to think differently as to their expediency; Mr. Burke wishes not hastily to determine, on a measure of such importance, agreed as to the end, yet thinking differently (with respect to one particular proposal) as to the means, he is craftily represented as opposing the end itself—but the artifice is too shallow to escape immediate detection on the first view. With regard to this point, Mr Burke *wishes to be open to conviction, and, if convinced*, to act accordingly.

Mr. Burke (we are next informed) is an enemy to government and an abettor of factious licentiousness.

Wonderfully consistent is this with the preceding charge! And how is this supported? Why, Mr. Burke has voted frequently against the Ministry—certainly he has—whenever measures have been adopted inconsistent with the proper ends of government, and the true interest of this nation, as in the case of the Boston Bill, the Quebec Bill, etc. His public conduct has for nine years been steadily uniform and consistent, neither adopting a measure (as so many have done) because it came by the ministry, nor rejecting it merely for the sake of opposition; and is not this the proper conduct of every free and independent representative, of every judicious and honest man?

To conclude, Mr. Burke is a steadfast friend of the established constitution in Church and State, on true *revolution* principles, equally remote from arbitrary oppression or factious licentiousness—and from his long tried steadfastness and integrity, his friends have the strongest reason to be assured that his future conduct will, equally with his past, be regulated by them. Such my fellow Citizens is the man, such are the measures which have been proposed to you; many of you have shewn your approbation of each, by your steadfast support; the writer of this congratulates you on the majority of numbers, *notwithstanding every act of undue influence has been put in practice* to deter some amongst you from voting according to the dictates of your own conscience. Go on and prosper.
PHILO-VERITAS.

A broadside, signed Tribunus, was issued in reply:—

[Copy reply to Philo-Veritas.]

Your name is a blunder—your performance so prolix and inconsistent, it needs no refutation. Ask *the two forward youths* if the Quakers (tho' very sensible men) had not a principal hand in bringing Mr. Burke hither, and pray who is this Mr. Burke? A man who has no consistency, but in opposing Government upon every question, whether right or wrong— who opposes triennial parliaments—who opposes limiting the number of placemen in the House of Commons. He says in page the 95th, line 21st: "I confess then, that I have no sort of reliance upon either a triennial "parliament or a place bill," and line 27th, "I should be fearful of com-"mitting, every three years, the independent gentlemen of the country "into a contest with the treasury." Excellent reasoning! The con- clusion however must be that the dependent candidates are always supported by the treasury. I believe his friends will be glad to find this true at the end of the present election.

His thoughts on a place bill are page 97th, line 22nd, "It is not easy "to foresee what the effect would be, of disconnecting with parliament "the greatest part of those, who hold civil employments, and of such "mighty and important bodies, as the military and naval establish-"ments. It were better, perhaps, that they should have a corrupt "interest in the forms of the constitution, than they should have none "at all." Mr. Burke, 'tis true, is not chargeable with "encreasing the power of the Crown," but we cannot help observing, that in his intended aristocratic Government to be formed by a combination of great men, he would not have short parliaments, nor be without the assistance of the military and naval officers, both in and out of the house, to make the King a cypher and enslave the people. For my own part, I think that the representatives of the people should be a controul on the Crown and the Lords, and that they will not be such, unless they themselves are controuled by the people. *That this cannot be without frequent elections.* That frequent elections will render all pecuniary influence vain and ineffectual and even dangerous, at certain periods, in the practice—that frequent elections is the constitutional right of the people, and that the restoration of that right, and limiting the number of placemen would remedy the causes of the present discontents.

TRIBUNUS.

October 24, 1774.

The following broadside was also issued :—

TO THE CITIZENS OF BRISTOL,

I am sorry to find you my brother Citizens so blindly imposed on by the false representations of Mr. Brickdale's tools. Mr. Burke that offers his service to represent you in Parliament is one of the greatest Orators we have in the Kingdom. His great abilities exerted for seven years past against the daring attempts to abridge and curtail that dearest object of our lives, our liberty, is a clear convincing proof. He is one that most nervously opposed a wicked, corrupt ministry who endeavoured to enslave us. He is the man that boldly stood forth against that vile Boston Act. He despised place or pension, his great abilities in Parliament were wholly exerted to defend our property, and protect us from the Shackles intended for us by an abandoned administration. In short he has a capacity sufficient, and I make not the least doubt but he will ever steadily exert it to protect and support our present happy constitution, as by law established. He will be a guard against any infringement of our liberty—will be the means of encouraging the Sinking Commerce of this opulent City—and in every other respect approve himself worthy of your choice :—Let us therefore stand forth and give our free suffrages for him.

A FREEHOLDER.

Desperate efforts were now made by the friends of Brickdale to make headway against Burke, as will be seen by an analysis of the figures. On Saturday, the 22nd of October, the poll closed with the following totals :—

Cruger.	Burke.	Brickdale.	Clare.
2769	2091	1740	197

At the end of each day the numbers were printed on small strips of paper and distributed by the "runners," or messengers attached to the Committees. On Monday, the 24th of October, a wag issued the following skit :—

Bristol, Monday, Oct. 24, 1774.

Cruger.	Burke.	Brickdale.	Clare.
2928	2172	1938	232
(Vagabond Tradesmen.)	(Scum of the Earth.)	(Court Sycophants.)	(Ministerial Tools.)

The following broadside refers to John, the brother of Matthew Brickdale, who had been engaged in suppressing a serious riot in the year 1753, caused by the knowledge that a quantity of wheat was about to be exported from Bristol, which had exasperated the Kingswood colliers, hence the appellation " Don John." The facts are set out in pages 303, 4 and 5 of Mr. John Latimer's ".Annals of Bristol in the Eighteenth " Century." It appears that at an inquest held by one of the Coroners of the County of Gloucester, a verdict of wilful murder was returned against John Brickdale and others.* The proceedings were quashed by certain proceedings in the Court of King's Bench and by granting a general pardon :—

> To all Electors of Bristol, who espouse the good old cause of the good old Church of Rome.
>
> You are requested to appear at Clifton to-morrow morning at eight o'clock, there to meet Don John Brickdale, who stands in need at this critical juncture, of your best advice and assistance, for his Brother, who will certainly lose his election, if not supported by his brethren of the X, being *hard push*d by the Rockingham party;* those Champions of Liberty, our inveterate enemies, who endeavoured to d—n the Quebec Bill, and thereby *prevent the establishment* of our ancient and holy religion, in North America. The holy standard is hoisted at Clifton, and those who attend early will be favored with a sight of Charley's portrait. If you heartily unite in the cause, it is not to be doubted but we shall overturn *the dissenting* Hereticks of all denominations.
>
> Our worthy Confessor Sc——d———e will attend to clear your conscience, and instruct you in the Charitable Doctrine of the now so much despised Society of J———ts.
>
> October 25, 1774.

In a broadside, purporting to be an announcement of a sale by auction, at the Three Queen's, St. Thomas Street, on the 25th of October, of certain "animals," the alleged partiality of Cruger for the society of the ladies was referred to in terms which It would be undesirable to re-print. At the 1774 election the attacks of the Brickdale party were almost exclusively directed towards Burke, but at the subsequent elections of 1780, 81 and 84, in which Cruger figured, his alleged amours were frequently referred to in anonymous publications, in which he was called "Doodle-doo," "American-doodle," and "Yankee-doodle." Richard Smith states that he was " a devotee to the ladies," and Chatterton hints at the same weakness in his (unpublished) " Exhibition."

---

* In all probability the man upon whom the inquest was held was killed near " Don John's Cross."

The friends of Brickdale now issued an important address :—

To the Citizens of Bristol.

GENTLEMEN,
If, among the many illiberal and violent publications which generally appear on the occasion of contested elections for Members of Parliament, the still voice of reason can at present be listened to by you, I will beg your attention and flatter myself that dispassionate argument will meet from the Citizens of Bristol with that respect it has ever a just claim to. Being an old man I remember, and my contemporaries may also recollect, the animosities which former struggles of this nature have been productive of in this City, animosities so injurious to individuals, so destructive of that friendly disposition which should always subsist between neighbours and fellow citizens, not to mention the sums lavished in support of riot and disorder which might have been of real service to the City in general and the industrious labouring part of it in particular. Of late we have happily been free from those evils, and I doubt not it is the wish of every sensible, cool and good citizen that such a blessing so particularly important in a large trading City has been continued to us, not that I would be understood to insinuate that our judgment in the choice of representatives should be sacrificed to a blind regard for the peace of the City. For, I only mean to set forth, and I will venture to assert, that it is our duty to endeavour that the peace of the City shall not be broken unless for some certain good, and on this head, Gentlemen, I would ask whether we can reasonably expect *from the person that now disturbs it better and more distinguished service than from our late members*, and I am not particularly attached to either of these gentlemen and would wish to support in anything I have and would say on this matter the dispassionate character I have adopted in the beginning of this address consistent with that I think that I may assert *that my Lord Clare has been as useful a member for the City as we have had these fifty years past*, and I might, perhaps, with truth add and more so he has been for three successive Parliaments diligently attentive to every application that has been made to him wherein the commercial interest of the City was concerned, and on every occasion his endeavours have been successfully employed. He has also been ever ready with his best assistance and support to any individual citizen that has been distressed and needed the hand of benevolence.

Our other member, Mr. Brickdale, has served us in one Parliament, and this I should consider to be a recommendation, for experience is as necessary to form a good Senator as to make a good man of business. During the last seven years Mr. Brickdale has closely attended to his duty. I hope not to incur the charge of partiality by saying that in no instance of his conduct in Parliament his integrity stands impeachable. On many occasions when respectable committees have been formed to sit on business of importance, he has been selected and considered a very useful member, and such men are as truly necessary in the Senate of a Commercial Kingdom, as the most polished orators. Rhetorical talents are indeed when properly applied an ornament to the possessor, but it is much to be regretted they are so frequently exerted to give a false colouring to a bad cause. Integrity is the sterling principle which must support every Government, and particularly that species of it which we happily live under. If therefore I am right, and our old members deserve what I have said of them, I would wish to know in what respect the new candidate can possibly stand superior in the eyes of any one citizen of Bristol, and if in none, why is the peace of the city unnecessarily disturbed ? In some respects I might perhaps point him out inferior, but tho' under an anonymous signature, I scorn to debase my pen with any illiberal personal reflection on him or any gentleman, but however improper and indefensible it is to investigate and hold up to public view the private character of any man, thus much I may remark that as there is a decency in appearance due to society whoever neglects to support such justly deserves and will certainly draw on him the public censure. But here I stop, and shall conclude with mentioning *no reason*, and that a public one, *why I deem the gentleman at this time totally unfit to represent the City* and that is *he is an American*. For I perfectly agree in the sentiments that a gentleman lately expressed on this head to a large meeting of Citizens nearly in the following words, which I beg his permission to use. That in the present unhappy disagreement between England and America it is the duty of every elective body in the Kingdom to be particularly attentive to send up to the next Parliament men cool and dispassionate, of honest hearts and sound understanding, which may be applied to the forming that necessary line and barrier between the Mother Country and its Colonies, which the former may look upon as the bulwark of the latter, and the colonies dutifully regard and never attempt to transgress.

CANDIDUS.

A Reply to Candidus and other Scribblers.

That generous disposition of soul, *Candidus*, which so much exalts human nature persuades me to make but a very slender distinction between him who actually states and him who tamely beholds the reputation of a fellow creature, labouring under the fangs of fell detraction. Under the influence of this doctrine (which I fear your heart is but too much acquainted with) I venture to reply to your cruel anonymous production. That void sanctimonious disguise so finely spun from a pretence to impartiality, serves but too ill to hide rancorous intention—it deepens the colour of your guilt and upbraids you with having lamentably abused the admirable signature you have the impudence enough to adopt. Surely you must blush (if so virtuous a feeling remains in you) to hear and to be conscious that you are neither liberal, impartial or anything else that entitles you to the least glimmering of that character, the dearest object of any honest heart, a just man, a feeling man, or a gentleman. I speak to you as the author of Candidus, and charitably hope the same portrait may not suit you in the more material concerns of life, whether professional or domestic, yet I would freely exculpate you by alleging that we do not always act from principle, that envy, malice, interest, and a thousand other unworthy passions sometimes becloud our better part and sink us beneath ourselves were it not too visible that your malignant aspirations originate in a heart badly—very badly—disposed. Your case is truly deplorable, and must be a sufficient torment to you, perhaps unconscious yourself of the sweets of unblemished reputation, you dangerously trifle with those to whom it is invaluable, and dare with sickly smiles and venal mouth and foulest license, mock the patriot's name. You declaim in favour of the peace of this great trading city, believe me, Sir, you who can so badly attempt to disturb the tranquillity of an amiable individual cannot be so deeply interested in that of a collective body, you pretend to that respect and decency due to society, who vitally stab it in a generous and noble hearted member of it. For shame, Sir! shrink from the recollection of your black, barbarous purpose.

Call to the aid of an evil heart the dictates of humanity the mild precepts of that religion, which you ought to be better acquainted with, that will teach you to drop every unfriendly passion to put on a merciful compassionating spirit.

If the inadvertency of you has unhappily betrayed the object of your illiberal invective into some venal disrespect to the duties of society and a noble warmth of heart (however it may struggle) cannot effect immediate release from a situation that cannot but oppress it, it was yours, Sir, it is humanity's part to forgive, or at least to take a less cruel mode of reproving. If you are one of that time-serving, venal set, ever yawning after emolument, you must have your share of stagnant shift and knavery so peculiar to you, to worm yourself into the favour of those who flatter so impertinently you pay them but an ill compliment indeed to build their merit on the airy basis of any other man's dismerit, if they have any delicacy or discernment they will discover you to be equally fulsome and injudicious. I sincerely believe my Lord Clare to be a worthy man, and my opinion of his understanding tells me he is far exalted above the servile homage you wish to pay him that he was a proper person to represent the City in Parliament, that he has it in his power and has it sometimes in inclination to benefit a few people, every-one who understands or feels the interest of it, or knows the man, will readily grant.

Mr. Brickdale it is true has (to use your expression) served us in one Parliament, and this which you strain into his favour is a very weighty if not a sufficient reason why he should not serve us again. Fatal experience has convinced us, and, I believe, the nation at large, of the evil effects of power invetering in the same hands. The only means we have left us of obviating *the bad consequences of long septennial Parliaments* is to be diligent to avoid returning the same members repeatedly, unless equally renowned for abilities and integrity, *such men, Sir, as Mr. Burke.* I mention him to give you some tolerable idea of what your letter proves you to be an utter stranger to abilities and integrity. For these reasons I sincerely wish both Lord Clare and Mr. Brickdale may be excluded from our representation, particularly as they have not opposed (if they have not swollen) the torrent of corruption that has sapped the very foundation of our liberty for almost these seven years past. Humanity is not less imature than weak, how far they have imbued the genius of a corrupt majority we need no great sagucity to perceive, and that they will become indolent (which has been the case already) if we return them again is more than probable.

Should long Parliaments be continued and a corrupt influence prevail, which will assuredly be the case if we make not a wholesome use of this glorious opportunity to prevent it by returning new worthy members, the sense of the house will not only be different from but directly contrary to the voice of the people. As to Mr. Brickdale's honor of being admitted a committee man, we know the nature of these secret juntos too well to consider that any recommendation of him, and we may fairly determine how conducive they are to the interest of the nation by the prodigiously fine efforts they have of late exhibited to us, I will not disagree with you on this point, Mr. Brickdale might have been a very useful member of them. You very gravely tell us that rhetorical talents are an ornament to the possessor when properly applied, and that integrity is the best support of all government. You are exceedingly clear indeed, you have thrown an amazing light upon affairs. I tell you, Sir, Mr. Cruger is equal in all and superior in some of these respects to the persons you are pleased to adorn with them. His sacred love of the constitution, his benevolence to mankind, his inviolable integrity and strong and natural sense, his particular attention to the interests of this city are equally an ornament to him, as they are a full justification of that almost universal favour which we cannot withhold from him. A moderate share of abilities, Sir, when faithfully applied to the great machine of government, and seconded by uprightness will bring it into and preserve it in its pristine plain sure course, from which it is to be lamented it has been obliged to deviate too much through the caprice and rascality of others. Mr. Cruger wants not ability nor fidelity for this good purpose, though perhaps not so deeply versed in the spirit of law and government as Mr. Locke, where will you find a Senator that is ?

While we wish to flourish as a great trading people, we cannot but feel the advantages of having Merchants in the Commons house, for want of this blessing our colonies have laboured much. I shall instance the restraint of paper credit in America. It is to be regretted that our representative house is filled with a set of hare-brained Nimrods, whose property is chiefly land (who understand commercial advantages just as much as they do the squaring of a circle) almost to the total exclusion of the mercantile and manufactural interest, the merchant is closely connected with the welfare of the nation, and cannot be separated from it but with the most pernicious consequences. *You say Mr. Cruger is an American*, futile disingenuous objection, hence he may have it more in his power to be instrumental to a happy reconciliation between the Mother Country and her aggrieved settlements, his connections are important on both sides of the water, and he knows—he cannot but know —the happiness of America to be precisely the same with that of England. I would say much more upon this subject, but as the same narrow prejudice which has embittered you against the man whom one day or other you will shudder to behold, must have hardened you to every cool and dispassionate feeling. I shall dismiss you with a slight return to my original purpose, whether you strut in the higher sphere or profession, *or sicken at the counting house morose obscurity*, you are cruel, mean and ungenerous, when you shall be oppressed with the candour and civilities of the man you have attempted to injure; beware lest an awkward consciousness betray your guilt. Should I ever discover you it may be the case. *I will be a vulture upon your liver*, if ever an envious cruel heart invite you again into public be discreet enough to spare the man to whom truth honour and generosity are ever dear and sacred.

Whose aim aspires to all diviner deeds
Whose tear for ever streams for others woes.

PHILANTHROPOS.

The results of the polling during the next few days, were as follow:—

	Cruger.	Burke.	Brickdale.	Clare.
25th October	3055	2277	2019	245
26th „	3168	2372	2075	250
27th „	3236	2433	2167	253

The following paragraph was inserted in the *Bristol Journal*, of Saturday, the 29th October:—

It was generally expected that our election would have ended on Thursday last; but the friends of Mr. Brickdale and Mr. Burke having agreed upon a meeting with intent to fix a time for the final close of the poll, accordingly attended—but to no purpose, neither party making any motion. The contest is still vigorously carried on by both parties, and the number of out-votes which are continually arriving, on whose account the books are kept open, render uncertain when it will end. The poll has lasted three weeks already, a longer time than was ever known. The numbers *last night* (Friday, the 28th of October) were:—

For Henry Cruger, Esq.	...	3270
Edmund Burke, Esq.	...	2462
Matthew Brickdale, Esq.	...	2234
Lord Clare	...	259

Felix Farley's Bristol Journal of Saturday, October 29, 1774, contains the following bit of news :—No poll for members to represent this city was ever known to continue so long as the present; it has been held three weeks already, and it is imagined will not be yet finally closed for some days. The number of voters that have been made free is incredible, being near two thousand, and a very considerable part of them since the poll began.

At the close of the poll on Saturday, the numbers were:—

Cruger.	Burke.	Brickdale.	Clare.
3325	2501	2314	261

On Monday, the 31st, there was a little life still left in the Brickdale party, and another squib was let off:—

[COPY.]
To the Citizens of Bristol.

Awake my Brethren, and be upon your guard. Yours is the second city in the kingdom—don't disgrace yourselves by suffering *a public incendiary* with his *two firebrands* like an *ignis fatuus*, to lead you to your ruin. You would now have been in a state of peace and tranquility, had not Mr. Champion and Mr. Harford, under the influence and direction of Mr. Peach, sown the seeds of discord among you. Will it be hereafter credited, that three such insignificant persons could raise such disturbances among so many sensible people? The *unprincipled* Patriot first set as *a Bill* of Rights man—now he vainly attempts to force upon you, Mr. Burke, a pensioner of the Rockinghams—*an Agent for New York*—one, who if not *a Papist,* can have no dislike to Popery, as he cannot deny *he married a rigid Roman Catholic.* He is a friend to *Aristocratic* Tyranny—an enemy to general freedom, neither short Parliaments nor place-bills are among his political Articles of Faith. In short, Mr. Burke's connections with the Rockinghams are such, as must for ever prevent his being *of any service* as a Member of Parliament, to this *or any other commercial city.* However, I don't blame him for accepting the invitation, but I can't help smiling that Mr. Peach should be so amazingly ignorant, as not to know of his connections, and that the *principles* of the Rockingham party are widely different from those of the Bill of Rights.

Mr. Peach is impudently striving to bring in two Representatives for the City, but happy it is for you, that he and his emissaries will fail in the attempt. The friends of the constitution and Mr. Brickdale who are yet unpolled, need only now step forwards—they will gain a complete victory and make their opponents sicken at the sound of

October 31, 1774.   OLD ENGLAND FOR EVER.

On this day a Freeman residing at Crediton, thought it desirable to give the men of Bristol a specimen of his poetic genius :—

To THE FRIENDS OF CRUGER AND BURKE,—

Hail to the man whose generous soul disdains
The golden clog of Ministerial chains;
Who! midst surrounding Sycophants of pow'r
(Machines of State; mere puppets of an hour),
Stands nobly steadfast in his country's cause,
And dares assert its Liberty and Laws;
Attacks corruption in each dark retreat,
And drags to view each cacus of the State;
Who rests the dagger from the desp'rate hand,
Held up to stab the vitals of the land.
This task, O Burke, has been and shall be thine,
And Cruger second every grand design;
Your timely aid immortal fame shall meet,
And Bristol lay glad tributes at your feet.
Tho' foes to Albion; for alarming ends,
Have drawn the sword of blood upon our friends;
Tho' all that's dear to British Hearts of Oak,
Now bends obsequious to the Papal yoke;
Cruger and Burke, with friends of manly zeal,
Shall rouse the Senate to a quick repeal!
And Bristol crown'd with commerce now shall see
Cruger and Burke have taught us to be free.

C. JONES.

Journeyman Wool-comber, a Freeman of Bristol, resident at Crediton, Devonshire.

Bristol, Monday Oct. 31, 1774.

The following squib was evidently intended as an intimation that Mr. Brickdale was badly in want of votes:—

WANTED.

As the election is getting towards the end, particulars of all dead men's copies, and the copies of persons beyond sea, should be immediately sent to the White Ass Club,* Broad Street. Particulars of the numbers and prices may be sent privately to Mr. B———e.†

October 31st, 1774.

The numbers at the close of the poll on Monday, the 31st October, and the following day were:—

	Cruger.	Burke.	Brickdale.	Clare.
31st October	3412	2579	2357	269
1st November	3496	2647	2412	276

The Poll finally closed on Wednesday, the 2nd of November, with the following result:—Cruger, 3565; Burke, 2707; Brickdale, 2456; Clare, 283.

---

* The White Lion Club   † Mr. Brickdale.

The number of votes recorded each day from the commencement to the close of the poll is appended:—

1774.		Day of Poll.	Cruger.	Burke.	Brickdale.	Clare.
Oct. 7	Friday	1	11	0	10	12
8	Saturday	2	5	0	15	0
10	Monday	3	95	71	46	0
11	Tuesday	4	233	164	110	1
12	Wednesday	5	205	168	122	4
13	Thursday	6	231	180	128	4
14	Friday	7	183	157	141	47
15	Saturday	8	201	164	121	11
17	Monday	9	244	194	121	4
18	Tuesday	10	326	260	154	3
19	Wednesday	11	278	223	165	14
20	Thursday	12	291	206	171	20
21	Friday	13	244	161	212	29
22	Saturday	14	222	143	224	48
24	Monday	15	159	81	198	35
25	Tuesday	16	127	105	81	13
26	Wednesday	17	113	95	56	5
27	Thursday	18	68	61	92	3
28	Friday	19	34	29	67	6
29	Saturday	20	55	39	80	2
31	Monday	21	87	78	43	8
Nov. 1	Tuesday	22	84	68	55	7
2	Wednesday	23	69	60	44	7
		Total	3565	2707	2456	283

SUMMARY OF THE TOTALS AT THE CLOSE OF EACH DAY.

Day of Poll.	Cruger.	Burke.	Brickdale.	Clare.	Majority of Cruger over Brickdale.	Majority of Burke over Brickdale.
1	11	0	10	12	—	—
2	16	0	25	0	—	—
3	111	71	71	0	—	—
4	344	235	181	13	163	54
5	549	403	303	16	246	100
6	780	583	431	21	349	152
7	963	740	572	68	391	168
8	1164	904	693	79	471	211
9	1408	1098	814	83	594	284
10	1734	1358	968	86	766	390
11	2012	1581	1133	100	879	448
12	2303	1787	1304	120	999	483
13	2547	1948	1516	149	1031	432
14	2760	2091	1740	197	1020	351
15	2928	2172	1938	232	990	234
16	3055	2277	2019	245	1036	258
17	3168	2372	2075	250	1093	297
18	3236	2433	2167	253	1069	266
19	3270	2462	2234	259	1036	228
20	3325	2501	2314	261	1011	187
21	3412	2579	2357	269	1055	222
22	3496	2647	2412	276	1084	235
23	3565	2707	2456	283	1109	251

Cruger's majority over Brickdale 1109.
Burke's   ,,   ,,   251

TABULATED STATEMENT SHOWING HOW MANY VOTED FOR EACH PARISH AND FOR WHOM.

Parishes, &c.	Persons polled.	Cruger.	Burke.	Brickdale.	Clare.
All Saints	37	22	12	25	6
St. Augustine	247	156	99	138	36
Castle Precincts	146	119	106	36	7
Christ Church	88	65	47	40	2
St. Ewen	11	9	5	5	1
St. James	853	625	511	323	60
St. John	91	61	43	41	9
St. Leonard	25	15	8	17	3
St. Mary-le-Port	52	42	28	24	1
St. Mary Redcliff	357	229	123	184	16
St. Michael	183	83	58	122	26
St. Nicholas	214	134	91	115	18
St. Peter	98	86	65	32	2
St. Philip and Jacob	585	478	364	170	17
St. Stephen	168	140	90	73	10
Temple	273	167	124	148	10
St. Thomas	182	113	78	99	7
St. Werburgh	28	18	12	16	3
Bedminster	132	89	35	67	0
Clifton	129	80	68	56	7
Out Voters	1485	834	740	725	42
Totals	5384	3565	2707	2456	283

The total number of persons polled was 5384.
1504 of whom voted for Brickdale only (plumpers).
220 ,, ,, Cruger ,, ,,
21 ,, ,, Burke ,, ,,
12 ,, ,, Clare ,, ,,
264 ,, ,, Clare and Brickdale.
2 ,, ,, Clare and Cruger.
5 ,, ,, Clare and Burke.
675 ,, ,, Brickdale and Cruger.
13 ,, ,, Brickdale and Burke.
2668 ,, ,, Cruger and Burke.

5384

The following members of the Corporation voted for Cruger and Burke :—Messrs. Levi Ames, John Anderson, Edward Brice, John Bull, Alexander Edgar, Thomas Farr, Thomas Deane, John Noble, Isaac Piguenit, Thomas Pearce, George Weare and Samuel Webb; Messrs. Andrew Pope and James Laroche voted for Brickdale and Cruger; Messrs. J. Bangh, W. Barnes, Wm. Miles, Henry Lippincott, George Daubeny and Jeremy Baker plumped for Brickdale; Messrs. Charles Hotchkin (the Mayor), Morgan Smith, Henry Mugleworth, Isaac Elton, E. Whatley, T. Harris. Henry Bright, Nathaniel Foy, Isaac Elton, jun., and Michael

Miller, jun., voted for Clare and Brickdale. Only two of the Aldermen, Thomas Deane, ward of Redcliff, and George Weare, ward of St. Thomas, supported Cruger and Burke. The other members of the Corporation *(including two of the candidates, Brickdale and Cruger)*, did not vote. An immense number of out-voters came to the poll at the expense of the candidates or their friends. [Burke was invited to contest the election free of expense to himself.] From London and Middlesex, 391; from Somersetshire, 449; from Gloucestershire, 355; many came from remote parts. The clergy who were entitled to vote in respect of freeholds or as freemen, with very few exceptions, voted against Burke and Cruger.

In the record of freeholders who voted at the election we find the names of various persons who held offices for life in connection with the Cathedral, such as Prebendaries, Minor Canons, "Schoolmaster of the Cathedral for life," two undermasters of the Cathedral School, the sub-Sacrist, the Chapter Clerk, several "patent pensioners," several "lay clerks," &c.

The trades or callings of the Freemen comprised:—Cordwainers, haberdasher-of-hats, vintners, chaise-drivers, anchor-smiths, hoopers, upholders, scriveners, weavers, skinners, peruke-makers, serge makers, mast makers, rope makers, stay makers, hoe makers, braziers, gingerbread bakers, lightermen, potters, sugar bakers, assayer of metals, felt makers, plush weavers, merchant tailors, soap makers, glassmen, landwaiter, tidewaiter, Serjeant-at-Mace, haberdasher of small wares, tobacco cutters, tobacco rollers, glass grinders, glovers, pump makers, watchmen, the Mayor's Serjeant, heel makers, bridle cutters, whitawers, lace-weavers, brandy merchants, block makers, leather dressers, riggers, silk dyers, hair merchants, bright smiths, bed joiners, barber-surgeons, well sinkers, crane masters, teamen, porters, pitchers, halliers, tin-plate-chasers, breeches makers, stocking-frame knitters, winehoopers, gallypot makers, saddle-tree makers, glaziers, vice makers, hot pressers, patten makers, patten and clog makers, patten-ring makers, file cutters, "chimsweepes," woolstaplers, whitners of woollen, flax-dressers, hair-sack weavers, salt refiners, millwrights, scribblers, mattmakers, chymists, wire-drawers, creatmakers, hemp dressers, bleechers, rug weavers, rough masons, woolcord makers, &c.

Not one of all the beneficed clergy gave a vote to Burke. Judging from the contents of an address to the electors (see ante pp 48-9) the clergy, or a considerable number of them, went in a procession to the poll. The Rector of St. Stephen's (the Rev. Josiah Tucker, D.D., who was also Dean of Gloucester), was one of Burke's active opponents. The cause is not far to seek. In the course of a speech in the House of Commons, on the 19th April, 1774, long before his name had been mentioned in connection with the representation of Bristol in Parliament, Burke had referred to Dean Tucker by name in reference to a tract the latter had issued, in which he alleged that the repeal of the Stamp Act had caused disturbances in America, and the worthy Dean probably thought, and perhaps not without cause, that he was included in a reference by Burke to "*this vermin of Court reporters;*" and as Burke went on, he said, " They say that the opposition made in Parliament to the
" Stamp Act at the time of its passing, encouraged the Americans
" to their resistance. This has even formally appeared in print
" in a regular volume, from an advocate of that faction, a Dr.
" Tucker. This Dr. Tucker is already a Dean, and his earnest
" labours in the vineyard will, I suppose, raise him to a
" Bishoprick." Later on, Dean Tucker addressed, " A letter to
" Edmund Burke, Esq., member of Parliament for the City of
" Bristol, and Agent for the Colony of New York," which commenced :—" Sir—As you have been pleased to bestow much
" abuse and scurrility on me in your public speech of the 19th of
" April, 1774; and also many commendations in private, both
" before and since that publication, &c., &c. . . . .
" *Therefore let Mr. Burke call me Court Vermin* as long as he
" pleases, *yet, as long as I can crawl,* I will ever maintain that
" the Rockingham Administration were the cause, the exciting

"cause I mean, of the present war, and of all the calamities "derived from it."

[This letter was published in pamphlet form, (58 p.p.), and was sold by T. Cadell, of the Strand.]

The Rev. Josiah Tucker took a very active part in the election of 1754, when Lord Clare (then Robert Nugent) was returned. In return for his assistance, his Lordship, a little later on, "out "of gratitude, obtained for him the Deanery of Gloucester."

It may not be amiss to mention that in 1778 Miss Mary Peloquin, the last survivor of one of the Huguenot families, by her will, left her house in Queen Square to be a residence for the Rector for the time being of St. Stephen's. The house was afterwards occupied by Dean Tucker. He died in December, 1799.

The next day, Thursday, the 3rd of October, about 12 o'clock, the Court was opened at St. George's Chapel, in the old Guildhall, when, after some altercation respecting the legality of the new-made votes, the Sheriffs declared Henry Cruger and Edmund Burke, Esqres., duly elected. After which Mr. Brickdale thanked his friends for the kind support they had given him, and told them that it was his intention to appeal to the House of Commons as to certain alleged irregularities connected with the election. [His objections were:—That Mr. Burke was improperly nominated after the poll had begun, and that the votes of the newly-admitted freemen were not legally admissable.] Mr. Cruger, as senior member—in accordance with custom—then addressed the assembled company:—

> GENTLEMEN AND FELLOW CITIZENS,
>
> The high honor you have done me, by electing me one of your representatives in the ensuing parliament, demands every possible return of personal gratitude and public fidelity.
> I am at a loss for words to declare, as forcibly as I could wish, the strong sense I feel of the dignity this day confirmed to me. My acknowledgments, though simple and unadorned, are as warm and sincere as though conveyed in the most refined expressions the most cultivated genius could suggest. What I have to say will be genuine, and from my heart,—a heart that this moment overflows with gratitude for the distinguishing marks of your regard and approbation, so generously manifested to its possessor. The unparalleled and respectable majority in my favor, does honor to the principle of the independent citizens of

Bristol. You have set a most noble example of independency to every elector in Great Britain. Indulge me in proclaiming to the whole world what you have done. You have, in spite of every effort to deter you from your virtuous purpose, gloriously dared to elect a man your representative in the grand council of the nation, whose highest title is that of merchant, and whose greatest boast is that of being an honest man.

It is my glory, gentlemen, to say, I have in this long contested election been as uninfluenced as unsupported by great men; so let it be your pride, O tradesmen, to promulge that you too have been uncontrolled and unbiassed by them. Your conduct shall be exemplary to me,—I, like you, will ever remain free and independent.

Gentlemen, permit me, at this favourable opportunity, to pay a little attention to a topic that has occasioned much altercation and uneasiness in this city: *I mean the legality and propriety of the people's instructing their representatives in Parliament. It has ever been my opinion that the electors have a right to instruct their members.* For my part, I shall always think it my duty in Parliament to be guided by your counsels *and instructions*. I shall consider myself *the servant of my constituents*, not their master. Subservient to their will, not superior to it. And let me add, I hold myself accountable to you for every action of my life which respects the public. By your upright judgment I desire to stand or fall.

It may be expected, gentlemen, that I should say *a few words* on the melancholy *subject of American affairs*. I will. They shall be few, but explicit. As far, fellow citizens, as the impulse of my power can be felt, it shall be exerted to *heal and conciliate* the unhappy differences, *not to foment them*. I consider the commercial interest of England and her colonies, as one and the same; they are reciprocal, and perfectly coincident. God and nature, and sound policy have linked them together in the strongest bonds of amity, mutual interest, and safety; the man that divides them, has either a weak head or a bad heart.

I will intrude no longer on your patience, than to assure you, I will carry to my grave the most ardent sentiments of affection and respect for my worthy friends of Bristol. And that I shall (with unshaken integrity) persevere to the last moments of my life, in every effort to promote the cause of liberty, and to render essential benefits to the trade and *commerce of this opulent* and flourishing City.

The following story is given in a work on Burke's life " by " Peter Burke, of the Inner Temple, and the Northern Circuit."—

> A humorous incident terminated the day's triumph. Mr. Cruger, Burke's colleague, a worthy Merchant in the American trade, and a Citizen of Bristol, *but no orator*, was *dumbfounded* by the eloquence of his mighty coadjutor. When his own turn came to thank the electors, he had recourse to a speech which though savouring of his countinghouse, was, under the circumstances, about the best he could make. He cried out, " *Gentlemen, I say ditto to Mr. Burke! ditto to Mr. Burke!* " *A roar of laughter and applause* marked the approval of his audience.

At this distance of time it is almost impossible to ascertain whether Peter Burke was imposed upon, or drew upon his imagination, for the story he has placed on record. Several generations of Bristolians have repeated it parrot like to one another, and it was lately repeated at the National Liberal

Club by Sir W. Vernon Harcourt, the Chancellor of the Exchequer. So far from being true, it will be seen that Cruger, who was the senior Member, in accordance with immemorial custom, was the first to speak. *He was followed by Mr. Burke,* who certainly spoke with great eloquence on this occasion. His speech for all practical purposes, may be divided into two parts, and for the benefit of the readers of this history of the contest, it has been thought advisable to give a few details by way of introduction to the matters referred to by Burke. After some preliminary complimentary references to everybody connected with the contest, he spoke on the subject of the admission to the freedom of the city of a large number of freemen—upwards of 2,000—after the date of the teste of the writ. Their claims to vote immediately after their admission had been admitted by the Sheriffs. Mr Brickdale, who had threatened to petition against the return of Cruger and Burke on the ground that the newly admitted freemen were not legally qualified to vote, had been informed by several old citizens that in 1734, the freemen—who were admitted after the date of the teste of the writ—were not allowed to vote, but he was probably, at the time, unacquainted with the fact that in 1734 *the agents of the two political parties had entered into an agreement* not to poll any freemen who had not been previously admitted. One of the persons who was the first to object at this (1774) election to the votes of the freemen who had been thus admitted, was Mr. Wm. Hart, a son of Mr. Wm. Hart who was a candidate in 1722, and he objected to the first newly admitted freeman when he presented himself at the hustings. When the Sheriffs allowed the vote *the man gave his vote for Brickdale,* so that Brickdale's friends (of whom Mr. Hart was one) brought the first newly-made voter to the poll, a matter which Burke made much of in his address to the electors. Brickdale polled 772 freemen whose votes had been created by their admission after the date of the teste of the writ. In reality the date of the teste of the writ had nothing to do with the question. Directly a freeman was

admitted, he was invested with the right to give his vote. In
Bristol only freeholders, in receipt of forty shillings or more
from a freehold, and freemen were entitled to the franchise.
Freemen were entitled to take up their freedoms by virtue of
servitude, birth, marriage to a daughter or widow of a freeman,
or by a special resolution of the Corporation. The son of a
freeman had to prove that he was born within the city
boundaries.* There was no register of voters, and the
voter might be resident in any part of the world. In
the year 1734 an attempt was made to reduce the
qualification of freemen to those who were resident and
paying scot and lot, but the proposal was not seriously
entertained. After the receipt of the writ by the Sheriffs on the
1st of October, 1774, the agents of the two political parties set
to work to find out the persons who were entitled to be made
freemen. The London agents of the Whigs and the Tories
respectively were actively engaged in tracing the freemen—
both those who had already been enrolled, but had left Bristol,
and those who were entitled to be enrolled—and communications
were opened with the most distant parts of England. Before
the close of the poll more than 2,000 new freemen had been
enrolled in the Corporation books. The fees for the admission
of the freemen were, with a few exceptions, paid by the
agents of the candidates, and the total perquisites of the
Town Clerk and the Chamberlain must have amounted to
a considerable sum. It was the custom for the agents to
take the men—who were decorated with the party colours—
in tallies—ten or five at a time—to the Town Clerk's
office, for the purpose of having their right to be admitted
inquired into, and if the Town Clerk was satisfied a
certificate was given to each applicant, which it was necessary
to take to the Chamberlain. By custom it was the duty of the
Mayor and two Aldermen to attend at the Town Clerk's office at

---

* A curious example is given by Mr. Latimer's in his "Annals of Bristol."—Mr. Jeremiah Osborne, solicitor, son of Joseph Osborne, a ship-wright, petitioned the Corporation for his admission as a freeman on the ground that the house in Limekiln Lane, in which he was born, was situated partly in Gloucestershire and partly in Bristol, and he alleged that he was born in that part of it which was in Gloucestershire. The Corporation granted him the freedom of the city.

a specified time to inquire into the qualifications of the persons claiming to be admitted, but, in practice, the duty was delegated to the Town Clerk or his deputy. The "Certificate"

City of Bristol.

The OATH of a Burgess.

YOU shall be good and true unto his Majesty King GEORGE 3ᵈ and to the Heirs and Successors of the said King, and to the Lieutenant, Master Mayor of the City of *Bristol*; and the Ministers of the same, in all Causes reasonable, you shall be Obedient and Assistant. You shall keep the Franchises and Customs of this City; and also the Kings Peace here you shall endeavour yourself to keep and maintain.

You shall be contributary to all manner of Summons as Watches, Taxes Lots Scots, and other Charges within this City to your power.

You shall know none unlawfull Assemblies, Riots, or Routs purposed to be made against the King's Laws or peace, but you shall withstand them to your Power, or warn Master Mayor for the Time being thereof, or some of the Head Officers of this City, as speedily as you can.

You shall not colour the Goods of any Foreigner, or Stranger, or know any Foreigner or Stranger to buy and sell with another Foreigner, within the precincts of this City, but you shall give Knowledge thereof unto the Chamberlain or his Deputy, without Delay.

You shall not implead or sue any Burgess of this City, in any Court out of this City; for any Matter whereof you may have sufficient Remedy within this City,

You shall not take any Apprentice that is bond of Blood, and none other except he be born under the King's Obeysance, and for no less Term than Seven Years, and that he be bound by Indentures to be made by the Town Clerk of this City for the time being, or by his Clerk: and at the end of his Term, if he have truly served you all his Term, you shall [if he require you to it] present him to Master Mayor, or to the Chamberlain, to be made a Burgess.

You shall not take or wear the Livery or Cloathing of any Lord. Gentleman, or other Person but only your own or your Crafts, or of Master Mayor, or of the Lord high Steward of this City, or of the Sheriffs of the same, so long as you shall be dwelling within this City.

You shall make no Oath or Promise by way of Confedracy, contrary to the King's Laws.

So help you GOD by the holy Contents of this Book.

John Lander, Weaver is admitted into the Liberties of this City, the *17* Day of *October 1774 Charles Hotchkin* Esq: Mayor, *John Durbin Junr. and James Hill* Esquires. Sheriffs, for that he *is the Son of Adam Lander, Weaver deceased Late* A Freeman of the same.

As appears by the Register Book of Burgesses, No. *15* Fol. *147* } *R. Hamswell* Chamberlain.

From a collection of original "copies," dating from the reign of Queen Anne to the present period, in the writer's possession. The four Sheriffs' marks on the above copy represent those used at the following elections, viz., 1774 (a heart), 1780 (a griffin), 1781 (a diamond), and 1784 (a crescent). his fac-simile of the original "copy" has been re-produced by the photo-zinco process.

was generally signed by the Mayor or by the Aldermen. The agents then accompanied the men to the Chamberlain's office, when the names were enrolled in the "Book of "Burgesses," and each of the newly admitted freemen received a "copy" or certificate of his admission on a form printed on parchment, and signed by the Chamberlain. [In the early part of the eighteenth century the form was printed on paper, signed by the Chamberlain, and sealed in wax, with the Chamberlain's official seal.] The voters were then taken in tallies to the poll. When the vote had been given, the "copy" was perforated by the Sheriffs with a stamp bearing a particular mark. The mark used by the Sheriffs at this (1774) election was a heart.

It was a matter of frequent occurrence for the agents of the candidates to trace out the widows or daughters of freemen who were entitled by marriage to confer the freedom of the city upon the "husbands of their choice"—even "grannies" and "biddies" in poor-houses were requisitioned, and husbands found for them by the agents. The "united" couples generally parted at the church door, but custom had provided for "conscientious couples" a short ceremony, which was supposed to represent death itself. The couple stood on either side of a grave and repeated the words "Death us do part." St. James' Churchyard was, it has been said, a favourite resort for the "conscientious couples." Dead men's copies were not unfrequently purchased, and men were hired—as a rule from a distance—to personate the voters. The London agents sometimes sent these men, who were known as "resurrectionists."* Sometimes men who were beyond seas—thousands of miles from the poll—suddenly turned up—at least their "copies" did—and their votes were recorded. These illegal practices were not unattended with risk, but the safeguard was the knowledge that both sides indulged in them, and if one side had instituted a prosecution the other would for certain have retaliated. Election petitions on the grounds of bribery and corruption only were rarely persevered with, as it was common knowledge that both sides paid and treated the voters. Besides, if either party had made an attempt to purify the election it would have been resented by the freemen on both sides, who claimed—as a right, and not wholly without cause—that they were entitled *by the custom of Bristol* to be paid for their votes.

It was usual to pay each freeman his "polling money," which custom had fixed at seven shillings and sixpence, but this payment did not always represent the amount of cash received by the voter. The voters were invariably indulged in the way of "refreshments," according to their wishes, to which tender regard was paid by the political agents, whose gratitude to the voter for services rendered was tinctured "with a lively sense of favours yet to come." The agents having paid for the admission of the freemen, frequently kept their "copies," and sometimes prominent citizens had hundreds of the "copies" in their possession, which they held as pledges for the fees paid for the freemen's admission.

It was quite usual when a bargain was struck at an election time between agent and voter, for the latter to hand over his "copy" as an earnest of his intention to fulfil the contract, upon the faith of which refreshments were given, or a payment on account made, by the agent. Without the "copy," the voter was unable to exercise the franchise, unless indeed he attended at the Council House and made oath that he had lost his "copy," in which event a duplicate was issued to him on payment of a small fee. During the progress of the poll it was usual to keep a certain number of men in reserve with a view to provide for any falling off in the supply of votes. This practice was called "bottling" the freemen, and the reserves, which included a certain number of men who would never record their votes until the poll had far advanced, were kept out of sight in the back rooms of hostelries, and in other places, and were accorded special treatment so far as "refreshments" were concerned.

The freemen were, as a rule, taken by the agents in tallies to

the poll—a "tally" generally speaking consisted of five or ten voters—and sometimes—when the election was a very disorderly one—they were accompanied by the "constables," armed with staves. These constables, otherwise designated "bludgeon men" were hired in considerable numbers by the agents of the candidates, and when the opposing bands came into conflict, fearful scenes of disorder ensued. Sometimes the principal meeting place of the Tories, the "White Lion" in Broad Street, was attacked; at other times the "Blues" attacked "The Bush," in Corn Street, which was the head quarters of the Whigs. Those two celebrated hostelries have been the scenes of great struggles, and sometimes they were pictures of desolation, not a single pane of glass being left whole. Occasionally the object of the attack was to secure the party coloured flag attached to the front of the house. During the progress of the poll at some of the earlier elections men were killed—murdered in fact. Sometimes a press-gang was hired from gun-boats lying at Kingroad, and used for the purpose of breaking up a meeting, or a procession of the freemen. But we must now return to our subject, and as the question of admission of new freemen afterwards formed the subject of an election petition it is to be hoped that this little diversion will not be thought irrelevant matter. We now propose to copy Mr. Burke's speech on his being declared duly elected one of the representatives in Parliament for the City of Bristol.

GENTLEMEN,

I cannot avoid sympathising strongly with the feelings of the gentleman who had received the same honor that you have conferred on me. If he, who was bred, and pass'd his whole time among you; if he, who through the easy gradations of acquaintance, friendship, and esteem, has obtained the honor, which seems of itself, naturally and almost insensibly, to meet with those, who by the even tenour of pleasing manners and social virtues, slide into the love and confidence of their fellow citizens; if he cannot speak but with great emotion on this subject, surrounded as he is on all sides with his old friends, you will have the goodness to excuse me, if my real, unaffected embarrassment prevents me from expressing my gratitude to you as I ought.

I was brought hither under the disadvantage of being unknown, even by sight, to any of you. No previous canvass was made for me. I was put in nomination after the poll was opened. I did not appear until it was far advanced. If, under all these accumulated disadvantages, your good opinion has carried me to this happy point of success, you will pardon me, if I can only say to you collectively, as I said to you individually, simply and plainly,—I thank you,—I am obliged to you,—I am not insensible of your kindness.

This is all I am able to say for the inestimable favor you have conferred upon me. But I cannot be satisfied without saying a little more in defence of the right you have to confer such a favour. The person that appeared here as counsel for the candidate, who so long and so earnestly solicited your votes, thinks proper to deny, that a very great part of you have any votes to give. He fixes a standard period of time in his own imagination, not what the law designs, but merely what the convenience of his client suggests, by which he would cut off at one stroke all those freedoms which are the dearest privileges of your Corporation; which the common law authorizes; which your magistrates are compelled to grant; which come duly authenticated into this court, and are saved in the clearest words, and with the most religious care and tenderness, in that very Act of Parliament which was made to regulate the elections by freemen, and to prevent all possible abuses in making them.

I do not intend to argue the matter here. My learned counsel has supported your cause with his usual ability; the worthy Sheriffs have acted with their usual equity; and, I have no doubt, that the same equity which dictates the return, will guide the final determination. I had the honor, in conjunction with many far wiser men, to contribute a very small assistance, but however some assistance, to the forming the judicature which is to try such questions. It would be unnatural in me to doubt the justice of that court in the trial of my own cause, to which I have been so active to give jurisdiction over every other.

I assure the worthy freemen, and this Corporation, that, if the gentleman perseveres in his intentions, which his present warmth dictates to him, I will attend their cause with diligence, and I hope with effect. For, if I know anything of myself, it is not my own interest in it, but my full conviction that induces me to tell you—I think there is not a shadow of doubt in the case.

I do not imagine that you find me rash in declaring myself, or very forward in troubling you. From the beginning to the end of the election I have kept silence in all matters of discussion. I have never asked a question of a voter on the other side, or supported a doubtful vote on my own. I respected the abilities of my managers. I relied on the candour of the Court. I think the worthy Sheriffs will bear me witness, that I have never once made an attempt to impose upon their reason, to surprise their justice, or to ruffle their temper. I stood on the hustings (except when I gave my thanks to those who favoured me with their votes) less like a candidate, than an unconcerned spectator of a public proceeding. But here the face of things is altered. Here is an attempt for a general massacre of suffrages; an attempt by a promiscuous carnage of friends and foes, to exterminate above two thousand votes, *including seven hundred polled for the gentleman himself*, who now complains, and who would destroy the friends whom he has obtained, only because he cannot obtain as many as he wishes.

How he will be permitted, in another place, to stultifiy and disable himself and to plead against his own acts, is another question. The law will decide it. I shall only speak of it as it concerns the propriety of public conduct in this City. I don't pretend to lay down rules of decorum for other gentlemen. They are the best judges of the mode of proceeding that will recommend them to the favor of their fellow Citizens. But I confess, I should look rather awkward, *if I had been the very first to produce the new copies of freedom, if I had persisted in producing them to the last; if I had ransacked, with the most unremitting industry, and the most penetrating research, the remotest corners of the Kingdom to discover them*, if I were then, all at once, to turn short and declare, that I had been sporting all this while with the rights of election; and that I had been drawing out a poll, upon no sort of rational grounds, which disturbed the peace of my fellow citizens for a month together. I really, for my part, should appear awkward under such circumstances.

It would be still more awkward in me, if I were to look the Sheriffs in the face, and to tell them. they were not to determine my cause on my own principles; nor make the return upon those votes, upon which I had rested my election. Such would be my appearance to the Court and Magistrates.

But how should I appear to the voters themselves? If I had gone round to the citizens entitled to freedom, and squeezed them by the hand—"Sir, I humbly beg your vote—I shall be eternally thankful—may I hope for the honour of your support? Well!—come—we shall see you at the Council House." [NOTE.—This refers to the attendance at the Council House for the purpose of being enrolled as a freeman.] If I were then to deliver them to my managers, pack them into tallies, vote them off in Court, and when I heard from the bar—"Such a one only! Such a one for ever! He's my man!" "Thank you good Sir.—Hah! my worthy friend! thank you kindly—that's an honest fellow--*how is your good family?*" Whilst these words were hardly out of my mouth, if I should have wheeled round at once, and told them—"Get you gone you pack of worthless fellows—you have no vote—you are usurpers! you are intruders on the rights of real freemen! I will have nothing to do with you! You ought never to have been produced at the election, and the Sheriffs ought not to have admitted you."

Gentlemen, I should make a strange figure, if my conduct had been of this sort. I am not so old an acquaintance as the worthy gentleman. Indeed, I could not have ventured on such kind of freedoms with you. But I am bound, and I will endeavour to have justice done to the rights of freemen; even then though I should, at the same time, be obliged to vindicate the former part of my antagonist's conduct against his own present inclinations.

I owe myself in all things, to all the freemen of the City. My particular friends have a demand on me, that I should not deceive their expectations. Never was cause or man supported with more constancy, more activity, more spirit. I have been supported with a zeal, indeed, and heartiness in my friends, which (if their object had been at all proportionable to their endeavour) could never be sufficiently recommended.

They supported me upon the most liberal principles. They wished that the member for Bristol should be chosen for the city, and for their country at large, and not for themselves.

So far they are not disappointed. If I possess nothing else, I am sure I possess the temper that is fit for your service. I know nothing of Bristol, but by the favour I have received, and the virtues I have seen exerted in it, I shall ever retain, what I now feel, the most perfect and grateful attachment to my friends—and I have no enmities, no resentments. I never can consider fidelity to engagements, and constancy in friendships, but with the highest approbation, even when those noble qualities are employed against my own pretensions. The gentleman, who is not so fortunate as I have been in this contest, enjoys, in this respect, a consolation full of honour both to himself and to his friends. They have certainly left nothing undone for his service.

As for the trifling petulance which the rage of party stirs up in little minds, tho' it should show itself in this court, it has not made the slightest impression on me. The highest flight of such clamorous birds is winged in an inferior region of the air. We have them, and we look upon them *just as you, Gentlemen, when you enjoy the serene air on your lofty rocks, look down upon the gulls, that skim the mud of your river, when it is exhausted of its tide.*

I am sorry I cannot conclude without saying a word on a topic touched upon by my worthy colleague. *I wish that topic had been passed by*, at a time when we have so little leisure to discuss it. But since he has thought proper to throw it out, I owe you a clear explanation of my poor sentiments on the subject.

He tells you, that " the topic of instructions has occasioned much " altercation and uneasiness in this City " (See Cruger's speech *ante* p, 79), and he expresses himself (if I understand him rightly) in favor of the coercive authority of such instructions.

[NOTE.—In the remainder of his speech, which is almost entirely devoted to the explanation of his views as to the duties of a Member of Parliament towards his constituents, the great orator rose to the occasion—he was here seen in his best form, as he had to reply to a passage in his colleague's speech on the spur of the moment—and his audience must have had their attention rivetted as they listened to one of his unstudied outbursts of oratory. This part of his speech has become historical, and has been frequently referred to by many of our greatest statesmen, both present and past.]

> Certainly, Gentlemen, it ought to be the happiness and glory of a representative to live in the strictest union, the closest correspondence, and the most unreserved communication with his constituents. Their wishes ought to have great weight with him; their opinions high respect; their business unremitted attention. It is his duty to sacrifice his repose, his pleasure, his satisfaction, to theirs; and above all, over, and in all cases, to prefer their interest to his own. But his unbiassed opinion, his mature judgment, his enlightened conscience, he ought not to sacrifice to you to any man, or to any set of men living. These he does not derive from your pleasure; no, nor from the law and the constitution. They are a trust from Providence, for the abuse of which he is deeply answerable. Your representative owes you, not his industry only, *but his judgment*, and he betrays instead of serving you, if he sacrifices it to your opinion.
> My worthy colleague says his will ought to be subservient to yours. If that be all, the thing is innocent. If government be a matter of will upon any side, yours, without question, ought to be superior. But Government and legislation are matters of reason and judgment, and not of inclination; and what sort of reason is that, in which the determination precedes the discussion; in which one set of men deliberate and another decide; and where those who form the conclusion are perhaps three hundred miles distant from those who hear the arguments?
> To deliver an opinion is the right of all men; that of constituents is a weighty and respectable opinion, which a representative ought always to rejoice to hear; and which he ought always most seriously to consider. *But authoritative instructions*, mandates issued, which the member is bound *blindly and implicitly to obey*, to vote, *and to argue for*, though contrary to the clearest conviction of his judgment and conscience; these are things utterly unknown to the laws of this land, and which arises from a fundamental mistake of the whole order and tenor of our constitution.
> *Parliament is not a congress of Ambassadors* from different and hostile interests; which interests each must maintain, as an agent and advocate against other agents and advocates; but Parliament is a deliberative assembly of one nation, with one interest, that of the whole; where not local purposes, *not local prejudices ought to guide*, but the general good, resulting from the general reason of the whole. You choose a member, indeed, but when you have chosen him, *he is not a member of Bristol, but he is a member of Parliament*. If the local constituent should have an interest, or should form a hasty opinion, evidently opposite to the real good of the rest of the community, the member for that place ought to be as far as any other from any endeavour to give it effect. I beg pardon for saying so much on this subject. I have been unwillingly drawn into it; but I shall ever use a respectful frankness of communication with you. Your faithful friend, your devoted servant, I shall be to the end of my life. A flatterer you do not wish for. On this point of instruction, however, I think it scarcely possible we ever can have any sort of difference. Perhaps I may give you too much trouble rather than too little trouble.
> From the first hour I was encouraged to court your favor to this happy day of obtaining it, I have never promised you anything, but humble and persevering endeavours to do my duty. The weight of that duty, I confess, makes me tremble; and whoever well considers what it is, of all

things in the world, *will fly from what has the least likeness to a positive and precipitate engagement.* To be a good member of Parliament is, let me tell you, no easy task; especially at this time, when there is so strong a disposition to run into the perilous extremes of servile compliance, or wild popularity. To unite circumspection with vigour is absolutely necessary; but it is extremely difficult.

We are now members for a rich commercial *City;* this City, however, is but part of a rich commercial *nation,* the interests of which are various, multiform and intricate. We are members for the great *nation,* which, however, is itself but part of a great *empire,* extended by our virtue and fortune to the farthest limits of the East and of the West. All these wide-spread interests must be considered; must be compared; must be reconciled if possible.

We are members for a free country, and surely we all know, that the machine of a free constitution is no simple thing; but as intricate and as delicate as it is valuable. We are members in a great and ancient monarchy; and we must preserve most religiously the true legal rights of the Sovereign, which form the key stone that binds together the noble and well constructed arch of our empire and our constitution. A constitution made up of balanced powers must ever be a critical thing. As such I mean to touch the part of it which comes within my reach. I know my inability, and I wish for support from every quarter. In particular I shall aim at the friendship, and shall cultivate the best correspondence of the worthy colleague you have given me.

I trouble you no farther than once more to thank you all; you, Gentlemen, for your favours: the candidates for their temperate and polite behaviour; and the Sheriffs, for a conduct which may give a model for all who are in public stations.

The two members were then chaired. The "Chairs" were richly ornamented, " and amid the acclamations of an innumerable "concourse of people, the procession passed through the principal "streets of Bristol. They were accompanied throughout the "whole procession by a very respectable number of gentlemen; "and the ladies, from the crowded windows of the houses in the "different streets, were not wanting in testifying their joy."

An Election procession in Bristol in those times was the subject of considerable preparation, and involved enormous expense. Thousands of men joined in it—a large number wearing hats specially made for the occasion, to which were affixed cockades, ribbons and special devices, all in the party colours, Sometimes the procession was headed by a cavalcade of gentlemen on horseback, followed by the candidates in the chairs, preceded, followed, and flanked on either side by men carrying long staves, the ends of which were painted in the party colour. Banners of an expensive kind, many of them specially prepared, together with an immense number of flags, ensigns, models of ships, and trade emblems of an indescribable character were carried. The services of all the available musicians in the city were requisitioned for the bands. The day was regarded as a holiday, and nearly all the persons who took part in the procession were liberally rewarded, both with money and refreshments.

The payments to the men and for the food and drink supplied to them at the various open houses, together with the cost of the banners, cockades, ribbons, &c., made up a formidable total.

The freemen who took part in the procession, which was not confined to voters, were paid a larger amount than other men taking part in it.

THE CHAIRING OF THE MEMBERS.

The apprentices—*the voters of the future*—were the objects of delicate attention on the part of the election managers.

The discovery that "every little boy ..... is either a little Conservative or else a little Liberal," is not a new one.

Sometimes a large employer of labour would be asked to permit the employment of the whole of the men and boys in his works, and the bill for the amount paid by or due to the employer for the attendance of the employees, and for refreshments, was paid direct to him.

Party feeling ran so high that it would hardly be possible for a Whig or a Tory employer to keep in his employ a freeman who was not prepared to vote according to his master's wishes. Of course it is possible that here and there might be found examples to the contrary, but substantially the allegation may be accepted as a true description of the then existing state of things. The procession, as a rule, ended with a dinner. On this occasion, Cruger and Burke with a great number of their respective friends dined together at the Coopers' Hall, where several popular toasts where drank; and the evening concluded with firing of cannon, and ringing of bells.

A rather funny editorial paragraph appeared in the *Bristol Journal*: "We hear Matthew Brickdale Esq.; the unsuccessful "candidate for this city, has ordered in notes of every expense, "incident to the Election.—*An example worthy of imitation.*"

The following report was sent to the *London Chronicle* by its Bristol correspondent :—

> "Notwithstanding the poll has continued 25 days, and the contest has "been so smart between Brickdale and Burke, there never was a contested "election carried on with less disturbance, and it is remarkable that "*Cruger* had a much larger number of votes *than any Candidate had* "*before in this City*, though when he declared himself several persons said "he would never get five hundred men to vote for him, And the majority "that Mr. Burke got over Mr. Brickdale is very extraordinary when it is "considered that he was not declared a Candidate till the second day of "the Poll, and that Mr. Brickdale's friends exerted every nerve."

Mr. Brickdale issued an address in which he stated his intention to petition Parliament against the sheriff's return, on two grounds, viz.: that the nomination of a candidate after the commencement of the Poll was illegal, and that the votes of the freemen who had been admitted subsequent to the date of the issue of the writ could not be received.

> To the Gentlemen, Clergy, Freeholders and Freemen.
>
> GENTLEMEN,
> The Poll being now finally closed, and this long and tedious contest brought to its final stage of decision, permit me to express the gratitude of my heart, for the disinterestedness, the strenuous and active support which my friends have honored me.
> The numbers declared by the Sheriffs upon their poll state not my determinations, and I am in consequence thereof, not less resolved to seek by appeal the decisions of an higher jurisdiction, *upon the admissibility of Candidates* and the legality of votes, than I was to count the majority of numbers.
> Upon what grounds voters, never received in this City before, have been by the Sheriffs deemed legal, is not mine to examine; this with other questions alike important to the law of parliament, shall now be carried to a superior tribunal; a tribunal which I glory to have concurred in establishing, and which, if I do not vainly prophecy, is a safer guard against venality and corruption, a surer palladium to the liberties of this nation, than the promises of modern patriots will readily afford you; I can only therefore at present wish, that my native City may gather sweeter and richer fruits from the services of any future representative, whom you may call to such station; *fully confident*, therefore, *that I am now constitutionally summoned to this honor*. I can only thank my friends for the honorable testimony they have borne to my past conduct by their recent suffrage, *and until I can see others legally vested with the same trust*, I take the liberty to subscribe myself, Gentlemen, your faithful and devoted servant   MATTHEW BRICKDALE.
> Bristol, Nov. 3, 1774.

The following addresses to the Electors were published by Messrs. Cruger and Burke :—

> GENTLEMEN,
> Impressed with the deepest sense of gratitude and regard, I return you my sincere thanks for the high honor you have this day conferred on me, by electing me one of your representatives in Parliament. I very sensibly feel, but cannot fully express, my obligations. I wish, however, to convey to you those ideas which may confirm the sincerity of the public declarations I have already made.
> Permit me, fellow citizens, to assure you, that it shall be the business of my life to support your rights and privileges, and to approve myself on every occasion,
>   Gentlemen,
>   Your most obedient,
>   And faithful humble servant,
>   HENRY CRUGER.
> Park Street, Nov, 3, 1774.

> GENTLEMEN,
> I humbly request your acceptance of my most hearty thanks for the high honor I have this day received, in being elected one of your representatives in Parliament.

Whatever advantage my public character may derive from the weight of so respectable a representation, you may be assured shall be employed in promoting to the best of my judgment the true interests of those from whom it is derived. I hope that, by your frequent advice and seasonable assistance, I may be enabled to execute the great trust you have reposed in me, in a manner in some degree equal to its importance and your wishes.

To my particular friends I owe the sincerest affection, to the City the most inviolable duty, to the Sheriffs who presided, my full testimony, that they have conducted themselves, thro' the whole of this long election, with the most liberal impartiality; with all the dignity of Magistrates; with all the politeness of gentlemen.

It is natural that an object, so important as the honor of representing this great city, should not be abandoned without reluctance. The gentleman, who has been unsuccessful in his pursuit, threatens a Petition. I submit with great cheerfulness my pretensions, and what are more important, your rights to the Committee of Election; the clearest cause to the justest tribunal. That tribunal, I am confident, will never authorize an attempt to render, contrary to the clear and express law of the land, the original, inherent, corporate rights of those entitled to freedom in this great City, dependent for their valid exercise on the occasional pleasure of a Minister, by dating their effect from the issuing of the writ. The time for issuing the writ, is entirely in the power of a Minister; and he may communicate his intentions to those, and those only whom he is inclined to favor; and upon this new doctrine enable them and disable all others from taking advantages of the right of freedom.

No care of mine shall be wanting to support the rights even of those freemen whom the gentleman, who threatens a petition, was the first to produce and encourage, and when they can no longer serve his purpose, he now endeavours to disfranchise by a retrospect.

I have the honor to be, with the highest veneration, esteem and gratitude,
           Gentlemen,
                Your most obedient
                    And ever obliged humble servant,
                              EDMUND BURKE.
Bristol, Nov. 3, 1774.

The two following broadsides were issued on the day after the declaration of the poll:—

To Mr. BRICKDALE,

Sir,—The mildness and candour with which you expressed yourself in the Common Hall, left upon my mind the most pleasing impressions in your favour. But how great was my astonishment afterwards to find all this mildness converted, in your printed address, into absolute menace and abuse. It may, indeed, be truly said, if I do not vainly prophecy, that this address was not penned by yourself, but by that haughty man, who so arduously attempted to render you odious, whilst he professed himself your friend, by his insolent speech yesterday relative to the late election. But as you have thought proper, Sir, to make this address your own, by giving it the sanction of your name, you are answerable for all the unparalleled insolences contained in it.

Upon what grounds, you say, voters never received in this city before, have been by the Sheriffs deemed legal, is not your's to examine, but you shall refer it to a higher tribunal to determine; expressing at the same time a vaunting, but if I prophecy right, a vain confidence, that the determination will be in your favour, for that you are fully confident you are now constitutionally elected. After such a pompous and highflown declaration, I almost fear it will be impossible for me to gain credence, whilst I announce it to all the world, as a well known fact, which you yourself cannot, dare not deny - that Mr. Brickdale was the man who at the last general election, made many hundreds free who were entitled to their freedom, and engaged them to vote for him when a contest was apprehended, that Mr. Brickdale was the man who first introduced this class of votes at the present election, actually putted them, and publicly thanked them for their suffrages, and that Mr. Brickdale is now the man who in his printed address to the citizens, has the effrontry to tell them, that upon what grounds the Sheriffs have admitted as legal such votes as he himself first introduced to them, he shall refer to a higher tribunal.

I am really pained at the shockingly disgraceful situation in which you are placed, by giving yourself up to be the passive tool of a very proud, but not very honourable party. If I was your enemy, which I solemnly declare I am not, I could wish you no greater punishment than the reflections of your own mind, upon your palpably absurd, treacherous and ungrateful conduct.

Wine Street, Nov. 4, 1774   ATTICUS.

To Mr. COUNSELLOR HOBHOUSE,

SIR, - In the true spirit of that proud, overbearing party to which you very properly belong, you said to us yesterday, that you would have us remember "who it was that first drew the sword, and t. at you were "now therefore determined to throw away the scabbard, and to fight it "out to the very last," with many other things equally menacing and hostile. If the angry bile is a little subsided, permit me cooly to ask you, Sir (for I am an Elector, as you were pleased, with pompous affectation to express it, as well as your very great self), what do you mean by these military phrases? In the name of common sense, Sir, at a professedly free Election, has not one Elector as good a right as another to propose a candidate? And if this candidate proves successful, must the citizens who thought proper to give him their free suffrages be insulted by you, Sir, in open court, that you are de ermined to throw away the scabbard; that is, that you will not rest till you have cut their throats for them? Is this fit language for the mouth of a lawyer, a gentleman, an Elector? If you have any sense of virtuous shame, you will blush at the recollection of your imprudence, your folly, your impudence.

But, meeting you on your own ground, in answer to what you say about first drawing the sword, I reply—You, yourself, Sir, or the party you presume to be the mouth of,—first drew the sword. At the last General Election, did not some of the High Party endeavour to introduce Mr. Combe, and others of them Mr. Brickdale? Mr. Combe, it is true, did not stand the poll; but I believe Sir, you will not contend that he declined the poll, because he chose to sheath the sword, but from motives of a different nature—for fear (to follow your own bloody phraseology) the sword should be sheathed in his bowels. And with respect to the late contest, has it been Party against Party? With what color of reason can this be pretended, when it is so well known, that many Dissenters of each denomination, and even several of the Quakers voted for Mr. Brickdale? You are very grateful to them for what they have done to be sure, by publicly telling them, as you have in fact, that they have only lent their aid for the destruction of the Brethren, whom you are determined to pursue with relentless fury. Great, indeed, Sir, is your malice, but then, happy for me and my fellow citizens, it is not greater than your impotence. Your rage and violence create only a smile, your haughty threats, contempt.

Impartial people must acknowledge, that the late Election has been strictly a popular Election, and the most free and unbiassed that was ever known in this City. It was undertaken with no hostile views, upon no sanguinary principles. Had your Party, Sir, proposed a gentleman tolerably popular and acceptable, I may venture to affirm he would have been cheerfully supported. But to attempt to force upon a free people, a gentleman who was, you well knew, generally unacceptable, was an outrage not to be borne with, and produced all the consequences that have followed. Glorious consequence, highly favourable to the liberties of this great City, and to this great Kingdom!—But to you, Sir, and your haughty Party surely never more sentiment more applicable than—"Quem Deus vult perdere, prius dementat."

I am, Sir, however inferior in
Pride and Violence,
Your Equal as an

Clifton, Nov. 4, 1774.   ELECTOR.

During Edmund Burke's stay in Bristol, he was the guest of Joseph Smith of Queen Square, an influential merchant, who was connected with the Presbyterians. He was one of the original promoters of the Bristol Library Society. Sarah Champion in her journal described Joseph Smith as " a gentleman of amiable " disposition and character; with a very pleasing person and " address; one of those few whose first appearance produced a " favourable sentiment of him; an opinion which a further " knowledge of him confirmed. He married Sally Pope, a pretty " sensible woman, with whom he appeared to be very happy." As a token of his appreciation of the hospitality he had received from the Smith family, Burke presented Mrs. Smith with a china tea-service, which had been specially manufactured at his request by Richard Champion. In Owen's work on " Two Centuries of Ceramic Art in Bristol," the following description of the Service is given:—"Each piece bears the arms of the Smith family, beautifully " emblazoned; and the initials of Mrs. Smith's name painted in " bright blossoms with rare precision and delicacy. The judgment " of the china painter is severely tested when using gold in " decoration. Although this seductive material is freely applied " on this service, the treatment of it is so broad and simple that " great richness has been obtained without gaudiness. Champion's

" artist depended on the effect of matted gilding. The shape is
" from a Dresden model with wreaths and festoons of laurel
" in green, and the painting is also of that Ceramic School, very
" delicately wrought with a burnished pattern, rather than on a

From a wood engraving in the possession of Mr. Hugh Owen, F.S.A.

" merely bright surface: and the contrast of the deep green and
" dead gold is charming." Owen also says:—" The purity and
" excellence of the paste as well as the beauty and execution of
" the elaborate ornamentation commanded special admiration,
" Champion also specially manufactured another tea-service in
" honour of Burke's return."

From Owen's work we learn that the most elaborately ornamented tea-service known was made by Champion, as the joint gift of himself and his wife to Mrs. Burke. The embellishments consisted of two figures representing respectively—Liberty, holding a spear surmounted by a Phrygian cap, and a shield bearing the Gorgon's head; and Plenty, with a cornucopia supporting a pedestal, on which stands Hymen, with a flaming torch. The pedestal bears a shield, emblazoned with the arms of Burke impaling Nugent, with a Latin inscription, of which the following is a translation :—" R. & J. Champion gave this as a

Specimens of the Burke Tea Service.—("Owen's Two Centuries of Ceramic Art in Bristol," p. 96.)

"token of friendship to Jane Burke, the best of British wives on "the third day of November, 1774." All the large pieces bear this design. The tea cups alone are somewhat different—the pedestal and arms remain, but the supporting figures are necessarily absent from want of space. All the cups bear also, on either side, a wreath of roses, from which hang the scales of *Justice*, crossed by a spear bearing the Phrygian cap, and a flaming torch—and the hands of *friendship*, clasping a caduceus Each piece has a rich border of arabesque gold, enclosing spaces of Byzantine pattern-work, on canary yellow; but there is less gilding than on the Smith set. The covered pieces have wreaths of modelled flowers, in white, round the lids. Taken as an effort of manufacture simply, the cost of labour must have been enormous, as the inscriptions, on the whole set, numbered no less than 2,400 letters. That this exquisitely imagined gift was highly appreciated by the lady to whom it was presented, cannot be doubted, and posterity has pronounced a remarkable verdict on the interest and beauty of the work—some of the pieces have realised thrice the value of their weight in pure gold.

However interesting these services may now be on account of the historical incidents with which they are associated, they are to be valued still more, as proving how excellent the manufacture had become. . . . . . . Executed moreover, without reference to either time, labour or expense, they afford indisputable evidence that had the Bristol works been adequately supported, they might have successfully rivalled the famous royal factories of Sèvres and Dresden.

The pieces forming these two magnificent services (upon which it has been truly said, that Champion almost exhausted the resources of his art) have been scattered.

Many years ago, the tea-pot of the 'Burke Service' realised £190 at a sale by auction, and was subsequently purchased by Mr. W. R. Callender, of Manchester, for £210. During a visit to Mr. Callender made by Mr. Disraeli, before or after he was made Lord Beaconsfield, he took tea from this historical tea-pot. At the Callender Sale in 1876, the same tea-pot was purchased by Mr. F. Rathbone for £215 5s. 0d., which is probably the highest price ever given for a porcelain tea-pot, and at the same sale a cup and saucer realized £91. For other pieces of this service, the following prices have been realised :—Cream ewer and cover £115, chocolate cup and saucer £93, tea-cup and saucer £80.

The 'Smith Service' was not considered to be so artistically finished as that presented by Champion to Jane Burke. In 1876 the tea-pot of this service realised £74 16s. 0d. At the 'Edkin's Sale,' a cup and saucer were sold for £55.

At the Industrial and Fine Art Exhibition, held in Bristol 1893-4, Mr. Alfred Trapnell exhibited the sucrier, cream jug and a cup and saucer of the 'Burke Service' and two tea cups and saucers of the 'Smith Service.'

In addition to the two services, Champion also manufactured an oval plaque in biscuit with the arms of Burke and Nugent in relief (commemorating the alliance of Edmund Burke with the daughter of Dr. Nugent), surrounded with wreaths of flowers of the most exquisite workmanship. This exquisite flower piece has been properly described a *chef d'œuvre*. A writer on the ceramic art says :— "The finest steel engraving is "inadequate to represent the ex- "quisite tenuity and delicacy of "these floral enrichments." A description of the beautiful plaque with the Harford-Lloyd arms in relief has already appeared (see ante p. 17).

The Harford Lloyd Plaque.

Quite apart from the tea services which have become historical owing to their connection with Burke's election as a Member for Bristol, it may be here mentioned that some pieces of the

BRISTOL HARD PORCELAIN FLOWER PIECE
ARMS — BURKE IMPALING NUGENT
IN THE BRITISH MUSEUM — PRESENTED BY HUGH OWEN ESQ: F.S.A.

1

Rich Champion

Engraved from a Miniature, in the possession of

Richard Champion Rawlins Esq

Judith Lloyd
See page 16.

Engraved from a Miniature, in the possession of
Richard Champion Rawlins Esqre

THE TEA-POT OF THE BURKE SERVICE.

Burke's Connection with Bristol. 109

SPECIMENS OF THE BURKE SERVICE,
IN THE POSSESSION OF ALFRED TRAPNELL ESQ.

Bristol China manufactured by Champion have fetched very high prices. A few examples are :—A set of four beautiful female figures £610; a vase of hexagonal form £305; a pair of compotiers £270; an oval plateau £105 : a flower plaque of hard porcelain, with a medallion portrait of Benjamin Franklin, £150.

Sometime after Burke had left the city, Joseph Smith requested him to become god-father for his infant son, whom the father was desirous to name Edmund Burke Smith, and it had evidently been suggested that Burke should appoint Richard Champion to act as his proxy. Burke was always quick to appreciate the ludicrous side of life, and a characteristic letter of his to Champion contains the following paragraphs :—" The purpose of this is so " whimsical that it breaks all rules. I am to desire a quaker to " become my proxy, as god-father, at the christening of a " presbyterian. This you will allow is pretty well, but the " substance is that you will pay the compliment of naming friend " Smith's little one in any way which their forms allow ; and give " for me five guineas to the nurse, if that be sufficient ; if not, " judge what it ought to be and give that : we will settle when we " meet." Burke's godson died in the year 1851. On the 23rd of August 1780, Mr. Joseph Smith was elected a Common Councilman and three weeks afterwards he was elected Sheriff. He was elected Mayor in 1794, and died January 17th, 1815.

Richard Champion also entertained Burke at his residence at Henbury, and he occasionally slept there. The bow-window of the dining parlour, from which there was a pretty look-out, was Burke's favourite seat, and Champion, in honour of his visitor, named it " Burke's Window."

Amongst other persons by whom Burke was entertained during his stay may be mentioned Mr. Thomas Farr of Blaize Castle, a member of the Bristol Corporation ; Mr. John Noble of Queen Square, a Newfoundland Merchant, a member of the Bristol Corporation ; at whose house he frequently spent his evenings. Mr. Noble afterwards became the leader of the Whig party in the Corporation. He was elected Common Councillor April 4th 1772;

Mayor 1791-2; and Alderman December 1792. He lost heavily in consequence of the stoppage of trade with the American Colonies. Alderman Noble subsequently removed from Bristol to London on receiving an appointment in the Audit Office, in the year 1806, but his name remained in the books of members of the Independent and Constitutional (Whig) Club* of Bristol for many years after he had left the city. He died January 9th 1828, aged 84.

MR. JOSEPH HARFORD.

Burke was also entertained by Mr. Joseph Harford, who was one of his constant companions during the progress of the poll.

* In the writer's possession.

Burke was a frequent visitor during the election at the house of Hannah More in Park Street (next door to Mr. Cruger's house). Miss More had been introduced to him during her stay in London in the early part of 1774 by Miss Reynolds. During the progress of the poll Burke made many short speeches at the hustings and lost his voice through hoarseness, whereupon Hannah More " sent him a wreath of flowers with the following " couplet attached conveying her mediocre esteem of her fellow " citizens :

> " Great Edmund's hoarse, they say, the reason's clear,
> " Could Attic lungs respire Bœotian air ? "

On one occasion a procession of the Crugerites in passing up Park Street, halted outside her house, and someone called out " three cheers for Sappho," and it is related that some of the mob imagined " Sappho " was the name of a new candidate. It was pretty well known that she had rendered practical assistance to Burke by using her pen on his behalf in replying to attacks made upon him during the election by anonymous writers. It is believed that several of the most important replies were written by her, and it is more than possible that she wrote at Burke's dictation. At the chairing of the members Burke wore a cockade adorned with myrtle, bay and laurel, and enriched with silver tassels, the gift of Hannah More and her sisters. A little later on, we find her mentioning, as a curious coincidence, that Edmund Burke, Dean Tucker, and Mrs. Macaulay called upon her in Park Street on the same morning, fortunately in succession, as they were all at that time writing against each other. When she next visited London she met Burke at one of the gatherings of the *literati* of the period, and he pleased her very much by repeating to her from memory, word for word, an epitaph which she had composed for a tablet to the memory of a friend in St. Mary Redcliff Church, the circumstances (so it was said) connected with the tablet having been brought to Burke's notice on the occasion of his visiting the church during his stay in Bristol. Burke was very favourably impressed with her, and on many occasions in the year following the Bristol election, they were brought together in London at the houses of Sir Joshua Reynolds and David Garrick, the latter being regarded by her as her most assiduous patron. To Garrick she owed her first introduction into the literary coteries of the metropolis, and to Sir Joshua Reynolds, Miss Reynolds, Horace Walpole, Edmund and Richard Burke, Sheridan, and others, she was indebted for the establishment of her name and fame as a writer. It is not generally known that she was very partial to the old Theatre in King Street, Bristol, but it is a fact that "before she became a saint" she was not only a constant visitor to the house, but was personally acquainted with, and took a personal and lively interest in the actors and actresses she met there. On one occasion she wrote the prologue of a piece for one of the actresses. Mrs. Siddons knew her, and it was destined that it should afterwards be in the power of that beautiful and gifted actress to secure, by her superb acting, the success of the tragedy of "Percy" written by Hannah More, and which had been ushered into the world at Covent Garden under the patronage of Garrick, who composed the prologue and epilogue for her. In all probability her visits to the King Street Theatre prompted her to write the tragedy. It appears, from the original plans of the Boxes and Dress Circle of the King Street Theatre for 1773 and 1774 (in the writer's possession), that Hannah More sometimes—on special occasions—secured seats for a large party of friends. In 1776, in describing a visit to a Theatre in London, during her stay in town, she wrote: "I found "myself not only in the best place, but with the best company in "the house, for I sat next the orchestra, in which were a number "of my acquaintances, Edmund and Richard Burke, Dr. Warton, "and Sheridan." She was rather proud of her acquaintances, and her letters frequently contain allusions to her meetings with persons of established reputation in the *beau monde*. In the same year (1776) she mentioned in one of her letters, that at a dinner party at Richmond she met Sir Joshua Reynolds, Mr. Gibbon,

Mr. Elliot, Edmund, Richard and William Burke, Lord Mahon, and David Garrick : and on another occasion she wrote that she met " the three Burkes " at a friend's house. During the time that Burke represented Bristol he took an interest in her, and she frequently met him when she visited London, and " when he " was rejected for Bristol in 1780, she moralized on the catastrophe " by the quaint reflection, that Providence has wisely contrived " to render all its dispensations equal, by making those talents " which set one man so much above another of no esteem in the " opinion of those who are without them."

An interesting letter sent by Edmund Burke to his sister, Mrs. French, is appended :—

[COPY.]

Bristol, November 2, 1774.

MY DEAR SISTER,

    I know it will give you both pleasure to hear that, after having been elected for Malton, in Yorkshire, several respectable people of this City invited me to stand a candidate here, and that I am elected by a majority of 251, after one of the longest and warmest contests that has been remembered. The party that has lost the election threatens a petition, but I am satisfied they have no solid ground to proceed upon. The election has lasted a month. I was put in nomination several days before I came hither. My absence gave the other party great advantages. My brother, who was in London when the messengers from this city arrived at my house there, came to Bristol and prevented our affairs from suffering so much as otherwise they would have done by my absence ; for I was then 220 miles from London, and 270 at least from Bristol. This event has given us all great satisfaction, and will give, I trust, a great deal to you. *This is the second city in the kingdom ;* and to be invited and chosen for it, without any request of mine, at no expense to myself, but with much charge and trouble to many public-spirited gentlemen, is an honour to which we ought not to be insensible.

In a letter to his wife, he wrote as follows :—

    I write from Mr. Noble's (of the Corporation), who is one of our very best friends, and this day gave us a very handsome dinner, to which the Committee and their ladies were invited. Two enemies, I think very willing to be reconciled, were invited also. I begin to breathe, though my visits are not half over. However, I dispatch them at a great rate. Two days more will, I think, carry me through most of them. The visits will then be over. The dinners would never end. But we close the poll of engagements next Saturday. That day Richard gives us a dinner at the Bush Tavern, to our Committee, but to no one else. Little Popham will call on you in town very shortly. He leaves this to-morrow. He has been friendly and serviceable here beyond expression, at much trouble, and at no small expense to himself. He gave us a grand entertainment ; by us I mean the two Committees, Cruger's and mine ; and invited the Sheriffs and several other gentlemen.

At a numerous meeting of the Society of Merchants, held on Thursday, the 10th of November 1774, it was resolved "That, "the thanks of this Society should, in the most respectful manner, "be returned to the Right Hon. Lord Viscount Clare for the many "important benefits that the commercial interests of this city had "for a series of twenty years, received by means of his Lordship's "constant attention, watchful care, and powerful protection, and "that the Society hope it shall hereafter be favoured with his "Lordship's friendly aid and assistance."

At a meeting of the Bristol Town Council, held on the 12th of November, the Council passed a vote of thanks to Lord Clare "for his important services to the city," and at the same meeting it was resolved to confer the Freedom of the City upon Edmund Burke. The following entry appears in the Book of Burgesses for the year 1774:—

14th November, 1774.

"Edmund Burke, Esq., is admitted into the liberties of this "city, by order of the Common Council, on the 12th day of "November, 1774."

This entitled him to a vote at Parliamentary Elections and to all other privileges at that time appertaining to the Freemen, notwithstanding his non-residence. It is believed, however, that he never exercised his right to vote.

[NOTE.—Admission as an honorary freeman does not now confer the right to vote.]

On Monday, the 14th November 1774, Burke attended at All Saints Church with the committee of the Grateful Society, to hear the sermon. He was accompanied by, amongst others, the two Sheriffs, Mr. John Noble, &c.

Cruger and Burke also attended the annual gathering of the Anchor Society, at the Assembly Room. The Mayor and Sheriffs were present. Richard Burke (brother to Edmund) was also present. "John Noble, Esq., was chosen president for the year "ensuing."

On the 16th of November, he bade adieu to his Bristol friends and left the city. On the 19th, he wrote a letter to Champion in which he said " Present me cordially to Mrs. Champion—her " worth, sense, and goodness of heart, make her deserving of what " she has—the best husband in the world. May your two sisters " hers and yours I mean, meet the like. . . . .
" I really parted from you as from friends of long standing, but " you have well filled a small measure of time."

By the way it may be mentioned that a letter was published in a local journal of the early part of December from Richard Shackleton, the son of Burke's old school-master, (see preface) to a Bristol Quaker. The letter is dated Baltimore, 20. 10 mo. 1776. " I this day (and not before) was informed that Edmund " Burke had offered himself a candidate to represent your city in " Parliament . . . . Having had a particular intimacy " with Edmund Burke from our early youth . . . . I think " then thou mayst with great truth assure our friends there, and " any one else in thy freedom, that Edmund Burke is a man of " the strictest honour and integrity ; *a firm and staunch* " *protestant* ; a zealous advocate (not an enthusiastic brawler) for " that which rightly deserves the name of liberty."

In pursuance of his threat, Brickdale presented a petition to the House of Commons, in which he complained of the postnomination of Burke ; of the admission of freemen after the date of the writ ; and that they were " illegally admitted to poll at the " said election for the said Henry Cruger and Edmund Burke " respectively"; and that Cruger and Burke were guilty of bribery " and corruption. There was also a petition signed by 383 of Brickdale's supporters, which contained an allegation " that the " aforesaid Matthew Brickdale had a great majority of legal and " undoubted votes upon the said poll." The petition alleged (interalia 'that great numbers of persons admitted to their " freedom after the date and issuing forth of the said writ of " summons to Parliament ; and also great numbers of persons not " lawfully or duly admitted to the freedom of the said city ; and

"also divers persons having no right to vote at the said election,
"were by the Sheriffs aforesaid, admitted to poll at the said
"election, whereby a majority of pretended votes was made out
"upon the poll aforesaid, for the said Henry Cruger and Edmund
"Burke, Esq., who thus procured a majority of votes, and caused
"themselves to be returned by the Sheriffs aforesaid, as citizens
"to serve in Parliament for the said city."

[NOTE.—No less than 772 freemen whose votes were created after the date of the issue of the writ, voted for Brickdale; a fact which placed him in a very awkward dilemma, when the matter was argued before the Committee of the House of Commons. Before Mr. Burke arrived in Bristol, Brickdale had polled 113 of the newly admitted voters. There is very little doubt that the real cause of Brickdale's discontent arose in consequence of the agents of Cruger and Burke having been more successful than those of Brickdale in tracing out the persons entitled to be admitted as Freemen. 1,030 "new votes" were recorded for Burke.]

In an advertisement in *Felix Farley's Journal,* a list of the petitioners was published, and it was stated that it contained the names of "paupers and others so exceedingly obscure, that their
"trades or places of residence cannot be discovered. Such are
"the persons who have been prevailed on to complain of an undue
"election, and to solicit the destruction of more than 2,000 of
"their fellow Citizen's Suffrages."

[NOTE.—As a matter of fact, the names of some of the most influential citizens were included in the petition.]

"Valerius Publicola" informed the editor of the *Bristol Journal* that the only Act of Parliament relating to the votes of freemen, referred to persons "who either purchased their freedom
"or are made honorary freemen," and in either case, it was necessary that the freeman should be admitted one year before he could legally record his vote.

[NOTE.—In the absence of an Act of Parliament, the freemen's rights would have had to be determined by evidence as to the ancient and established customs and usages in Bristol. It was provided by Magna Charta that the City of London . . . . and all other cities, boroughs, towns, &c. . . . shall have all their liberties and free customs.]

In *Farley's Bristol Journal* there appeared an address, signed " A subscriber to the petition," and dated December 30th 1774, in which the writer said :—" Mr. Burke's friends have "industriously circulated that 'the petitions presented to Parliament " on behalf of Mr. Brickdale, were framed purposely to deprive " nearly two thousand free burgesses of this city, of their just " rights and privileges.' " . . . .

" It has been said by Mr. Burke's friends, that persons entitled " to their freedom by birth, servitude, &c., are free the day they " are of age, or their apprenticeship expires, that their copy is " only a certificate of such freedom, and that they are therefore " qualified to vote immediately."

[NOTE.—The contention of " Mr. Burke's friends " was afterwards upheld by the committee of the House of Commons.]

Shortly after the election, two very remarkable poetical effusions bearing distinct traces of the style of Churchill, were published by James Thistlethwaite. They were of a scurrilous nature, and singularly illustrative of the license allowed at the period, to those who were inclined to indulge in personalities. Thistlethwaite, a former resident of Bristol, was, at the date of the election, residing at Little Newport Street, Soho, and was following the trade of a book-binder. It seems certain that he was under the impression that he had some "old scores " to pay to certain Bristol citizens; and the proceedings at the election were apparently seized upon with a view not only to gratify a spirit of revenge for some real or fancied grievance, but to make the victims contribute what people in these days would call blackmail. It was well known to Thistlethwaite, that a very vain purse-proud person named Henry Burgum, a rich pewterer, then in partnership with Catcott, at " 2 Bridge Foot,"* had been one of the earliest victims of Chatterton's precocious

---
* Bristol Bridge Parade.

genius. With a keen insight of human nature, the youth had made a shrewd guess that it would be possible to obtain a few shillings from Mr. Henry Burgum, an important local personage, by representing to him that he was descended from an ancient family—the de Berghems. Accordingly, Chatterton produced to Burgum a pedigree, which he alleged had been discovered among the old documents preserved in the ancient Church of St. Mary Redcliff. The bait took, and the boy received his reward. Thistlethwaite, commenced his "Mock Heroic in four cantos," with an "Epistle dedicatory to Henry Burgum, Esq., *Lord of the Manor of Glastonbury, &c.*," with the following addition "We *great men* love to be called by our *titles* (Otway)." Burgum was held up to ridicule in the dedication, but he was only one of a very large number who suffered from Thistlethwaite's scurrilous production. But the unfortunate Burgum was apparently still further victimized by a rumour that the work had been dedicated to him with his consent; thereupon advertisements were inserted in the local papers, in which he declared he was not made acquainted with the work till after the publication thereof, and an intimation was given that he would take steps to stop the publication. There is very little doubt that Burgum "bought up" all the copies he could find—(a copy of the first edition is very rarely met with.) The work soon passed into a second edition, and Thistlethwaite found it so profitable that he issued another pamphlet entitled "The Tories in the Dumps." On this occasion the chief sufferers from his venomous pen, were Matthew Brickdale the defeated candidate, and Henry Burgum, but a considerable number of citizens were lampooned. It was stated at the time that Thistlethwaite walked about the city with the butt ends of pistols protruding from his pockets. A writer in the *Bristol Journal,* described the first production as "the most infamous, gross, and vilest libel that ever disgraced the press." At the present time, the publication taken as a whole, would be regarded as "unprintable matter." In connection with these publications however, we must in fairness, not forget that most disgraceful personalities were indulged in by the other side.

In writing to Champion on the 10th of January, 1775, as to the draft of a petition to the House of Commons, Burke casually refers to Thistlethwaite's first publication. He acknowledged that there were "a great many good verses in his poem," adding, "if he " is too rough a player, he is a player against our adversary, but, "as I judge by his preface not on our part. At any rate it is " certainly not right in you to encourage such things: but then " it is not necessary you should be anxious about these publications. " You do not direct. *I do not find that the other party has ever " made an apology for any of their scurrilities."*

The interval between Burke's election as M.P. for Bristol in 1774 and his rejection at the same place in 1780, comprises a period memorable in English history. When the new Parliament— the writ for which had been made returnable for the 29th of November 1774—settled down to business, the King's ascendancy was made apparent in one of the earliest divisions—taken on an amendment to the address—the division showed only 73 against and 264 in favour of the original address—and it will thus be seen that the minority in favour of a policy of conciliation towards the American Colonists was infinitesimally small. Before the recess both Burke and Cruger spoke on the American question. On the 16th of December 1774, the latter addressed the House in a speech which proves that he was a fair speaker, and quite able to give expression to his views. On another occasion when he addressed the House in 1775, in connection with Lord Barrington's motion for the employment of troops, he was complimented for his speech in the *Gentleman's Magazine* (vol. 45, p. 6). In the course of his speech on the 16th of December 1774, he argued that if the colonists had committed indiscretions they had been hurried into them "not by a rebellious " spirit, but by that generous spirit of freedom which has often " led their own ancestors into indiscretions. Acts of severity are " far from having a tendency to eradicate jealousies; on the " contrary, they must produce new fears and weaken the " attachment which kindness might have ensured. No country,

"Sir, has been more happy in her Colonies than Great Britain;
"cemented by mutual interests, (till the æra of that fatal Stamp
"Act) they flourished in an intercourse of amity, protection and
"obedience—supporting and supported by each other . . .
"but they ever loved liberty; that passion is coeval with their
"first emigration to America; they were persecuted for it in
"this country—they sought a sanctuary in the unexplored
"regions of that; there they peacefully cleared their inhospitable
"wilds—*cultivated their lands*—and cheerfully poured the first-
"fruits of their industry into the bosom of their Mother
"Country. You protected them in their infant state, and they
"returned it by confining to you the sole benefits of their trade,"

At this time there was a singular if not an unusual unanimity between the Corporation, the Merchant Venturers, and the traders generally as to the necessity for joint action with regard to the American difficulties. At a meeting of the Merchant Venturers, held on the 11th day of January, 1775, "at which "were present many merchants and traders not members of that "hall," it was decided to petition Parliament as to the many and great hardships expected to ensue to the commercial and trading interest of the Kingdom in general, "and of the city in particular" through the differences subsisting between Great Britain and the Colonies, and to quote certain statistics as to the volume of traffic, the number of ships and seamen employed, together with the results of the interruption of traffic caused by the Stamp and other Acts, and the benefits which had accrued by the restoration of trade after the repeal of the Stamp Act. A petition was accordingly prepared for presentation to the House of Commons. As an illustration *of the trade still unaffected, it may be here mentioned* that in the ten days preceding the 14th day of January, 1775, one firm (Messrs. Cruger and Mallard) "had no less than five ships arrived from New York; "two of them loaded with wheat and flour, one with timber, "the other two with rich assorted cargoes of rice, oil, &c."

In the following week there were imported into Bristol from Maryland 15,448 bushels of wheat and 2,039 barrels of flour.* It was publicly stated that at this period if a balance of account were taken it would be found that the Colonists were indebted to persons in Great Britain to the extent of two millions, by far the greater portion of which would be sacrificed on the outbreak of hostilities.

In addition to the petition to the House of Commons, prepared in pursuance of the decision come to at the meeting of the Merchants Hall, there was another petition to the like effect from Bristol. Mr. Cruger presented one and Mr. Burke the other. It was proposed to refer these petitions to a Committee appointed to discuss and enquire into certain matters relating to the American Colonists, but the motion was defeated by the supporters of the Government on a division being taken. A petition from Dudley to the same purport as the Bristol petition was presented, and the House was about to divide on the question of referring it to the before-mentioned Committee, when Burke said he would "not " trouble Lord North and his train *to walk out every five minutes* " *in funeral pomp* to inter petitions."

Burke in a letter dated Friday, January 20th, 1775, to a committee at Bristol, referring to certain proceedings in the House of Lords, as to the affairs of America, said " I have received the " petition, which Mr. Cruger and I will deliver on Monday. " Ministry wishes that our petitions should be deferred to that " day, and we could get nothing by refusing it. The London " petition stands for the same time. When they are delivered, we " shall acquaint the Merchants' Hall of our obedience to their " commands."

On the 20th of January, 1775, an address, in which he was thanked for his services to the city, was transmitted to Lord Clare. It was signed by about 220 inhabitants of Bristol, " gentlemen, clergy, merchants and principal traders," " one half

---

* During the year 1774 a few consignments of American flour and rice were sold by the importers for the benefit of the poor people at retail prices.

of whom," (according to the statement of a correspondent of the *London Chronicle*,) "are said to possess property to the amount " of three millions sterling.

The hearing of the election petition, commenced on the 11th of February, 1775. The real points at issue were :—

1.—" The legality of the post nomination of Burke, as to which several cases were quoted by his counsel to prove that (as the law then stood) it was quite legal to nominate a person at any time before the close of the poll. Counsel urged "that the history of " our law has no such word as candidate ; that it was of modern " introduction, and borrowed from the *candidati or toga candida*, " in which a Roman was habited when suing for a civil office ; " that the commonwealth has a right to every man's service, " therefore, the electors can return a burgess without his consent, " and insist on his services."

2.—The admission by the sheriffs of the votes of the freemen, who were "admitted to their freedom after the date and issuing " forth of the writ of summons," as to which evidence of a very interesting nature as to the custom at former contested elections was given by many aged citizens ; and

3.—There was an allegation of corruption, but as both sides paid the voters, nobody treated this part of the petition seriously, and it was withdrawn. There were several adjournments of the hearing, and the committee without much consultation declared Cruger duly elected, and ultimately agreed to meet again to discuss the matter on Saturday, the 18th day of February at 11 o'clock. About 4 o'clock in the afternoon, they declared Burke duly elected.

The news of the decision was announced to the city by the ringing of bells and the discharge of cannon. On Monday, the bells of several churches rang all day, and in the evening there were hugh bonfires.

On Monday, the 27th February, 1775, a procession of citizens comprising not less than a thousand horsemen and a considerable number of vehicles, met Cruger at Keynsham, and escorted him to Temple Gate, at which place they were joined by a procession of freemen, craftsmen, sailors, &c., from whence they proceeded viâ the Borough Wall, St. Thomas Street, the Bridge and High Street to the Council House; where they halted while Mr. Cruger paid his compliments to the Mayor, then down Corn Street, Clare Street, Drawbridge, College Green, Park Street to Mr. Cruger's house. Burke declined to take part in the procession, which he regarded as "a foolish piece of pageantry."

A Bristol newspaper, after a brief reference to the procession, said:—" Such a concourse of people was assembled as 'tis "supposed was never seen in this city before." In the evening Mr. Cruger dined with his leading supporters and friends at the Assembly Room in Prince's Street.

It appears that a portion of a triumphal arch erected in Clare Street by the Crugerites, was constructed in such a way as to obscure the name of Clare, and reference was made to the fact in some lines written for the occasion :—

> The friends of liberty to show their spleen,
> Clare Street no more in capitals is seen,
> A gaudy gallows there offends the eye,
> With pendant rope, which threatens from on high.
> Shameful act; act of eternal shame;
> The man rejected, why insult his name.

[NOTE.—When Burke's election for Bristol was assured, he withdrew his name as member for Malton, and the vacancy was filled up on the 28th of February, 1775. It was destined, however, that Burke should have occasion at the next general election to be again returned for this pocket borough.]

The Society of Merchant Venturers, on the 13th of March, 1775, elected Burke a member of the Society.

Some little time after the result of the petition was known, a pamphlet containing many references to the election and the election petition was issued, probably in the interests of Cruger and Burke. It contained the following dedication :—

> To the Free, Independent and Worthy Electors of the
> City of Bristol.
> GENTLEMEN,
> The noble struggle you made on a late occasion, in the glorious cause of true liberty, is of the greatest moment to this country, and deserves

our highest praise: Your unsullied and unadulterated principles have put you in possession of what is infinitely preferable to the transient honours of a day; and for which your names will be dear and venerable to succeeding ages.

> Hail those patriots on whose tongue
> Persuasion in the Senate hung
> Whilst they the sacred cause maintain'd.
>
> CHURCHILL.

> Here let those reign, whom pensions can excite
> To make a Patriot black, a Courtier white;
> Explain their country's dear bought rights away
> And ———————
>
> JOHNSON.

"Embellished with an engraving of that justly celebrated "Patriot, Edmund Burke, Esq."

This Pamphlet also contains a report of the maiden speech of Mr. Cruger, in the House of Commons, on American Affairs, on Friday, the 16th December, 1774.

On the 22nd March, 1775, Burke, in the House of Commons, moved certain resolutions (thirteen in number) for conciliation with the colonies in a characteristic speech, which was afterwards printed by Dodsley (112 p.p.). Upon the first resolution being introduced the previous question was put and carried: for the previous question 270 against 78. The three following resolutions were served in the same way and the others were negatived. In the course of a truly surprising oration, he said: "The proposition "is peace. Not peace through the medium of war: not peace "to be hunted through the labyrinth of intricate and endless "negociations; not peace to arise out of universal discord, "fomented, from principle, in all parts of the empire; not peace "to depend on the judicial determination of perplexing questions; "or the precise marking the shadowy boundaries of a complex "government. It is simple peace; fought in its natural course, "and in its ordinary haunts.—It is peace fought in the spirit of "peace; and laid in principles purely pacific. I propose, by "removing the ground of the difference, and by restoring the "former unsuspecting confidence of the colonies in the mother "country, to give permanent satisfaction . . . . My

"plan, therefore, being formed upon the most simple grounds
" imaginable, may disappoint some people when they hear it. It
" has nothing to recommend it to the pruriency of curious ears.
" There is nothing at all new and captivating in it. . . . .
" I mean to give peace. Peace implies reconciliation; and where
" there has been a material dispute, reconciliation does in a
" manner always imply concession on the one part or on the
" other. In this state of things I make no difficulty in affirming
" that the proposal ought to originate from us. . . . . The
" superior power may offer *peace with honour* and with safety.
" Such an offer from such a power will be attributed to
" magnanimity."

At the close of his speech, which even at this distance of time
is well worthy of a careful study, he said, " All this I know well
" enough, will sound wild and chimerical to the profane herd of
" those vulgar and mechanical politicians, who have no place
" among us; a sort of people who think that nothing exists but
" what is gross and material; and who therefore, far from being
" qualified to be directors of the great movement of empire, are
" not fit to turn a wheel in the machine. But to men truly
" initiated and rightly taught, these ruling and master principles
" which, in the opinion of such men as I have mentioned, have
" no substantial existence, are in truth everything and all in all.
" Magnanimity in politics is not seldom the truest wisdom; and a
" great empire and little minds go ill together. If we are
" conscious of our situation, and glow with zeal to fill our places
" as becomes our station and ourselves, we ought to auspicate all
" our public proceedings on America, with the old warning of the
" church, *sursum corda!* We ought to elevate our minds to the
" greatness of that trust to which the order of providence has
" called us. By adverting to the dignity of this high calling, our
" ancestors have turned a savage wilderness into a glorious empire;
" and have made the most extensive, and the only honourable
" conquests; not by destroying, but by promoting, the wealth,
" the number, the happiness of the human race. Let us get an

"American revenue, as we have got an American empire. English "privileges have made it all that it is. English privileges alone "will make it all it can be." In moving the first resolution, he said "I now lay the first stone of the Temple of Peace." Dr. Tucker issued a reply to this speech in pamphlet form.

Benjamin Franklyn, just about this time, came to the conclusion that the King was not prepared to meet any real concessions, and he determined to return to America. Dr. Fothergill wrote to him on the eve of his departure from London to Philadelphia, "Whatever specious pretences were offered, they were all hollow, "and that to get a larger field on which to fatten a herd of "worthless parasites, was all that was intended."

On Wednesday, the 19th of April, 1775, the king's troops commenced hostilities. At the latter end of May, it became known in London that a skirmish had taken place in the province of Massachusetts, but the government intimated that no news of the event had reached them; thereupon Mr. Lee, agent for the House of Representatives of the Massachusetts Bay, published copies of affidavits, detailing certain alleged excesses by the soldiery. There was also published in the London and provincial papers, a manifesto from the Provincial Congress, in which, representatives of the colonists, declared that "appealing to heaven for the justice "of our cause, we determine to die or be free."

During this Session Burke moved that a remonstrance and representation of the General Assembly of New York should be brought up for consideration, but the motion was rejected.

As the result of the outbreak of hostilities, the commercial prosperity of Bristol was affected to an extent unparelleled in any previous period of its history. Remittances ceased to be made, the blockade prevented the landing of cargoes afloat, and the vessels were compelled to return; the trade with the colonies and the West Indies became practically annihilated, owing to the fitting out of privateers, and many of the best commercial houses were at a stand, and after a time vessels were prohibited from making voyages without a convoy. The African trade ceased to be profitable; the ships were laid up, and numbers of seamen were thrown out of employ. Some idea may be formed of what the suspension of traffic meant. The various shipbuilding yards and cooperages also ceased to afford employment, and thus added to the general dearth. It has been stated upon apparently reliable authority that the poor rates increased nearly 150 per cent.

In June, 1775, in was announced in the *Bristol Journal* that Henry Cruger, senior (the father of the M.P.), had arrived in Bristol from New York. It appears that Mr. Cruger, sen., left New York, the place of his nativity, where he had served several important public offices, to take up his residence in Bristol. He died at St. James's Square, on the 5th February, 1780.

Richard Penn, brother to the governor of Pennsylvania,[*] quaintly described as "The Hon. Richard Penn, Esq.," arrived at Bristol from America on Sunday, the 13th of August, 1775, and made a short stay in the city. He published in the local journals, a copy of the declaration of the American General Congress, and "an address to the inhabitants "of Great Britain." He was the bearer of a petition to the king from the American Congress, urging the necessity of conciliatory measures, which petition it was said, was "couched in such "respectful terms, that it cannot fail to have effect." He afterwards went to London for the purpose of presenting the petition to the king. In a letter from London, dated the 5th September, it was stated that the king had asked Lord Dartmouth to say that no answer would be given to the petition.

Burke, at the request of some of his Bristol friends, visited the city in September, 1775. "He found the corporation divided; "half were Tories, and of the rest, half were of his party and half "'were languid.' . . . . The citizens generally believed "that 'things would come right of themselves,' and accordingly "the merchants bought freely, and exhausted their capital; a

---

[*] Pennsylvania and Maryland were under proprietary governments.

"mistake for which they suffered heavily."* Burke himself knew that the war would be long and bitter.

When the Parliament met again on the 26th of October, 1775, there was a considerable degree of excitement caused by the apparent difficulties the king's troops were experiencing in America. It was gradually dawning upon the nation that the colonists would not be overcome in such an easy manner as the government had anticipated. An animated address on an amendment to the address took place, but the government received the support of 278 members as against 108 for the opposition. On the 16th of November, Mr. Burke, in the House of Commons, again took up the matters in dispute between the mother country and the American colonies, and he moved for leave to bring in a bill to acknowledge that Great Britain had no right to tax the colonies without the assent of their representatives, to repeal all the acts of taxation tending to raise a revenue without their consent; and to limit the jurisdiction of the British Parliament over the Colonies to commercial regulations only. In the course of his speech, which he commenced a little after three, and continued till past seven, and which was described as "a most elaborate and eloquent oration," he pointed out what appeared to him to have been the sources of the unfortunate and impolitic breach between Great Britain and her colonies; commencing with the Stamp Act, and ending with the coercive, oppressive measure of the last and present year (1775). He justified the repeal of the Stamp Act, and the subsequent Declaratory Act, with which, he asserted, he was quite satisfied. He also pointed out that independent of the right of taxation without their consent, they acknowledged the legislative authority of the Parliament of Great Britain. He received the support of 105 members as against 210 for the government. It will be observed, however, that the number of the supporters of the government had fallen off considerably.

Notwithstanding the difficulties of his position, he continued indefatigable in his exertions to induce the King and his

---
* Hunt's Bristol.

Ministers to listen to reason; the agents of the colonies did their best to propagate the views and sentiments of the colonists; but all to no purpose. The King remained both blind and deaf as to matters pertaining to the colonies; arguments were treated with contempt; petitions, representation, and protests were regarded, as fit only for the receptacle for waste paper. How significant are the references to the indifference of the English in the Declaration of Independence of the 4th July, 1776. "Nor " have we been wanting in attention to our British brethren. " We have warned them, from time to time, of attempts made to "extend an unwarrantable jurisdiction over us. We have " reminded them of the circumstances of our emigration and " settlement here. . . . . . We have conjured them, by the " ties of our common kindred. . . . . . They, too, have " been deaf to the voice of justice and consanguinity."

In the month of November, 1775, the anniversary of the election was commemorated. A considerable number of the friends of Cruger dined together at the Tailors' Hall, in Broad Street. They were favoured with the company of the Right Worshipful the Mayor and Sheriffs, the Hon. George Berkeley (candidate for the County of Gloucester), and several other gentlemen of distinction. After dinner many constitutional toasts were drank; particularly the King, Queen and Family; the Representatives of the City in Parliament; the Mayor; the Sheriffs; prosperity to the City of Bristol; and speedy restoration of the trade thereof; reconciliation between Great Britain and her colonies; liberty to every subject of the King, and peace to the whole Empire; the immortal memory of King William the Third, our glorious deliverer from Popery and slavery; Lord Berkeley, Lord Lieutenant of the County of Gloucester; the Hon. George Berkeley; Lord Rockingham; Lord Effingham; the Lord Mayor of London; the minority in both Houses of Parliament, and success to their patriotic endeavours; with many others. Mr Sheriff Noble and Mr. James Jones were chosen Stewards for the next year. The bells of several churches rang during the day, and the evening was concluded in the utmost harmony.

Towards the close of 1775, the Rev. John Wesley became an active supporter of the king's policy, and a pamphlet written by him, entitled "A calm address to our American colonies," was extensively circulated in Bristol. His brother Charles, was, at the time, a resident in the city. This brochure caused a literary warfare, and John Wesley was reminded by one writer, that he had formerly expressed an opinion that " the Americans were an " oppressed, injured people, and that if they submitted to taxation " they must be either fools or knaves." It will be remembered that Wesley had in his early life, for a short period, officiated as a clergyman of the Church of England, in the American plantations. Some of the supporters of Cruger and Burke were evidently caused some anxiety as to the probable effect of the pamphlet on the Bristol followers of Wesley, and every effort was made to counteract it. The reverend gentleman was charged in a local journal " that he had been guilty of the most palpable forgery, " in offering to the world under his own name, and without the " slightest acknowledgment, *the work of Dr. Johnson.*" It is not at all improbable that Burke lost a few of his non-conformist supporters through the change in the opinion of Wesley.

In the early part of January, 1776, it was announced that Matthew Brickdale, the defeated candidate at the last election, had distributed £105 among the poor of the various parishes. In a paragraph in one of the local journals, the citizens were reminded of Lord Clare's former generous donations to the poor. This was followed by an announcement, that it was rumoured that the sitting members had distributed some money through an agent, but in a subsequent issue, a distinct contradiction of the rumour was given.

[NOTE.—This little transaction tends to prove that it was Brickdale's intention to take the earliest opportunity to try and obtain the seat he had lost.]

In consequence of urgent representations made to Burke by many of his principal supporters—including Messrs. Harford, Champion and Farr—he, in August 1776, resolved to visit his constituents. On the 15th of August, 1776, William Burke wrote to Champion to the effect that his kinsman had just set off for Bristol. During his stay, he visited his principal supporters, but as far as can be ascertained, he made no attempt to ingratiate himself with the freemen. He appears to have attended a dinner of the Herefordshire Society, (a society of natives of the County of Hereford) on the 22nd of August, at the Assembly Room in Prince Street. In an account of a society formed for the purpose of obtaining the release of poor persons who were kept in Newgate for debt, his name appears as a donor of five guineas.

On the 23rd of August, there was a gathering of his friends and supporters, at Champion's house, and he afterwards returned to London. It may not be considered uninteresting to here note that a Bristol journal in the month of August, quotes from a letter dated from America, on the 24th of June, that "General " Carleton had summoned a meeting of 500 Indian chiefs who were " described as friends to government." It was also stated, that these " friends to government " had sent in the scalps of the "rebels," which the writer assumed " must have a vast effect on the Yankees."

This reference to the meeting of the Indians, reminds us that at a later period, when Burke "in the course of a great oration " parodied Burgoyne's invitation to the Indians to repair to the " King's standard, the wit and satire of it almost suffocated the " prime minister, Lord North, not with shame but with laughter. " His heart had long ceased to be in the matter, and everybody " knew that he only retained his post in obedience to the urgent " importunities of the King." (Morley's Burke, p. 87.)

In October 1776, through the instrumentality of Burke, Champion received permission for one of his vessels, the " Lloyd," commanded by Capt. Pocock, to proceed to the West Indies without a convoy, Champion agreeing of course to take all risks.

[Captain Nicholas Pocock, who resided in Prince Street, voted at the 1774 election for Cruger and Burke. He was admitted a freeman after the issue of the writ for this election. He was a very clever draughtsman, and some of his log-books, illustrated with views of the harbours, cities, &c., visited during the voyages, contain splendid specimens of his work. One of his illustrated log-books is in the possession of J. H. Rawlins, Esq., of Liverpool, one of the surviving grandsons of Richard Champion, and there is another in the British Museum. In the Jefferies' collection at the Bristol Museum and Library there is a book containing many beautifully executed drawings by Pocock of Privateers belonging to Bristol. After his retirement from the Mercantile Service he became an Artist, and was employed as a Landscape painter by King George the Third.]

From an intimation contained in the *Bristol Journal*, of the 12th of October, 1776, it appears that at a dinner party at a house in Redcliff parish, the disloyalty of the gentlemen present "excited them to drink success to the cause of General Washington," and a reference was made to a "Captain of a ship in the Barbadoes trade," who was present, and it was asked, "what the insurers must think, &c.," which, in effect, meant that it might be possible for a captain, under certain circumstances, to offer facilities for the capture of his vessel by the American Privateers.

On the 5th of November, 1776, "the friends of Cruger and Burke celebrated the day on which they were elected Members of Parliament," by dining together at the Coopers' Hall, King Street. The tickets for the dinner were issued from the Lamb, in Broadmead, a celebrated hostelry at that period. The two members wrote to the effect that they were detained in London by their Parliamentary duties. Cruger, in his letter, referred to "the awful situation of public affairs."

During this month (Nov. 1776) Burke made a telling speech in the House of Commons, in which he said that the administration was "guilty of all the blood shed," and he drew a picture of the horrors of the war. Referring to the day proposed to be set apart for a general fast, on account of the war, he said "the "purposes of religion were to be inverted; for they were to go "to church in a most impious manner, to accuse our American "brethren of being deluded into acts of treason, by specious "falsehoods." This he condemned as blasphemous, and "converting "the house of God into the tabernacle of Satan." He spoke with great vehemence, and at the close of his speech, during which he was called to order on two occasions, he became quite exhausted.

In December, 1776, Champion invited a large number of Burke's friends to a dinner, at "The Bell", in Broad Street—Burke had intimated to Champion that he would defray all expenses. The dinner must have commenced pretty early, as it was afterwards stated that the party broke up before 6 o'clock, notwithstanding that there were no less than 14 toasts proposed. —The thirteenth toast, "Every opposition to a ministry whose "tyranny has lost us an empire, and obliged a *virtuous* people to "an unwilling separation,"—and the fourteenth, "A full sense of "their condition, to the deluded people of Britain, that they may "see the dangerous designs of their arbitrary ministerial leaders," will give some idea of the post prandial proceedings.

[NOTE.—"The Bell" was one of the gathering places of Burke's friends—a kind of political club was held there. The friends of Cruger had a meeting place of a similar kind, at the "Three Queens," in St. Thomas Street.]

The Bristol Whigs were charged in the early part of 1777, that they had instigated a scheme for setting fire to the shipping in the harbour. The Whigs retorted that the incendiaries had been employed by the Tories. A large number of warehouses were destroyed by fire, caused by persons unknown. Amongst other rewards for the discovery of the offenders, the King offered £1,000 and Burke £50. The fires afterwards proved to be the work of James Aiken, alias Jack the Painter.

In February 1777, Burke wrote to Champion giving him his explanation for staying away from Parliament:—"I stay away .... because I know I can do no sort of good by attending; but think, and am sure, I should do the work of that faction which is ruining us, by keeping up debate, and helping to make those things plausible for a time, which are destructive in their nature."

At this time, many of the Rockingham Whigs, including Burke, had come to the conclusion that their opposition to the King's policy was of no avail, and for a time they ceased to be active opponents, and practically withdrew from Parliament. Burke's opponents in Bristol, seized this as a pretext for a suggestion that he had actually retired from Parliamentary life.

On the 3rd of April 1777, he wrote a long letter to John Farr and John Harris, the Sheriffs of Bristol, on the affairs of America, with which he enclosed "the two last Acts which have been "passed with regard to the troubles in America." In the commencement he said "If I have the misfortune of differing "with some of my fellow citizens on this great and arduous "subject, it is no small consolation to me that I do not differ "from you. With you, I am perfectly united. We are heartily "agreed in our detestation of a civil war. We have ever expressed "the most unqualified disapprobation of all the steps which have "led to it, and of all those which tend to prolong it. And I have "no doubt that we feel exactly the same emotions of grief and "shame on all its miserable consequences." .... "Of the "first of these statutes (that for the letter of marque) I shall say "little. .... The other (for a partial suspension of the "Habeas Corpus) appears to me of a much deeper malignity." He then entered into the details of his objections to the partial suspension of the Habeas Corpus—He pointed out that to bring a man from America to try him in England (which was what the Act aimed at) was to take away "all that is substantial and "beneficial in a trial by jury." "A person is brought hither in "the dungeon of a ship's hold, thence he is vomited into a dungeon

"on land; loaded with irons, unfurnished with money, unsupported
"by friends, three thousand miles from all means of calling upon,
"or confronting evidence, where no one local circumstance that
"tends to detect perjury, can possibly be judged of:—such a
"person may be executed according to form, but he can never be
"tried according to justice." . . . . , ... "I suppose nobody
"has . . . . conceived so strange an idea of English dignity,
"as to think the defeats in America compensated by the triumphs
"of Tyburn. If the colonies are reduced to the obedience of the
"crown, there must be under that authority, tribunals in the
"country itself, fully competent to administer justice. But if
"these are not, and that we must suppose a thing so humiliating
"to our government, as that all this vast continent should
"unanimously concur in thinking, that no ill fortune can convert
"resistance to the royal authority into a criminal act, *we may
"call the effect of our victory peace, or obedience, or what we will;
"but the war is not ended, the hostile mind continues in full
"vigour, and it continues under a worse form.* If your peace
"be nothing more than a sullen pause from arms; if their quiet
"be nothing but the meditation of revenge, where smitten pride
"smarting from its wounds, festers into new rancour . . . . . it is
"not the judicial slaughter *which is made in another hemisphere
"against their universal sense of justice,* that will ever reconcile
"them to the British Government."

.   .   .   .

"I have not debated against this Bill in its progress through
"the house, because it would have been vain to oppose, and
"impossible to correct it. It is some time since I have been
"already convinced, that in the present state of things *all
"opposition to any measure,* proposed by ministers, *where the
"name of America appears, is vain and frivolous.* . . . .
"Preserving my principles unshaken, I reserve my activity for
"rational endeavours; and I hope that my past conduct has given
"sufficient evidence, that if I am a single day from my place, it
"is not owing to indolence or love of dissipation. The slightest

"hope of doing good is sufficient to recall me from what I quitted "with regret."

In a postscript to the letter he intimated that the Sheriffs might communicate the letter " in any manner you think proper to my "constituents." He had previously been in communication with Champion as to the circulation of the letter. It was printed in pamphlet form (79 p.p.) by William Pine of Bristol, also by Dodsley of Pall Mall. Pine's pamphlet has now become rather rare owing to its having been so frequently applied for by persons in America. The letter, which has become historical, was criticised in a pamphlet by " H. C. of Lincoln's Inn "; and subsequently by the Earl of Abingdon, a less hostile critic than H. C.

[NOTE.—Owing to the position of affairs in America there is very little doubt that the English national pride had been aroused to an extent that was calculated to make the advocates of the colonist's interests less popular than they had been previously.]

In the month of July, 1777, his misgivings as to the wane of his popularity was mentioned by him in a confidential letter to his staunch friend, Champion :—

" No man can serve with any success, those who do not look " upon him with some degree of partiality. For my part I shall " endeavour to omit nothing to help the most trifling business, " or the most insignificant person in Bristol. This I shall most " certainly do from a sense of duty and of great obligation ; but " if we think that, by any means, we can keep up an interest " there, in the present state of things, by any attention of ours, " we are idly amusing ourselves. I see that any mistake or " neglect of mine is so heavily taken, *and my service so coldly* " *regarded, or soon forgotten, or even so totally misconceived,* " that I am perfectly convinced, that unless I can contrive *to* " *apply to the interests of individuals,* Bristol is for some more " fortunate person at the next election."

Not long after the last letter had been written, he was waited upon at Beaconsfield, by a deputation of persons from Bristol, who were interested in the glass trade, on their way to London, in order to obtain some concession for their trade interests. He wrote to Champion informing him that he sent a letter by the deputation, "to Commissioner Pownell, who returned me an "obliging answer, and seems well disposed to do for them what-"ever can be done. I have had a letter from Mr. Cowles, who "seems well satisfied with my endeavours." In a letter written at a later period of his connection with Bristol, to a friend who was not engaged in business, he intimated in confidence that the applications from his constituents sometimes interfered with his comfort, instancing that on one occasion when he was absorbed in the consideration of an important matter, he was compelled to accompany a gentleman from Bristol, to see someone on his behalf with regard to a matter—rather urgent—relating to a fishery in Newfoundland.

The anniversary of the return of Cruger and Burke was again celebrated on the 3rd November, 1777, by a dinner, at which Cruger attended—Burke did not attend. It is significant that the anniversary was not again celebrated.

The difficulties experienced by the British in America during the year 1777, were followed by the news of the surrender of General Burgoyne's army to the Americans. It will be remembered, that it was in November 1777, before the news of the surrender had reached England, that Chatham exclaimed "But yesterday, and England might have stood against the world: now none so poor to do her reverence." These words had no effect, and an amendment to the King's address proposed by Chatham, with a view to stop hostilities and to restore peace and liberty, was rejected.

In the early part of December, 1777, the news of Burgoyne's surrender reached England. The pride of the nation was sensibly hurt, and in some of the large towns of Great Britain, regiments were raised. In Bristol, a considerable sum was paid or promised in the way of subscriptions for assistance in carrying on the war.

On the 6th of February, 1778, Burke introduced in the House of Commons, a motion for papers relating to the employment of

Indians, by a magnificent speech *which lasted three hours and a half*; a length of time which no other orator except Burke had ever yet ventured to occupy. Quite as much from his rich and teeming fancy, as from facts, he drew a most striking and ghastly picture of Indian warfare. Strangers were shut out from the debate. The speech was never published. The motion was negatived by a majority of 223 against 137.

In March 1778, it became known that the French had entered into a treaty with the American colonists, and it will be remembered that it was due to the terrible plight the nation was in, that caused Chatham—whose end [was fast approaching—to enter the House of Lords wrapped up in flannel, and having all the appearance of a dying man, when he made that celebrated speech—which proved to be his last—in which he replied to the motion made on behalf of his (Chatham's) own party.

In April 1778, serious differences of opinion existed between Burke and his constituents as to certain proposals for legislation as to the trade of Ireland. To Champion, who was perhaps the only one of his active supporters who stood by him, he wrote "Do " not be afraid, the things pretended to be done for Ireland are " frivolous. . . . . They are intended to keep Ireland from " diverting you without another rebellion." This letter was dated the 11th of April, 1778, and on the 14th of the same month, he wrote again to Champion, to the effect that the proposed legislation was " merely to satisfy the minds of the people there, to show " a good disposition in this country, and to prevent the spread " of universal discontent and disaffection." He then refers to the fact that one of his principal supporters had taken offence, and afterwards refers with dissatisfaction, to the views taken by " the rest of my friends." . . . . " But I shall go on my " own way, and they will find the error of theirs in the long run."

On the 23rd of April, 1778, he wrote to Mr. Samuel Span, the Master of the Society of Merchants, in answer to a letter received from him on the Bills depending in Parliament relative to the trade of Ireland. He informed Mr. Span, who was one of his friends and supporters, that the propositions in question did not originate with him, or from his particular friends, but when things were so right in themselves, he held it his duty, not to enquire from what hands they came. . . . . . "There is a "dreadful schism in the British nation. Since we are not able "to reunite the empire, it is our business to give all possible "vigour and soundness *to those parts of it which are still content* "*to be governed by our councils.* Sir,—it is proper to inform "you, that our measures *must be healing.* Such a degree of "strength must be communicated to all the members "of the State, as may enable them to defend themselves, "and to co-operate in the defence of the whole. Their "temper, too, must be managed, and their good affection "cultivated. They may then be disposed to bear the load with "cheerfulness, as a contribution towards what may be called, "with truth and propriety, and not by an empty form of words, "*a common cause.* But we all know, that our resolutions in "favour of Ireland are trifling and insignificant when compared "with the concessions to the Americans. At such a juncture, I "would implore every man, who retains the least spark of regard "to the yet remaining honour and security of this country, not "to compel others to an imitation of their conduct; or by "passion and violence, to force them to seek in the territories of "the Separation, that freedom, and those advantages, which they "are not to look for whilst they remain under the wings of their "ancient Government. . . . . . . To say that Ireland "interferes with us, and therefore must be checked, is, in my "opinion, a very mistaken, and a very dangerous principle " . . . . . Indeed, Sir, England and Ireland may flourish "together. The world is large enough for us both. Let it be "our care, not to make ourselves too little for it. . . . . . "It gave me inexpressible concern to find, that my conduct had "been a cause of uneasiness to many of my constituents. Next "to my honour and conscience, I have nothing so near and dear "to me as their approbation. However, I had much rather run "the risk of displeasing than of injuring them;—if I am driven "to make such an option." . . . . . Of the true position of a member of Parliament, he said, "He is in Parliament to "support his opinion of the public good, and does not form his "opinion in order to get into Parliament, *or to continue in it.*"

John Noble had written to Burke urging him to come to Bristol. On the 24th of April, 1778, he wrote to Noble intimating that "for various reasons, this is not a moment in which I can "indulge in that gratification, ... I would, however, "very willingly give up my rest, and sacrifice my private affairs, "but I fear that a visit from me at this time, and in the present "temper of the city of Bristol, would do much more harm than "good." Noble, one of his most intimate friends, had been pointing out that he was acting against the almost unanimous wishes of his constituents, but he was obdurate. His answer was "I confess I cannot see this sort of unanimity with any "degree of satisfaction. . . . . To represent Bristol, is a "capital object of my pride at present; indeed I have nothing "external on which I can value myself but that honourable "situation. . . . . I do not wish to represent Bristol, "or to represent any place, but upon terms that shall be "honourable to the chosen and the choosers. I do not desire to "sit in Parliament for any other end than that of promoting the "common happiness of all those who are in any degree subjected "to our legislative authority; and all together in one common tie "of civil interest and constitutional freedom, every denomination "of men amongst us. . . . . What interest, my dear "sir, have my friends in Bristol, that I should oppose myself by "a dereliction of every opinion and principle that I have held "since I first set my foot in Parliament."

Referring to his letters to Mr. Span, the master of the Merchants' Society, he said "I have written my letter to the hall, "to my constituents of all denominations. This (the letter to "Noble) and my former, I have written to my own particular

"friends; and I wish these letters, if you please, to be read at
"the 'Bush,' and the 'Bell' club." *

On the 30th of April, 1778, he wrote: "My dear Champion,
"the people of London show something of a more sound mind
"than, I fear, will be discovered amongst us. Was it not enough
"that our forward zeal in the subscription, has made America
"abhor the name of Bristol, without endeavouring to make
"Ireland to detest us ? Ireland, with whom we have so many
"connections, and with whom, if we were in our senses, we ought
"to cultivate many more."

On the 12th May, 1778, he addressed another letter to Samuel
Span, Esq., the Master of the Merchants' Society, who had written
with a view to alter his opinions on the subject. Mr. Span was
not an unfriendly critic, he was one of Burke's supporters. In
his reply, Burke says, "With regard to my opinions, I may be
"very wrong in them, but be assured that my error arises neither
"from ill will or obstinacy, or a want of the highest regard for
"the sentiments of those from whom I have the misfortune to
"differ."

But to add to his embarrassment he now found himself acting
in opposition to the wishes of one of his best friends, Joseph
Harford. The firm of Harford, Cowles & Co., Iron Merchants, also
sent him a letter by express, urging him to adopt the views of
his constituents. His answer intimated that he was obliged to
act rather from his conviction, than from his inclination, and that
it gave him "great pain to write a line which can tend to keep up
a moment's difference between us."

In a speech in the House on the Irish Bills, he referred to the
opinions of his Bristol constituents, and said "If from the conduct
"I shall forfeit their suffrages at an ensuing election, it will stand
"on record, *an example to future representatives of the Commons
"of England*, that one man, at least, has dared to resist the desires
"of his constituents, *when his judgment assured him that they
"were wrong.*"

---

* The two Whig meeting places or clubs.

In a letter written by Edmund Burke on the 9th December, 1779, as to proposals for Irish Legislation, he said, "The "propositions, in substance, are, that Ireland is to trade, not only "to all independent nations, but Africa, America, and the West "Indies, subject, however, with regard to the three latter, to the "same restrictions, limitations, and regulations, that now affect the "commerce of Great Britain, and that the direct importation into "Ireland of sugar, and other West India commodities is to be made "liable to duties equivalent to those paid on the entry of the same "commodities into England. . . . . That the woollen export "trade to the places above mentioned be free from restriction."

In the early part of 1780, Burke was in communication with some of his constituents on the subject of economical reform, with a view to obtain a petition in support of a scheme which he had prepared. On the 24th January, 1780, he wrote to Richard Champion as follows :—" You will, therefore, be so good "as to talk over this matter with Mr. (Alderman) Merlott, Mr. "Harford, Mr. Noble, and the rest of our friends who are men "of weight in the Corporation. I think to make my motion as "soon as possible after the call of the House."

In a local paper it was stated that Burke's scheme, if carried into effect, would be the means of saving £161,500 per annum. The Bristol Corporation forwarded a petition in favour of Burke's proposal.

The Bristol petition was prepared on the model of a form received from York, with some slight alterations. The inhabitants of Westminster, to the number of 4,000, met for the purpose of framing a petition on similar lines. At this meeting it was stated that £60,000 had been paid to the American Indians, either in cash or in presents, and serious allegations were made as to the *real* destination of the money. A division on the subject of this petition was taken at the meeting of the Corporation, with the following result :—For—Messrs. Gordon, Pope, Dean, Baugh, Smith, Brice, Harford, Bull, B. Loscombe, Edgar, J. Farr, Wm. Weare, J. F. Weare, Merlott, Pearce, Hill,

Harris, Morgan, Noble.   Against—Messrs. M. Miller, Harris, Durbin, Miles, Daubeny.

On the 11th February, 1780, Burke, on presenting to the House of Commons, "A plan for the better Security of the "Independence of Parliament, and the Economical Reformation "of the Civil and other Establishments," made one of his most famous speeches, a speech which many persons considered raised him above the greatest orators of the period. He had been engaged for a long time in drawing up a scheme for the suppression of a large number of sinecure offices, and certain useless appointments connected with the King's household, and with the collection of the Royal revenues. It need hardly be said that the measure was of a nature not calculated to please the Royal Family, nor was it likely to be regarded with favour by the numerous persons who were interested in maintaining the then existing state of things. In opening his speech, he dealt with some of the difficulties. He said:—" I enter perfectly into the nature and "consequences of my attempt; and I advance to it with a tremor "that shakes me to the inmost fibre of my frame. I feel that I "engage in a business, in itself most ungracious, totally wide of "the course of prudent conduct. . . . . . But it is much "more easy to reconcile this measure to humanity, than to bring "it to any agreement with prudence. . . . . . Besides "this, the private enemies to be made in all attempts of this "kind, are innumerable; and their enmity will be the more "bitter, and the more dangerous too, because a sense of dignity, "will oblige them to conceal the cause of their resentment. "Very few men of great families and extensive connections, but "will feel the smart of a cutting reform, in some close relation, "some bosom friend, some pleasant acquaintance, some dear "protected dependent. Emolument is taken from some; patronage "from others; objects of pursuit from all. Men, forced into an "involuntary independence, will abhor the authors of a blessing "which in their eyes has so very near a resemblance to a curse." He laid down seven fundamental rules, under one or other of which he justified his proposals for reform. In dealing with the delicate matter of the sovereign jurisdiction, he made the following remarks in comparing certain proceedings of the monarchy with certain theatrical companies in which they are obliged to throw a variety of parts on the chief persons: "So our sovereign condescends "himself to act, not only the principal, but all the subordinate "parts of the play. He condescends to dissipate the royal "character, and to trifle with those light subordinate lacquered "sceptres, in those hands that sustain the ball representing the "world, or which wield the trident that commands the ocean. "Cross a brook, and you lose the King of England; but you "have some comfort in coming again under his majesty, though "'shorn of his beams,' and no more than Prince of Wales. Go "to the north, and you find him dwindled to a Duke of Lancaster; "turn to the west of that north, and he pops upon you in the "humble character of Earl of Chester. Travel a few miles on, "the Earl of Chester disappears; and the King surprises you "again, as Count Palatine of Lancaster. If you travel beyond "Mount Edgecombe, you find him once more in his incognito, "and he is Duke of Cornwall. . . . . In every one of "these five principalities, duchies, palatinates, there is a regular "establishment of considerable expense, and most domineering "influence. As his majesty submits to appear in this state of "subordination to himself, his loyal peers, and faithful commoners "attend his royal transformation; and are *not so nice as to refuse* "*to nibble at those crumbs of emoluments*, which console their "petty metamorphoses. Thus every one of those principalities, "has the apparatus of a kingdom, for the jurisdiction of a few "private estates; and the formality and charge of the Exchequer. "of Great Britain, for collecting the rents of a county squire." His speech, which was of considerable length, dealt exhaustively with the landed estates of the Crown, the forest lands, &c. In dealing with the Royal household, a somewhat delicate matter for anyone to handle, he ridiculed an ancient court called the Green Cloth—" composed of the marshal, treasurer, and other "great officials of the household, with certain clerks." In referring to a former attempt by Lord Talbot, to reform the royal establishment, he said :—" Lord Talbot attempted to reform the "kitchen, but such, as he well observed, is the consequence of "having duty done by one person, whilst the others enjoyed the "emoluments, that he found himself frustrated in all his designs. "On that rock his whole adventure split—his whole scheme of "economy was dashed to pieces.—Why ? It was truly from a "cause, which, though perfectly adequate to the effect, one would "not have instantly guessed. *It was because the turnspit in the* "*King's kitchen, was a member of Parliament.*"

In dealing with certain names on the exchequer list, he referred to the Duke of Newcastle, who was in receipt of certain emoluments, and whose dining room was "under the House of "Commons," as follows :—" It was in one of these lines (referring "to certain families) that the immense and envied employment "he now holds, came to a certain duke, who is now probably "sitting quietly at a very good dinner under us ; and acting high "life below stairs, whilst we, his masters, are filling our mouths "with unsubstantial sounds, and talking of hungry economy over "his head."

In criticising the action of the Board of Trade and plantations he asserted that it had "not been of any use to the Colonies, as "Colonies ; . . . . The province of Nova Scotia "was the youngest and the favourite child of the board. Good "God ! What sums the nursing of that ill-thriven, hard-visaged, "and ill-favoured brat, has cost to this wittol nation ? Sir, this "colony has stood us in a sum of not less than £700,000."

In further references to the proposed reductions of salaries of persons connected with the King's household, he said, "It will "fall, as it ought to fall, upon offices of no primary importance "in the state ; but then it will fall upon persons, whom it will be "a matter of no slight importance for a minister to provoke— "It will fall upon . . . . . . those who are nearest to the "King, and frequently have a more interior credit with him than "the minister himself. . . . . . A rebellion of the thirteen "lords of the bed-chamber would be far more terrible to a minister, "and would probably affect his power more to the quick, than a "revolt of thirteen colonies. What an uproar such an event would "create at court! What petitions, and committees, and associations "would it not produce! Bless me! what a clattering of white "sticks and yellow sticks would be about his head—what a storm "of gold keys would fly about the ears of the minister—what a "shower of Georges and Thistles, and Medals, and collars of S.S. "would assail him."

On Monday the 14th February, 1780, leave was given to Mr. Burke to bring in three bills dealing with the matters referred to in his speech.

During the month of March, 1780, an advertisement was inserted in the local papers, in which reference was made to Burke's support of the Bill to relieve persons under arrest for debt, and it was alleged that he had used his earnest endeavours to effect the ruin of the credit, the trade, and the fortune of his constituents.

On the 4th April, 1780, in a letter addressed to Joseph Harford, Burke tendered his thanks for the judicious petition on the subject of economical reform sent by the Corporation of Bristol. In the same letter, he refers as follows to the contemplated dissolution of Parliament: "Before I close permit me to say a word or two "on the election which approaches in its ordinary sense, I mean "as far as regards Bristol. Mr. Cruger tells me that he has "secured his particular and personal interest there beyond a doubt, "and I have heard something to the same effect from others. I "hear, too, that Mr. Combe and Mr. Brickdale have declared that "they mean to offer their services. It was reported that you "intended to stand with Mr. Cruger, but Mr. —— tells me that "you had authorized him to say that this report was without "foundation."

"Two or three gentlemen, on a report that I declined serving "any longer for Bristol (I know not how the report arose), asked "me whether I intended to appear again as a candidate. This is

"a point which my friends at Bristol are better able to give an
"answer than I am. You know that I neither had originally, nor
"have I now, anything of what is called a natural interest in that
"city. I was called thither merely upon public ground, and
"have no other to stand upon at this moment. The business of
"Parliament occupies me for a great part of the year, and the
"effect of it afterwards make a residence at home necessary
"both to my health and my family affairs.

"*I myself am not in a condition to supply any part of the
"expense.* I was not rich at the last election, and my fortune has
"by no means improved by my parliamentary labours. *I cannot
"look back without pain at the expense of the last contest, nor
"forward without horror,* at the probable renewal of it; and I
"do not speculate on such scenes of expense with the less
"uneasiness because they have fallen, and may fall, on the
"purses of other people.

Burke wrote to Alderman John Merlott, of Bristol, from Beaconsfield, on April 4th, 1780, in which he deprecated the resentment of some of his constituents on account of his having voted in favour of concessions to Ireland in the matter of commerce. He points out that the Ministers who opposed these concessions, had subsequently proposed and enacted much more extensive ones. "I thought I ought rather to lighten the ship "in time than expose it to a total wreck."

In the early part of June, 1780, the petition of the so called "Protestant Association" was presented to the House of Commons, and was immediately followed by the destruction of a number of Roman Catholic chapels and other buildings. Burke's house had been marked, with the houses of several prominent supporters of the Bill for giving relief to the Roman Catholics, for destruction, but it was saved by the military. Comparatively few persons in Bristol signed the petition, but the minds of a considerable number were inflamed with prejudices against the Roman Catholics, and against those who had supported the measures for their relief.

On the 23rd June, the Bill relating to economical reform, in the preparation of which Burke had taken such great pains, was lost. [NOTE.—In 1781 the matter was again brought before the house, and eventually, with considerable modifications of the original proposals, an Act of Parliament was obtained.]

In a letter dated August 10, 1780, from Burke to Mr. Job Watts, at that time carrying on the business of a hosier, in High Street, he refers to certain rumours and "religious prejudices" which were likely to affect his popularity. On the same day that he despatched the letter to Job Watts, he wrote to John Noble, in which he says :—" Mr. Harford was with me last night, and " he is of opinion that I ought to lose no time in showing myself " at Bristol. I shall be there in a day or two after him, and " have accepted of his obliging invitation to make use of his " house. Paul Farr, I have not seen."

[COPY LETTER TO MR. WATTS.]

DEAR SIR,

I am very much obliged to you for your very kind remembrance of me on the present occasion; as on former occasions I have been obliged to you for your hearty and effectual services.

I do not know by what means a report should have prevailed so contrary to truth, and so injurious to me, as that I do not intend to repeat the offer of my humble services to Bristol for another Parliament. I cannot conceive why it should be thought that I now undervalue an honour which for several years past I have taken such pains to merit; and I should pay an ill compliment to Bristol, if I thought that to serve them without regard to my own ease, pleasure, or profit, were the way to lose the favour of my constituency.

I cannot deny that there is great truth in what you say of the number of employments which have been at the disposal of our opponents, and of the prudent use they have made of them to the advancement of their interest and the depression of ours. But you knew from the beginning, that the cause which I pursued in publick was no certain road to the disposal of the favours of the Crown; and I beg leave to say, that if I have not obtained any more places for my friends than I have for myself, I have not disappointed the just expectations of any citizen. As, therefore, none has been deceived by me, it remains to be seen whether there be enough independence among us to support a representative who throws himself on his own good behaviour and the good disposition of his constituents without playing any little game, either to bribe or to delude them. I hope to put this to the proof within a few days, when I hope to have the pleasure of taking you by the hand. I shall certainly make the experiment. It must have a good effect one way or the other, for it is always of use to know the true temper of the time and country one lives in.

You tell me besides, that religious prejudices have set me ill in the minds of some people. I do not know how this could possibly happen, as I do not know that I have ever offered either in a public or private capacity, an hardship or even an affront to the religious prejudices of any person whatsoever. I have been a steadily friend, since I have come to the use of reason, to the cause of religious toleration, not only as a Christian and a Protestant, but as one concerned for the civil welfare of the country in which I live, and in which I have for some time discharged a public trust. I never thought it wise, my dear Mr. Watts to force men into enmity with the State by ill-treatment, upon any pretence, either of civil or religious party; and if I never thought it wise in any circumstances, still less do I think it wise when we have lost one half of our empire by one idle quarrel, to distract, and perhaps to lose too, the other half by another quarrel, not less injudicious and absurd.

No people ought to be permitted to live in a country who are not permitted to have an interest in its welfare, by quiet in their goods, their freedom, and their conscience. These are not my particular sentiments. If they were, I should not be ashamed of them; but they are the unanimous sentiments of all who are distinguished in this Kingdom for learning, integrity, and abilities, of all parties and descriptions of men, and it is neither safe nor honest to the country to attempt to enforce plans of tyranny against any particular persons, contrary to the uniform judgment of all the wise and informed people that are in it.

For one, I would not consent to a tyranny though all the parts, and all the dignity of a country were in favour of a scheme of oppression; but when they are all against it, to grow fond of oppression in defiance of everything respectable in a nation, is a thing so monstrous that there is no danger that you and I should be ever so deplorably fanatick as to fall into such a delusion.

Therefore if any gentleman chooses to quarrel with me on that ground, he perfectly knows, that he cannot find any respectable person in the Kingdom, or who is able to serve him with credit or effect, as his member. The two houses are next to unanimous in this business, for which they attempt to make me obnoxious; and they can scarcely find a person to give their vote to who ever sat in this Parliament, if they except to me; as hardly one has ever spoken their sentiments, nor has anyone attempted a division on them. All this, therefore, my dear Sir, is only a paltry pretence made by those who wish to quit the grounds they formerly stood on; and to gratify some personal interest, or subordinate faction, at the expense of every public and manly principle. Those who pretend to go off on these pretences, in their minds were gone before.

As to what you say of Mr. Harford, I perfectly agree with you. A man of more honour and more ability in every respect, is not of my acquaintance. He it was, that with Mr. Champion, first invited me to Bristol. Without his encouragement I should not think of Bristol now. I shall have the honour of being at his house when I pay you my intended visit. Believe me, with the sincerest regard, &c., &c.,

Charles Street, August 10, 1780.   EDM. BURKE.

Pray remember me cordially to all our friends,

Mr Harford is just gone from hence. He is very earnest that I should be as little time as possible in going to Bristol, and I shall be there in a day or two after him.

It may not be considered out of place to pause and consider some of the causes that led to the unpopularity of Burke.

In his speech upon the hustings in 1774, in returning thanks for his election, he gave his colleague Cruger, a mild rebuke (see ante p. 89) for declaring that it was his intention to vote not in accordance with his judgment, but according to "instructions" —to be received from time to time from Bristol—he gave the Bristol Whigs an idea that they would have to reckon with a man whose lofty style of address must have caused misgivings to at least a few of them. Just imagine a declaration of independence—a declaration that he would vote in accordance with his mature judgment—being flung at the heads of those who had been attacking Lord Clare, for voting in accordance with his mature judgment against the repeal of the obnoxious Stamp Act, and in other matters refusing to act upon "instructions." It is impossible to avoid the contemplation of the ludicrous element in the proceedings. And they had squeezed themselves almost dry, or at least some of them found themselves so, in connection with the large amounts subscribed to return Burke free of charge. Did any of them look ahead? On the American questions, they knew that he would need no "instructions," but what about the future?—the other matters that would demand his attention? He ridiculed a procession he was invited to join very shortly afterwards (see ante p. 125) and designated it as "a foolish piece of pageantry." There can be no question as to the truth of his description, but was it wise of him to take such a lofty position? He must have known that many of the freemen —the bulk of them—were venal; that a considerable number of obscure persons would be given a chance of self-glorification, by joining in the "foolish piece of pageantry," that the Whigs, from the highest to the lowest, would look upon the procession as a means of gratifying their revenge, and at the same time likely to cause humiliation to their opponents. Would the Tories appreciate the high sense of chivalry involved in Burke's answer? An intelligent—shall we say an ordinary—election agent, would probably have advised him to come down from his lofty pedestal, and gratify and delude the "swinish multitude." He had thus early sown the seeds of discontent.

John Wesley's interference in the American questions in 1777, was not calculated perhaps to do very much injury to Burke, but it could hardly fail to have affected the minds of a few of the followers of the High Priest of Methodism.

Then came the differences of opinion between him and certain sections of his constituents on various matters, including the proposed concessions to the Irish traders, the proposal for legislation with regard to persons who were kept in gaol for debt, the repeal of certain penal laws affecting Roman Catholics, which estranged many of the Low Church party, and caused many protestant dissenters to regard him with suspicion.

From the date of his election in 1774 down to the time he appeared in Bristol in 1780, to seek re-election, the rumour that he had received his education at St. Omer's, and was a Jesuit in disguise, had been continuously kept in circulation. The masses, and a very considerable number of those who fondly imagine themselves to be "superior persons," are prone to take other than a judicial view of charges made against a man either in the course of casual conversation and passed on from one mouth to another, or when made by innendoes and veiled suggestions circulated in a plausible manner; and incorrect and inapposite opinions are formed upon specious appearances of truth having no real foundation, in fact; sometimes mere coincidences are eagerly seized upon, and persons bring themselves to believe that they have grasped the truth. In matters calculated to arouse prejudices against one's neighbours by reason of their supposed erroneous religious views, or, in some cases, supposed absence of religious views, the human mind would seem to be always in a state of receptivity. Burke's political opponents knew that his support of the Bill for relieving the Roman Catholics from the disabilities they were suffering, was calculated to give colour to the assertion that he was a Roman Catholic in disguise, so they industriously set to work to warn the electors against him. The Protestant Association was also very active; and the Lord George Gordon riots— the origin of the agitation which led to the terrible scenes which involved the destruction of Roman Catholic chapels, and the houses of Roman Catholics, was clearly traceable to Lord George Gordon, who was afterwards proved to be insane—had combined to affect many low Churchmen and Protestant Dissenters with the notion that the obnoxious Bill was part and parcel of a Roman Catholic conspiracy. It will thus be seen that there were many causes at work to lessen his influence, and to estrange some of his former supporters. He had taken little or no trouble to maintain his popularity; he had failed to resort to the various arts and devices—the wheedlings, the flatteries, the treatings—which were then necessary to ensure a member's popularity with the freemen; he had not visited the city for four years; many of his former supporters had been ruined, or had become very much reduced in circumstances owing to the war with the colonies. During his absence his political opponents—of whom Brickdale, the defeated candidate at the 1774 election, and who had again announced himself as a candidate, was the most active—had been carrying on a canvass against him, the voters were being carefully looked after, and applicants for the many minor offices which were then in the gift of the Government, were not sent empty away; and, to crown all, his opponents had caused a rumour to be circulated that he would not again attend at Bristol to seek re-election.

A writer in one of the local journals, after enumerating the manly part Burke had taken, in the face of great difficulties, said:—" *Yet no man has been requited by a greater torrent of* " *abuse,* . . . . . *and the most artful means have been* " *used to prejudice him in the opinion of some among you.*"

Burke's letters clearly indicated that grave doubts had arisen in his mind as to his reception as a candidate. He was well aware of the narrow views of life which were entertained by many of his nonconformist friends, including the quakers, from whom he had received so much support in 1774, and he knew how easily their prejudices were aroused. Lord Clare, when member for Bristol, had incurred the displeasure of a considerable number, for not taking an active part in the attempt that was made, to prevent the licensing of the theatre in King Street.

Just after the election of 1774, Burke is reported to have said " that though he had great respect for the good men of Bristol, " he should prefer not to live amongst them ; as it would be " necessary for him to be always on his best behaviour."

The Parliament, which had been prorogued, on the 8th of July, 1780, was dissolved by a sudden and unexpected proclamation, on the 1st of September, 1780.

It had been known in Bristol for a considerable period, that whenever the Parliament should be dissolved, Cruger and Burke would be opposed by Mr. Matthew Brickdale, the defeated candidate at the 1774 election, and Mr. Richard Combe, quite recently appointed Treasurer of the Ordnance. Mr. Combe had announced himself as a candidate in 1768, and had unsuccessfully endeavoured to break the compact, which had been entered into between the leaders of the two political parties. [See ante p. 13]

The following paragraph appeared in the *Bristol Journal* of August 19th :—" We have the pleasure to inform our fellow " citizens, that our worthy member, Edmund Burke, arrived in " this city last night, with a determination to offer his services, " to be our representative at the ensuing election."

The same newspaper contained Mr. Burke's address :—

GENTLEMEN,

It is at the earnest request of several of the most respectable persons in this city, that I take the liberty of soliciting your votes at the approaching General Election. My friends are so indulgent, as to think that I have not wholly fallen short of the expectation upon which they brought me here some years ago ; a stranger, and recommended only by my public conduct.

I have served you through one Parliament, with fidelity and deligence, both in your public and private affairs, If it should be your pleasure to continue me for another Parliament in the same trust, I shall endeavour to execute it in the same manner. I shall certainly receive that renewed mark of your confidence, as a favour of very high value, and with very sincere gratitude,

Your most obedient and most humble Servant,

Bristol, Sept. 1st, 1780.   EDMUND BURKE.

The addresses of Brickdale, Combe and Cruger soon followed.

Messrs. Brickdale and Combe issued a card :—

> TO THE WORTHY ELECTORS OF BRISTOL,
> Your vote, interest, and poll if needful, are earnestly requested for
> MATTHEW BRICKDALE
> AND
> RICHARD COMBE
> } ESQUIRES,
>
> to be your representatives in the ensuing Parliament. Being gentlemen intimately connected with you by birth, as well as inheritance; *firmly attached to His Majesty, King George,* and the glorious constitution of Old England, in Church and State, and whose interest and inclination it is to be the promoters of your trade and commerce.

All the old stories of the alleged amours of Burke and Cruger were revived. On the 4th of September, Cruger issued a second address to the electors, in which he said :—" I need not apprize " you that party virulence scruples not to use every artifice to " calumniate those who are objects of its envy."

On the 6th of September, 1780, he addressed a meeting of his friends and supporters, at the old Guildhall, Broad Street; the Mayor and several members of the Corporation being present.

> MR. MAYOR AND GENTLEMEN,
>
> I am extremely pleased at the appearance of this large and respectable meeting. . . . . I have been backward to begin my canvass. The dissolution of Parliament was uncertain; and it did not become me by an unseasonable opportunity, to appear diffident of the effect of my six years endeavours to please you. I have served the City of Bristol honourably; and the City of Bristol had no reason to think, that the means of honourable services to the public, were become indifferent to me.
>
> I found on my arrival hence, that three gentlemen had been long in eager pursuit of an object which but two of us can obtain. I found that they had all met with encouragement. *A contested election in such a city as this, is no light thing.* I paused on the brink of the precipice. These three gentlemen by various merits, and on various titles, I make no doubt, were worthy of your favour.
>
> . . . .
>
> I am sensible that no endeavours have been left untried, to injure me in your opinion.
>
> . . . .

In this speech, which for lucidity of argument and for its dignified tone, ranks rather above than below any other speech of his, of which we have any record, he divided the charges against him—said to be four in number—and dealt with each in due course.

The first charge was, that he had neglected his constituents; the second, his conduct on the affairs of the first Irish Trade Acts; the third, his action on the Debtors' Bill; the fourth, the removal of Roman Catholic Disabilities.

It is proposed to give a few extracts from the speech under each head.

As to the first charge, he said:

> "I live at an hundred miles distance from Bristol; and at the end of a session I come to my own town fatigued in body and in mind, to a little repose, and to a very little attention to my family and my private concerns. A visit to Bristol is always a sort of canvass; else it would do more harm than good. . . . . My canvass to you was not on the change, nor in the county meetings, nor in the clubs of this city. It was in the House of Commons; it was at the Custom House; it was at the council; it was at the Treasury; it was at the Admiralty. I canvassed you through your affairs, and not your persons. I was not only your representative as a body, I was the agent, the solicitor of individuals; I ran about whereever your affairs could call me; and in acting for you, I often appeared rather as a shipbroker, than as a member of Parliament . . . . If I had a disposition, or a right to complain, I have some cause of complaint on my side. With a petition of this city in my hands, passed through the Corporation without a dissenting voice; a petition in unison with almost the whole voice of the kingdom (with whose formal thanks I was covered over) whilst I laboured on no less than five Bills for a public reform, and fought against the opposition of great abilities, and of the greatest power, every clause and every word of the largest of these Bills, almost to the very last day of a very long session; all this time, a canvass in Bristol was as calmly carried on, as if I were dead."

In connection with the charge that he had not visited his constituents, he refers to the effect of the outbreak of hostilities on the trade of Bristol.

> "In that public storm too, I had my private feelings. I had seen blown down, and prostrate on the ground, several of those houses to whom I was chiefly indebted for the honour this city has done me. I confess, that whilst the wounds of those I loved were yet green I could not bear to show myself in pride and triumph in that place, into which their partiality had brought me; and to appear at feasts and rejoicings, in the midst of the grief and calamity of my warm friends, my zealous supporters, my generous benefactors. This is a true, unvarnished, undisguised state of the affairs, you will judge of it."

In dealing with the Irish questions and concessions which he had at first advocated, but which were at the time rejected, he told his audience that in the part he had taken, he was true to his old standing invariable principle, that all things which come from Great Britain, should issue as a gift of her bounty and beneficence.

> . . . . not as things wrung from you with your blood, by the cruel gripe of a rigid necessity. The first concessions, by being (much against my will) mangled and stripped of the parts which were necessary to make out their just correspondence and connection in trade, were of no use. The next year, a feeble attempt was made to bring the thing into better shape. This attempt (countenanced by the Minister) on the very first appearance of some popular uneasiness, was, after a considerable progress through the House, thrown out by *him*.
> What was the consequence? The whole Kingdom of Ireland was instantly in a flame. . . . .
> What! Gentlemen, was I not to foresee, or foreseeing, was I not to endeavour to save you from all these multiplied mischiefs and disgraces? Would *the little, silly, canvass prattle of obeying instructions, and having no opinions but yours*, and such idle, senseless tales, which amuse the vacant ears of unthinking men, have saved you from the pelting of that pitiless storm, to which the loose improvidence, the cowardly rashness of those who dare not look danger in the face, so as to provide against it in time, have exposed this degraded nation, beat down and prostrate on the earth, unsheltered, unarmed, unresisting? . . . .
> I did not obey your *instructions*. No, I conformed to the instructions of truth and nature, and maintained your interest against your opinions, with a constancy that became me. A representative worthy of you, ought to be a person of stability. . . . . I know that you chose me, along with others, to be a pillar of the State, *and not a weathercock on the top of the edifice, exalted for my levity and versatility, and of no use but to indicate the shiftings of every fashionable gale.*

[He next dealt with his conduct with regard to the proposals for reform, concerning imprisonment for debt. As the law then stood, it was open to a creditor to imprison his debtor for an indefinite period. The gaols were frequently filled with unfortunate persons, quite unable to find the money necessary to enable them to obtain their discharge. The merchants and traders doubtless at times managed to squeeze money from the relatives of persons incarcerated for debt, but it had long been known that the law was extremely unjust and hard, and that an alteration was necessary. A Bill dealing with the subject had been brought in by Lord Beauchamp, and Burke had given his support to the principle of the Measure. The traders of Bristol had sent Burke a petition against the Bill, and on receipt of it, he took steps to gain time for a further consideration of the matter and his action had caused the Bill to be thrown out—at least for that session. His enemies had actually circulated a rumour that he had treated the Bristol petition with contempt.]

In defending his support of the Bill, he said;—

> "The operation of the old law is so savage, and so inconvenient to
> "society, that for a long time past, once in every Parliament, and lately
> "twice, the legislature has been obliged to make a general arbitrary gaol-
> "delivery, ... by which, not for humanity, not from
> "policy, but merely because we have not room enough to hold these
> "victims of the absurdity of our laws. We turn loose upon the public,
> "three or four thousand naked wretches, corrupted by the habits, debased
> "by the ignominy of a prison."

In the course of his speech, he said :—

> "Holland understands trade, as well as us, and she has done more
> "than this obnoxious Bill intended to do. There was not, when Mr.
> "Howard visited Holland, more than one prisoner for debt, in the great
> "city of Rotterdam. Although Lord Beauchamp's act, (which was,
> "previous to this Bill, and intended to feel the way for it) has already
> "preserved liberty to thousands ; and though it is not three years since
> "the last Act of Grace was passed, yet by Mr. Howard's last account,
> "*there were near three thousand again in gaol.*"

Of Mr. Howard he said :—

> He has visited all Europe,—not to survey the the sumptuousness of
> palaces . . . . but to dive into the
> depths of dungeons : to plunge into the infection of hospitals, to survey
> the mansions of sorrow and pain ; to take the guage and dimensions of
> misery, depression and contempt ; to remember the forgotten ; to visit the
> forsaken, and to compare and collate the distresses of all men in all
> countries. His plan is original, and it is as full of genius as it is of
> humanity. It was a voyage of discovery : a circumnavigation of charity.
> Already the benefit of his labour is felt more or less in every country. I
> hope he will anticipate his final reward by seeing all its effects fully
> realized in his own.

The part of his speech relating to the Catholic question is too long for reproduction, but it may be well to give a few quotations to illustrate the unjust treatment to which the Roman Catholics were subjected.

> It is but six or seven years since a clergyman of the name of Maloney,
> a man of morals, neither guilty nor accused of anything noxious to the
> state, was condemned to perpetual imprisonment for exercising the
> functions of his religion ; and after lying in gaol for two or three years,
> was relieved by the mercy of Government from perpetual imprisonment,
> on condition of perpetual banishment. A brother of the Earl of Shrews-
> bury, a Talbot, a name respectable in this country, whilst its glory is any
> part of its concern, was hauled to the bar of the Old Bailey among
> common felons, and only escaped the same doom, either by some error in
> the process, or that the wretch who brought him there could not correctly
> describe his person ; in short, the prosecution would never have relented
> for a moment, if the judges, superseding the strict rule of their artificial
> duty, by the higher obligation of their conscience, did not constantly
> throw every difficulty in the way of such informers.

> *But so inefficient is the power of legal evasion against legal iniquity,* that it was but the other day that a lady of condition, beyond the middle of life, was on the point of being stripped of her whole fortune by a near relation, to whom she had been a friend and benefactor, and she must have been totally ruined, without a power of redress or mitigation from the courts of law, had not the legislature rushed in, and by a special Act of Parliament rescued her from the injustice of its own statutes.

[NOTE.—The penal laws against Roman Catholics were not always enforced, but, under one of the Acts, a person who was proved to be a Roman Catholic was to forfeit his or her property to his or her nearest Protestant relation.]

> One of the Acts authorising such things was that which we in part repealed, knowing what our duty was; and doing that duty as men of honour and virtue, as good Protestants, and as good citizens. *Let him stand forth that disapproves what we have done.*
> Gentlemen, bad laws are the worst sort of tyranny, ... For very obvious reasons you cannot trust the Crown with a dispensing power over any of your laws.
> However, a Government, be it as bad as it may, will, in the exercise of a discretionary power, discriminate times and persons; and will not ordinarily pursue any man, when its own safety is not concerned. A mercenary informer knows no distinction. Under such a system, the obnoxious people are slaves, not only to the Government, but they live at the mercy of every individual; they are at once the slaves of the whole community, and of every part of it; and the worst and most unmerciful men are those on whose goodness they most depend. In this situation men will not only shrink from the frowns of a stern magistrate, but they are obliged to fly from their very species. The seeds of destruction are sown in civil intercourse, in social habitudes. The blood of wholesome kindred is infected. Their tables and beds are surrounded with snares. All the means given by Providence to make life safe and comfortable, are perverted into instruments of terror and torment. This species of universal subserviency, that makes the very servant who waits behind your chair, the arbiter of your life and fortune, has such a tendency to degrade and debase mankind, and to deprive them of that assured and liberal state of mind, which alone can make us what we ought to be, that I vow to God I would sooner bring myself to put a man to immediate death for opinion I disliked, and so get rid of the man and his opinions at once, than to fret him with a feverish being, tainted with the gaol distemper of a contagious servitude, to keep him above ground, an animated mass of putrefaction, corrupted himself, and corrupting all about him. [NOTE.—The Bill for the relief of the Roman Catholics was proposed by Sir John Savile, and seconded by Mr. Denning, M.P., the Recorder of Bristol.]

Towards the end of his brilliant speech, he said:—

> I would not only consult the interests of the people, but I would cheerfully gratify their humours. We are all a sort of children, that must be soothed and managed. I think I am not austere or formal in my nature. . . . . . But I never will act the tyrant for their amusement. . . . . . But if I profess all this impolitic stubbornness, I may chance never to be elected into Parliament. It is certainly not pleasing to be put out of the public service. *But I wish to be a member*

of Parliament, to have my share of doing good, and resisting evil.* . . . .
And now, Gentlemen, on this serious day, when I come, as it were, to make up my account with you, let me take to myself some degree of honest pride on the nature of the charges that are against me. I do not stand before you accused of venality, or of neglect of duty. It is not said that, in the long period of my service, I have, in a single instance, sacrificed the slightest of your interests to my ambition, or to my fortune. It is not alleged that to gratify any anger, or revenge of my own, or of the party, I have had a share in wronging or oppressing any description of men, or any one man in any description. No! the charges against me are all of one kind, that I have pushed the principles of general justice and benevolence too far; further than a cautious policy would warrant; and further than the opinions of many would go along with me. In every accident which may happen through life, in pain, in sorrow, in depression, and distress, I will call to mind this accusation, and be comforted.

Gentlemen.—I submit the whole to your judgment, Mr. Mayor, I thank you for the trouble you have taken on this occasion. In your state of health, it is particularly obliging. If this Company should think it advisable for me to withdraw, I shall respectfully retire; if you think otherwise, I shall go directly to the Council-house and to the Change, and without a moment's delay, begin my canvass."

It was thereupon resolved—

(1) That Mr. Burke, as a representative for this City, has done all possible honour to himself as a Senator and a man, and that we do heartily and honestly approve of his conduct, as the result of an enlightened loyalty to his Sovereign, a warm and zealous love to his country, through its widely extended empire; a jealous and watchful care of the liberties of his fellow subjects, an enlarged and liberal understanding of our commercial interest; a humane attention to the circumstances of even the lowest ranks of the community; and a truly wise, polite and tolerant spirit, in supporting the National Church, with a reasonable indulgence to all who dissent from it; and we wish to express the most marked abhorrence of the base arts which have been employed, without regard to truth and reason, to misrepresent his eminent services to his country. That this resolution be copied out, and signed by the Chairman, and be by him presented to Mr. Burke as the fullest expression of the respectful and grateful sense, we entertain of his merits and services, public and private, to the Citizens of Bristol, as a man and a representative.

(2) That the thanks of this meeting be given to the Right Worshipful the Mayor, who so ably and worthily presided at this Meeting.

(3) That it is the earnest request of this Meeting to Mr. Burke, that he should again offer himself a candidate to represent this City in Parliament; assuring him of that full and strenuous support which is due to the merits of so excellent a representative.

Mr. Burke afterwards went to the Exchange, and offered himself as a candidate in the usual manner. He was accompanied to the Council-house, and from thence to the Exchange, by a large body of most respectable gentlemen, amongst whom were the following members of the Corporation, viz.: Mr. Mayor, Mr. Alderman Smith, Mr. Alderman Deane, Mr. Alderman Gordon,

---

* This passage in Burke's speech appears on the pedestal of the statue lately erected in Bristol.

Messrs. William Weare, Samuel Munckley, John Merlott, John Crofts, Levy Ames, John Fisher Weare, Benjamin Loscombe, Philip Protheroe, Samuel Span, Joseph Smith, Richard Bright, and John Noble.

He subsequently issued the following address :—

> To the Gentlemen, Clergy, Freeholders, and Freemen of the City of Bristol.
>
> GENTLEMEN,
>
> My general conduct in Parliament, and my humble endeavours to serve the City and the Citizens of Bristol in their particular affairs, having been honoured by the unanimous approbation of a very large and very respectable meeting at the Guildhall this day; in conformity with the desire of that meeting, and under the sanction of their weighty authority, I beg leave to renew to you my humble solicitation for your votes at this election, and the favour of your early appearance at the poll on Friday next; and if I have the honour of being again chosen to represent you, I trust that I shall not shew myself less deserving of your favour than formerly, or less sincerely grateful for it. I have the honour to be, with the most perfect respect and esteem, Gentlemen, your most obedient and most obliged servant,
>
> Bristol, Sept. 6th, 1780.   EDMUND BURKE.

The Sheriffs had fixed Friday the 8th September 1780 for the nomination. All the Candidates were nominated, but news arrived to the effect, that Mr. Combe had died suddenly at a house in College Green.

[It was this sad incident that caused Burke to exclaim "What shadows we are, and what shadows we pursue."]

The Tories hurriedly summoned a meeting of their supporters at the Tailors Hall, and it was resolved to put Sir Henry Lippincott, Bart., in nomination, jointly with Brickdale. Thereupon, Sir Henry Lippincott issued an address to the electors, asking for their support. In a postcript to the address, he intimated that as the poll had begun, the electors would have to excuse his personal attendance and solicitation.

As the result of careful inquiry, it soon became apparent to Burke, that so far as he was concerned, the contest would be a hopeless one; he had alienated from his interest small sections of the constituency; the Crugerites held aloof, and it became known that a very considerable number of them intended to plump for their candidate; it was rumoured, with a certainty of truth, that the Tory candidates had large funds at their disposal, to which the King himself would largely contribute; a large number of Burke's former supporters were not now in a position to afford him financial help, and he was personally unable to pay the enormous cost of a hotly contested election. Under the circumstances he wisely determined to intimate that he would withdraw from the contest. He had, however, been nominated therefore his name could not be withdrawn. He thereupon attended at the Guildhall, and, in a speech on the hustings, announced his withdrawal.

GENTLEMEN,

I decline the election. It has ever been my rule though life, to observe a proportion between my efforts and my objects. I have never been remarkable for a bold, active, and sanguine pursuit of advantages that are personal to myself.

I have not canvassed the whole of this city in form. But I have taken such a view of it as satisfies my own mind, that your choice will not ultimately fall upon me. Your city, gentlemen, is in a state of miserable distraction; and I am resolved to withdraw whatever share my pretensions may have had in its unhappy divisions. I have not been in haste; I have tried all prudent means; I have waited for the effect of all contingencies. If I were fond of a contest, by the partiality of my numerous friends (whom you know to be among the most weighty and respectable people of the city) I have the means of a sharp one in my hands. But I thought it far better, with my strength unspent, and my reputation unimpared; to do, early and from foresight, that which I might be obliged to do from necessity at last.

I am not in the least surprised nor in the least angry at this view of things. I have read the book of life for a long time, and I have read other books a little. Nothing has happened to me but what has happened to men much better than me, and in times and in nations fully as good as the age and country that we live in. To say that I am in no way concerned, would be neither decent nor true. The representation of Bristol was an object on many accounts dear to me; and I certainly should very far prefer it to any other in the kingdom. My habits are made to it; *and it is in general more unpleasant to be rejected after long trial*, than not to be chosen at all.

But, gentlemen, I will see nothing except your former kindness, and I will give way to no other sentiments than those of gratitude. From the bottom of my heart I thank you for what you have done for me. You have given me a long term, which is now expired. I have performed the conditions, and enjoyed all the profits to the full; and I now surrender your estate into your hands, without being, in a single tile, or a single stone, impaired or wasted by my use. I have served the public for fifteen years. I have served you in particular for six. What is passed is well stored. It is safe, and out of the power of fortune. What is to come is in wiser heads than ours; and he, in whose hands it is, best knows whether it is best for you and me, that I should be in Parliament, or even in the world.

Gentlemen,—The melancholy event of yesterday reads to us an awful lesson against being too much troubled about any of the objects of ordinary ambition. The worthy gentleman (Mr. Combe) who has been snatched from us at the moment of the election, and in the middle of the contest, whilst his desires were so warm, and his hopes as eager as ours, has feelingly told us *what shadows we are, and what shadows we pursue.*

It has been usual for a candidate who declines, to take his leave by a letter to the Sheriffs; but I received your trust in the face of to-day, and in the face of to-day I accept your admission. I am not—I am not at all ashamed to look upon you; nor can my presence discompose the order of business here. I humbly and respectfully take my leave of the Sheriffs, the candidates, and the electors, wishing heartily that the choice may be for the best, at a time which calls, if ever time did call, for service that is not nominal. It is no plaything that you are about. I tremble when I consider the trust I have presumed to ask. I confided, perhaps, too much in my intentions. They were really fair and upright; and I am told to say, that I ask no ill thing for you, when, on parting from this place, I pray, that whoever you choose to succeed me, may resemble me exactly in all things, except my abilities to serve, and my fortune to please you.

He afterwards issued an Address to the Electors:

To the Gentlemen, Clergy, Freeholders, and Freemen of the City of Bristol.
Gentlemen,

A very large and most respectable meeting of the principal Citizens did, by an unanimous vote, authorize me to offer myself once more to your service. My deference to that authority was my sole motive for giving you one moment's trouble. On my canvass, so far as it has proceeded, I found that my pretensions were well received, and even with a degree of warmth in many of the Electors. But on a calm and very deliberate view of the state of the City, I am convinced that no other consequence can be reasonably expected from my continuing a candidate, than a long, veratious, and expensive contest. Conscious that no difference between my services and that of any other man, can be worth the inconveniences of such a struggle,—I decline the election.

I return you my best thanks, for having at any time, or for any period, condescended to think of me for your representative. I have done my duty towards you, and towards the nation as became me. You dispose of the future trust, (as you have a right to do), according to your discretion. We have no cause of complaint on either side. By being returned into the mass of private Citizens, my burthens are lessened; my satisfactions are not destroyed. There are duties to be performed, and there are comforts to be enjoyed in obscurity, for which I am not without a disposition and relish. I am sure there is nothing in the retrospect of my public conduct, which is likely to disturb the tranquility of that situation, to which you restore me. I have the honour to be, with the utmost possible respect.

Gentlemen,
Your much obliged and most obedient humble servant,

Bristol, Saturday Morning,   EDMUND BURKE.
9th Sept., 1780.

On the announcement of Burke's retirement, the Crugerites nominated Mr. Samuel Peach. This nomination was made in order to catch the votes of persons who might otherwise have given their second vote to one or other of the Tory Candidates.

The friends and supporters of Burke withdrew from the contest and refused to vote for Cruger. After the poll had been open for nine days, Cruger came to the conclusion that it would serve no good purpose to keep it open any longer, and he gave notice of his withdrawal, and the poll closed. The numbers at the declaration on the 20th September were:—Brickdale, 2771 ; Lippincott, 2518 ; Cruger, 1271 ; Peach, 788 ; Burke, 18. After the declaration of the poll the procession at the "Chairing" of the two members was on an unusually grand scale, and in the evening "the Members and their friends retired to the White Lion in Broad Street."

Notwithstanding the dignified tone in which Burke took leave of Bristol, there is very little doubt that he was provoked at the way his explanations of his conduct had been received.

Referring to his desertion by the Crugerites, he expressed himself as follows in a letter to Richard Champion : " The fact " is, Mr. Cruger's friends took it for granted that they could take " in or exclude whom they pleased, *and that Bristol was their* "*advowson*. When it came to the trial, it proved that they had " only the power of doing mischief." In a letter to Joseph Harford, he said, " As to the event of the Election it has been " just what it ought to be. It was the natural result of the " conduct of all parties, and it may have a tendency to reform " the conduct of some."

One of Burke's biographers relates that he felt "hurt by the " reception he had so undeservedly experienced," and said, " Do " not talk to me of a Merchant — a Merchant is the same " in every part of the world--his gold his God, his invoice his " country, his ledger his bible, his desk his altar, the Exchange " his church, and he has faith in none but his banker."

Charles James Fox wrote, " Indeed, my dear Burke, it requires " all your candour and reverse of selfishness (for I know no word " to express it) to be in patience with that rascally City, for so " I must call it, after the way in which it has behaved to you."

Hannah More expressed her opinion : " Methink I envy Burke " that consciousness of his worth, which he must feel on consider- "ing himself rejected, only because his talents were a crime."

Referring to the noble language in which Burke addressed his constituents on the 6th of September, 1780, John Morley says, " We can only wonder that a constituency which could suffer " itself to be addressed on this high level, should have allowed the " small selfishness of local interest to weigh against such wisdom " and nobility."

Subsequently the Corporation passed a vote of thanks " to "Edmund Burke, Esq., for the faithful discharge of his duty in "Parliament. . . . . . And, resolved, that though he ceases " to be the representative of this City in Parliament, yet this " Corporation will always retain for him the strongest sentiments " of friendship and regard."

In consequence of the death of Sir Henry Lippincott, Bart., which happened on the 1st of January, 1781, there was another contest. . Mr George Daubeny, a sugar refiner, and a member of the Corporation, was selected as the Tory candidate, and Cruger was again nominated. Many of the supporters of Burke still held aloof from the Crugerites. A suggestion was made directly Lippincott's death became known that Burke should be nominated, but Cruger's friends declared that unless Burke could obtain a promise that Cruger should be given the seat at Malton, they would nominate him in opposition. Burke, when applied to, declined to be a party to the proposal, consequently there was a split in the Whig camp. The poll was kept open from the 31st of January to the 24th of February. Daubeny was ultimately declared elected by a majority of 372. The Sheriffs allowed the votes to be taken in tallies. Cruger's supply of voters became exhausted on the 18th day of the poll, and the success of Daubeny was assured. Cruger alleged that he had lost the election by bribery, but this was only a half truth. Cruger, was, however, elected for Bristol at the General Election of 1784, as the colleague of Brickdale, and Daubeny was ousted. Cruger was in America during the contest, but his cause was championed by his brother, Col. Cruger, and the money, or the greater part of it, was no doubt found by Mr. Peach. This was one of the most hotly contested and the most protracted of all the Bristol elections; the polling was continued for five weeks; excluding Sundays, the poll was actually kept going for 31 days. On his return Cruger issued an address, thanking the electors. It was dated from Trinity Street, July 21, 1784. In 1785 an act of Parliament was passed limiting the duration of the poll at a contested election to 21 days. The Parliament was dissolved on the 10th of June, 1790, and both Cruger and Brickdale retired from Parliamentary life. Cruger had, prior to the dissolution, left Bristol for New York, his native city, having determined to spend the remainder of his days in America. He was elected a Common Councillor on the 23rd of July, 1766; he filled the office of Mayor in 1781 (in the same year he was Master of the Society of Merchant Venturers); he was made an Alderman July 25th, 1782, on the death of Alderman Mugleworth, but resigned in 1792 (being succeeded December 1st, 1792, by John Noble), retaining his seat in the Council, notwithstanding his absence in America, until his death, April 24th, 1827. Cruger's son took the name of Peach, on his succession to the fortune of his maternal grandfather. The estate at Tockington, which he inherited, has quite recently changed hands.

Matthew Brickdale was elected a Common Councillor, August 15th, 1767, and was discharged January 17th, 1784; he died September 8th, 1831. The enormous sums he had expended in the election contests supplemented by other losses, left him in reduced circumstances in his old age. His son was Collector of the Customs in Bristol, and his daughter filled the position of housekeeper at the Custom House, in Queen Square. (The Custom House was destroyed during the Bristol Riots of 1831). For many years the old man spent the greater part of his time sitting in a chair which had been assigned to him in the Long Room, at the Custom House, and he generally appeared to be in a drowsy condition. It was thus that Matthew Brickdale ended his days.

Burke was elected for Malton on the 7th December, 1780, vice Savile Finch, who had been elected at the General Election, and who accepted the Stewardship of the Manor of East Hendred, County Berks, in order to enable Burke to take his seat in Parliament. In consequence of a resolution, deprecating further action against the Americans, having been carried against the Government, Lord North on the 20th March, 1782, announced his own resignation and that of his colleagues. To the Marquis of Rockingham was entrusted the arrangement of a new administration, and Burke was appointed Paymaster-General. The following entries relate to the representation of Malton. "Edmund Burke, "Esq., re-elected after appointment as Paymaster-General of the "Land Forces, 4 April, 1782." "Edmund Burke, Esq., re-elected "after appointment as Paymaster-General of the Land Forces, "11 April, 1783."

The last two entries serve to call attention to an act of friendship which Burke was able to perform towards his old and constant friend Richard Champion, whose fortune had been sensibly affected by losses connected with the American struggle. In a letter dated 9th April, 1782, Champion wrote that he had been appointed "joint "deputy Paymaster General with young Richard Burke, " but Edmund Burke's appointment was only held for about four months, as the death of the Marquis of Rockingham caused the resignation of several of the leaders of the party, including Edmund Burke, and of course Champion's appointment ceased on the resignation of his principal.

The coalition ministry of Lord Shelburne (which lasted for nine months) succeeded, and Champion was requested to remain in office. He declined, but was, notwithstanding, allowed during the nine months to continue his occupation of the official residence in Chelsea Hospital. The Duke of Portland's administration succeeded, Burke was reinstated as Paymaster, and Champion was again appointed Deputy.

Champion afterwards emigrated to America, and died at his residence, County Branch, near Camden, South Carolina, on the 7th October, 1791. Champion was far in advance of his time in all political matters, especially as to free trade, which he strongly advocated in a work on American commerce, a second and enlarged edition of which was published in 1786.

It now only remains to add a few brief references to Burke. At the General Election of 1784, he was returned for Malton, and again at the next General Election, in June 1790; he subsequently resigned the seat in favour of his son Richard, who was elected *on the 18th July, 1794.*

.   .   .   .   .

An inscription on a tablet in the south aisle of Beaconsfield Church, speaks for itself :—

Near this place lies interred all
That was mortal of the
Right Honourable Edmund Burke,
Who died on the 9th of July, 1797, aged 68 years.

In the same grave are deposited the remains of his only son, Richard Burke, Esq., representative in Parliament for the Borough of Malton.

Who died the 2nd August, 1794, aged 35.

Of his brother, Richard Burke, Esq., Barrister-at-Law,
And Recorder of the City of Bristol,
Who died on the 4th February, 1794;
And of his Widow, Jane Mary Burke, who died
on the 2nd April, 1812, aged 78.

.   .   .   .   .

In conclusion we may well repeat again Burke's own words:—
" What shadows we are, and what shadows we pursue."

FINIS.

Burke's Connection with Bristol.

SUMMARY OF CONTENTS.

	Page.
The Prorogation of Parliament in June 1774. Rumours of Dissolution. Opposition threatened to the sitting Members (Lord Clare and Matthew Brickdale).	1
References to the trade between Bristol and the American Colonies, the West Indies, &c.	2—9
The situation of the political parties in Bristol. References to Robert Nugent, M.P. (afterwards Lord Clare.)	9—11
The Candidates at the General Election in Bristol, 1754. Sir John Philipps, Bart., and Richard Beckford (Tories), and Robert Nugent, Esq. (Whig). Election of Nugent and Beckford.	11
Death of Beckford in 1756. Return of Jarrit Smith (Tory), after a contest with the Hon. John Spencer (afterwards Earl Spencer).	11
Agreement between the Tories and the Whigs to divide the representation of the City between them for three General Elections. Return of Nugent (Whig), at a bye-election in 1759, and of Nugent and Smith (Tory) at the General Election of 1761 (in pursuance of the agreement between the two political parties.)	12
Return of Nugent (now Lord Clare in the Irish Peerage) and Matthew Brickdale (nominated by the Tories in the place of Sir Jarrit Smith) at the General Election of 1768.	13—14
Re-election of Lord Clare at a bye-election in 1768	14

Page.

Reference to the agreement as to the division of the representation of the City. Lord Clare no longer a Whig. Symptoms of discontent in 1769. A Meeting at the Guildhall. Petition to Lord Clare and Matthew Brickdale, calling upon them to vote in accordance with "instructions." References to Richard Champion, Joseph Harford, Henry Cruger, and Samuel Peach. - -   15

References to the Champions, the Lloyds, the Harfords, &c.   16—17

Edmund Burke's name in connection with Bristol first mentioned by Dr. Wilson. References to Dr. Wilson and to Burke's early visits to Bath and Bristol. - - - - 18—19—20

References to Henry Cruger as a candidate. - - - 21—22—23

Dissolution of the Parliament in September 1774. The candidate's addresses. Nomination of Lord Clare, Brickdale, and Cruger. Retirement of Lord Clare. Subsequent nomination of Edmund Burke. Full particulars of the contest. Daily records of the poll. The broadsides and other election literature. Incidents connected with the contest. The close of the poll (p. 73.) Summaries and Tabulated Statements as to the votes. Notes as to the votes of the members of the Corporation. Notes as to certain Votes in respect of Freehold Offices, and as to the Trades or Callings of the Freemen. Notes as to the Clergy, Dean Tucker, &c.   23—78

Declaration of the Poll. Henry Cruger and Edmund Burke, Esqres., duly elected. Speeches of Cruger. The "I say ditto to Mr. Burke," story. - - - - - 78–99

Mr. Brickdale's petition against the return. The customs at previous elections. The admission of Freemen after the issue of the writ and during the progress of the poll. *Facsimile* of a freeman's copy, with the Sheriffs' marks. Details as to the admission of freemen. Taking the freemen in tallies to the poll. - - - - - - 80—86

Burke's Speech on his Election. - - - - 86—90

Chairing the Members. - - - - - 91—92

Addresses by Brickdale, Cruger, and Burke - - - 92—94

The celebrated Burke-Smith and Champion-Burke Tea Services, and other Bristol China - - - - - 96—111

References to Joseph Smith (p. 111), Richard Champion's residence at Henbury (p. 111.) Thomas Farr (p. 111), John Noble (p. 111), Joseph Harford (p. 112), Hannah More (p.p. 113, 4, 5.) - 111—116

References to the election petition. - - - - 117

Publication of scurrilous pamphlets by Thistlethwaite - 119—21

The new Parliament. The American questions. Speech of Cruger in the House of Commons on the 16th December 1774. Notes as to petitions from Bristol - - - - 121—23

Summary of Contents.

	Page.
Address of thanks to Lord Clare	123
The hearing of the election petition—the decision.—Cruger and Burke declared duly elected—Procession to celebrate the event	124—25
Burke elected a Member of the Society of Merchant Venturers	125
Publication of a pamphlet as to the election and the petition	125—26
Burke's proposals for conciliation with the American Colonists.—Extracts from his Speech, &c.	126—28
Commencement of hostilities against the American Colonists.—The trade of Bristol seriously affected	128
Arrival in Bristol of Mr. Henry Cruger, senior (the father of the M.P.) from New York, and of Richard Penn, from Pennsylvania	129
Visit of Burke to Bristol in September, 1775	129—30
Burke's Speech in the House of Commons in November, 1775	130
The Rev. John Wesley's pamphlet on the American difficulties	132
Visit of Burke to Bristol in August, 1776	133
Dinner at "The Bell" in Broad Street, in December, 1776	135
Reference to the burning of Warehouses in Bristol, by Jack the Painter	135
The withdrawal of the Rockingham Whigs from active opposition	136
Letter from Burke to the Sheriffs of Bristol, dated the 3rd April 1777	136—38
Letters to Champion in July, 1777	138—39
Burke's motion in the House of Commons as to the employment of Indians against the Colonists	140
References to the differences of opinion existing between Burke and his constituents as to proposals for Irish Legislation.	140—42
Letters to Noble, Champion, Samuel Span (the Master of the Merchants Society), Harford, Cowles & Co., as to the Irish Bills.	142—43
Burke's proposals for economical reform in 1780, his speech in the House of Commons, &c.	144—48
Letter from Burke to Alderman Merlott, of Bristol, dated 4th April, 1780	149
Letter from Burke to Mr. Job Watts, of Bristol, dated 10th August, 1780, as to certain rumours and "religious prejudices" which were likely to affect his popularity	150—51
References to some of the causes that led to the unpopularity of Burke with his constituents	151—54
Dissolution of Parliament on the 1st September, 1780.	155
Matthew Brickdale and Richard Combe, the Tory candidates, in opposition to Cruger and Burke.	153
Arrival of Burke in Bristol. His address to the electors. His celebrated speech at the Guildhall.	156—61

Summary of Contents.

	Page.
Burke's second address to the electors. The nomination of candidates. Death of Mr. Combe, one of the candidates. ("What shadows we are, and what shadows we pursue.") Sir Henry Lippincott, Bart., nominated in the place of Combe. - -	162
Burke came to the conclusion that the contest would be a hopeless one. He declines the election. His speech on the hustings. His subsequent printed address to the electors. -	162—66
The nomination of Samuel Peach (Cruger's father-in-law). Burke's friends decide not to vote for Cruger. The result of the poll. Return of Brickdale and Lippincott. - - -	164—65
Letters from Burke to Cruger and Harford as to the result of the election. The opinions of Charles James Fox, Hannah More, and others, as to the result of the election. . - -	165—66
Vote of thanks to Burke by the Corporation of Bristol.	166
Death of Lippincott on the 1st of January, 1781. - -	166
Henry Cruger (Whig) and George Daubeny (Tory) candidates. Election of Daubeny. - - - - -	166
The general election of 1784. Candidates—Brickdale and Daubeny (Tories), and Henry Cruger (Whig.) Return of Brickdale and Cruger. - - - - -	166—67
Dissolution of Parliament in 1790. Retirement from Parliamentary life of Brickdale and Cruger. - - -	167
Brief references to Cruger, Brickdale, Champion and Burke. -	167—69

Errata.

Preface, p. ix., "Garrard" should read "Gerrard."

Page 1, line 2, for "nearly a year" read "more than a year."

Page 12, line 14, "ia" should read "in."

Page 33, (There is no proof that William Franks was connected with the China manufactory.)

Page 42, "Burk's' should read "Burke."

Page 123, "retail" in the foot-note should read "wholesale."

Page 128, line 7, "meet" should read "make."

Page 129, line 8, "in was announced" should read "it was announced."

Page 136, line 32, "Anerica" should read "America."

Page 169, line 2, "county" should read "rocky."

[NOTE.—*The Author will be glad to receive notes of any discrepancies in dates, &c.*]

www.ingramcontent.com/pod-product-compliance
Lightning Source LLC
Chambersburg PA
CBHW021733220426
43662CB00008B/831